*Blandine Kriegel*

# The State and the
# Rule of Law

*Translated by Marc A. LePain and Jeffrey C. Cohen*

*With a Foreword by Donald R. Kelley*

 NEW FRENCH THOUGHT

PRINCETON UNIVERSITY PRESS · PRINCETON, NEW JERSEY

Copyright © 1995 by Princeton University Press
Published by Princeton University Press, 41 William Street,
Princeton, New Jersey 08540
In the United Kingdom: Princeton University Press, Chichester, West Sussex

Translated from the French edition of Blandine Barret-Kriegel, *L'État et les esclaves:
Réflexions pour l'histoire des états* (Paris: © Editions Payot, 1989).

*Library of Congress Cataloging-in-Publication Data*

---

Barret-Kriegel, Blandine.
[Etat et les esclaves. English]
The state and the rule of law / Blandine Kriegel ; translated by Marc A. LePain
and Jeffrey C. Cohen ; with a foreword by Donald R. Kelley.
p.   cm. — (New French thought)
Includes bibliographical references and index.
ISBN 0-691-03291-2 (cl. : alk. paper)
1. Civil rights. 2. Human rights. 3. State, The. I. Title. II. Series.
JC571.B35815   1995
320.1′1—dc20       95-17976

Published with the assistance of the French Ministry of Culture

This book has been composed in Adobe Bauer Bodoni

Princeton University Press books are printed on acid-free paper and meet the guidelines
for permanence and durability of the Committee on Production Guidelines for Book
Longevity of the Council on Library Resources

Printed in the United States of America

10 9 8 7 6 5 4 3 2 1

# Contents

# Foreword

A SPECTER has been haunting European intellectuals in our century—the specter of "anti-statism." All the forces of ideology—right, left, liberal, and uncommitted—have entered into an unholy alliance to protect this specter. This is the first message of Blandine Kriegel's *The State and the Rule of Law*, a book published first in 1979, then (still more opportunely) in 1989, and now in translation, at a time when cultural critics are still trying to find a way out of the ideological chaos left by the decline (if not disappearance) of the Left, new as well as old.

In France since the advent of Mitterrand, this has meant, for the non-communist Left, the discrediting of revolution and coming to terms with power, that is, with the old nemesis of the state, and considering the possibility that human liberty may still find its best, or least objectionable, guarantee in this old institution, rightly understood. Such a political turn has also meant reconsidering a more conventional, historical, and conservative (at least, as Marxists used to say "objectively" conservative) view of French and European history. Finding another "master narrative" in which the revolution does not figure as historical icon is another impulse underlying this book in its original form.

The state has long been regarded as the medium of modern forms of enslavement. Indeed, "from the Platonic utopia to the absolutist state to the Stalinist nightmare," the vision and experience of authoritarian government has given cause for such fears, and since the later eighteenth century the abstraction of "civil society" has been set up in opposition to the state. For Kriegel, however, this is an unfortunate error arising from a perverse tradition that would do away with the Western institution we have come to call the state. This tradition arose from liberal and democratic ideas of civil society, was embodied in the romantic apotheosis of the purely and metapolitically social, was radicalized by Marxist designs for a society without a state, and culminated in Nazism and communism. It has survived in our times in the illusions of the Left, exemplified most notably in the crisis of 1968 in France. In fact and in a still longer perspective, however, the "classic state" of the West was not despotic except in aberrant forms. On the contrary, it has arguably been, since the later Middle Ages, the major vehicle of human liberty and a sanctuary for political critics as well as historical scholars.

This impassioned work offers a remedy as well as a diagnosis. It endorses a conservative philosophical and historiographical canon that also represents an essential moral choice that may save us from the threat of slavery traditionally, if often inadvertently, encouraged by anti-statists. For Kriegel, whose political sympathies lie with Mitterrand's Socialist Party, it is tragic as well as ironic that champions of liberty against the state have, in fact if not by intention, contributed to the persistence and renewal of master-slave relationships. Political philosophers have always celebrated "liberty," of course, but too often they have done so in the name of a spurious individualism that glorifies a subject that is not only autonomous but also isolated, desocialized, and so defenseless in a society in which complete self-reliance is actually self-destructive. Naive "Robinson Crusoe myths," from the state of nature to the *homo economicus*, have reinforced this antagonism between individual and state and utopian dreams of its abolishment, and so has any historical method or social science seeking to ground reality in socioeconomic analysis divested of human relations and divorced from political context. Marx was wrong to follow the liberal tendency of basing a philosophy on purely material interests, turning Hegel on his head, and consigning politics and ideology to a so-called superstructure. Now, after a century and a half, Hegel has finally been restored to an upright position.

"Economics does not explain everything," Kriegel argues. We are, socially, not just what we eat or work at but also what we have dreamed and built. She wants us to keep this in mind as we try to analyze our current predicament, and so what she proposes is "the restoration of a historical perspective on the question of the state."

In order to carry on this "uphill battle" against economic and social historians, she proposes a return to the almost forgotten classics of French legal and institutional history, including the works of Rodolphe Dareste, Adolphe Chéruel, Ernest Glasson, Jean Declareuil, François Olivier-Martin, and Michel Villey. In keeping with this traditionalist stance, she calls for a political or "juridico-institutional" method rather than the invidious identification of supposedly deeper social structures or economic mechanisms, inspired directly or indirectly by Marxist notions of superstructure and by the fateful eighteenth-century formula, "Society *versus* the State!" (recalling Herbert Spencer's formula, "The Man *versus* the State").[1] This turn to the past had been just the move made by the great romantic historians of the Restoration period—Guizot, Mignet, Thierry, and the "new historians" of that day—and like them Kriegel looks back across a period of radical illusions and terminological abuse in order to follow and to reassess the slow and "sedimentary" workings of the historical process.

It should be noted that during the decade between the two editions of the present book Kriegel has herself undertaken just such a scholarly reevaluation in an impressive four-volume work published under the general title of *Les Historiens et la monarchie* and based on a doctoral thesis directed by Michel Foucault.[2] In this study of the Enlightenment, Kriegel turns from the empty skepticism of the philosophes to the rich scholarly efforts of the royalist *érudits* (especially her three "heroes," Jean Mabillon, Nicolas Fréret, and Jacob-Nicolas Moreau), from the salons to the academies of history and the archives, in order to understand the neglected tradition of learning that promoted, legitimized, and publicized the French monarchy of the Old Regime. These scholars were fighting a losing battle against the reforming rationalists of the Enlightenment, but their contributions were in some ways more enduring, and they may be recovered from the scholarly sediment that Kriegel, following her unfashionable canon, examines and interprets.

Excavating this sedimentation, Kriegel finds a new—or rather an old, mistakenly discredited, or forgotten—interpretation of key concepts of the Western political tradition, which have been distorted by neglect of history and by modern socioeconomic reductionism, especially the state, sovereignty, and the rights of man (we do not hear of women except as subsumed under this traditional rubric). What she examines and celebrates above all is the "state under the rule of law." The state in this idealized sense is a legal, institutional, and moral construct and cannot be reduced to economic or social interests as such Marxists as Perry Anderson have tried to do; nor is it to be identified with despotism as such early modern critics as Pierre Bayle and even Montesquieu tended to do. The natural development of the state, she argues, is in the direction not of absolutism but of the rule of law, in which the state is not an irresponsible wielder of power but rather a protector of human liberty against the ever-recurring threats of despotism and enslavement.

Kriegel views the state and its development, in Weberian—and implicitly Hegelian—fashion, as an "ideal-type," although for her this ideal is by no means value-free. The statist paradigm is founded, she tells us, on the three principles: the final value of the individual human being, the legal expression of this value, and its political and institutional guarantees. The Western intellectual tradition that produced this paradigm is also threefold, and equally schematic: first, the ancient concept of natural law associated with Greek science; second, that of civil law, which is the Roman legacy; and third, the Judeo-Christian tradition, which added a moral vision to the abstract and often brutal views of classical antiquity. Kriegel retells the story of state building and state conceptualizing in terms of the interplay of these political traditions as reflected in the writings of selected

Western legal and political philosophers, who are set in dialogue with one another on this issue.

The key to the modern state is "sovereignty," a concept that was given its classic form by Jean Bodin in the sixteenth century and radicalized by Thomas Hobbes in the seventeenth. Bodin identified sovereignty with the Roman-law idea of "majesty," which was the original power bestowed by the Roman poeple on the *princeps* through the legendary *lex regia*. For Kriegel, however, this sovereign power was far different from the *imperium* that identified law with the king's will. Nor was sovereignty to be confused with fuedal *dominium*, or suzerainty, the brutal product of feudal anarchy: "Feudalism is war . . . , sovereign power is peace," aphorizes Kriegel. "Feudalism was servitude; the sovereign state heralds enfranchisement."

"Sovereignty," according to Kriegel, has nothing to do with Roman despotism, with the rule of fear and force; rather, as the very form of the state, it represents the legitimate, rational, and responsible exercise of power. This was the view not only of such political writers as Machiavelli, Bodin, Locke, and even Hobbes, but also of such theologians as Luther, Calvin, and Suárez and such liberals as Locke, Burlamaqui, and Barbeyrac. In the early modern period, however, political theory was overwhelmed by state-building practices. Under pressures of imperial expansion, colonialist greed, and attendant ideologies, the sovereign state slid down what Kriegel calls the "slippery slope" to the absolutist and then to the totalitarian state, finally to the concentration camp and the gulag. In the anti-statist backlash to these phenomena, the original ideal of limited government has been lost.

Corresponding to Roman imperialism in public law was the notion of property (*dominium*) in the private sphere, and this, too, was a dehumanizing expression of power and a threat to liberty in the sense (which the Romans never knew) of subjective rights. Personal liberty, which is the first of all rights, has been threatened from two quarters. One is private property, which allows human beings to be treated as things and which is the premise of slavery in all of its forms. Whether regarded as theft or the very essence of civilization, property was radically politicized in the nineteenth century. The formula of Linguet appropriated by Marx—"The spirit of the laws is property"—signaled the misguided effort to identify the political with the economic, morality with greed, legality with force, and liberty with property, and in all of these ways to discredit the state. The other threat is associated with the natural-law worship of the contract, which allows the alienation of human liberty. But freedom of contract to the contrary notwithstanding, human beings are not things; their humanity is not for sale or contract except in a speciously "free" market; and only the sovereign state can insure this first inalienable right.

"The rights of man" had a very different nature and progeny than anti-statists have argued.[3] This concept was the product neither of enlightened liberalism nor of modern democracy—nor certainly of the forests of Germany invoked by Montesquieu—but rather of an older, ultimately biblical concept that is far from the individualism of ancient Roman, medieval feudal, and modern natural law and that emphasizes not the human will but the human right to self-preservation and subsistence. While feudal aristocrats may have promoted their own "liberties," Kriegel remarks, they could not discover the New World, abolish slavery, guarantee individual security, or invent habeas corpus. As for natural lawyers like Hugo Grotius and Samuel Pufendorf, their abstract, unsocial, and unpolitical conception was precisely what encouraged modern forms of alienation and enslavement; and so, in other ways, did the utopian visionaries who imagined communities outside of conventional political and institutional structures.

For Kriegel, as for Montesquieu, English government furnishes the model of a state under the rule of law, and indeed achieves centralization through its common law. In this idealized picture, she follows the century-old works of Émile Boutmy and the Germanist view of the English constitution of such Victorian scholars as Bishop Stubbs and E. A. Freeman. The French monarchy, too, shared some of these admirable features before being diverted in the direction of absolutism through fiscal and administrative deformations, the movement toward codification, and finally the Revolution. This contrasts sharply with the political experience of Eastern Europe, where despotic government and serfdom lasted much longer and where communism flourished. These tendencies have been intensified by the totalitarian creations of the past century, whose inhumanity was intensified by modern technology and by the "public-opinion machine" that magnifies defects and confounds criticism.

In Kriegel's story, the villains are the German romantics. Much of the evil in our world, she argues, can be traced to the egoism and totalitarianism that issued from their political values and that produced the modern "nation-state." It was not in France but in Germany that doctrines of populism and civilism took an anti-statist turn, exalting the social and the *völkisch* above the liberal and the political. As the French revolutionary armies set out on a series of wars, Kriegel writes dramatically, "Fichte was just around the corner," ready to launch the "romantic juggernaut" on its path to new forms of despotism and slavery—from the nation-state to the party-state and between the milestones of *Reden an die deutsche Nation* and *Mein Kampf*. This is part of the explanation of "how Germany went mad."

According to the diagnosis of Kriegel, following the judgments of Goethe and Lukacs, romanticism was a sort of sickness in which new breeds of despotism and slavery were produced by an unholy marriage of irrationalism and nationalism. In the sleep of reason encouraged by what has been called the German "counter-Enlightenment," monsters were born. Identifying the nation with the *Volk* made politics in effect into a popular religion and introduced terror into social relations. The result, according to Kriegel, is that for Fichte the nation takes the place of the state, education takes the place of justice, faith takes the place of law, and the imperatives of society take the place of the rights of man.

Others were complicit in this sinister project, including members of the German historical school, led by the great legal historian Savigny. As he raised history above philosophy, so Savigny raised custom and the social above law and the state; and some of his students pushed these antipolitical attitudes to a more dangerous extreme, the most conspicuous such student being the young—anti-Hegelian and "romantic"—Karl Marx, who was the ultimate anti-statist and "anti-juridist." Marx's mission was to replace law and the state, which were both antique creations of Old Regime ideology, with a new religion of the social, based on economic analysis and social action based in turn on opposition to the state, to law, and to individualism. The Soviet civilization without law—and so without rights—was the end product of Marx's antipolitical vision.

What appeared finally in the wake of this hyperromantic anti-statism was a new religion—a religion that took a secular form as a sort of mystical and racialist "immanence," in which man was assimilated to God, or at least the gods. Here Kriegel finds still another villain "around the corner"—in this case Wagner. The monster that was born out of this dream of unreason was the German Empire, which again arose in war and which gave despotic form to the new ideology. Other, still more menacing figures continued to lurk "around the corners" of the historical drama, whose denouement came in the still more horrifying political monsters that have appeared in our century as a result of this treason of the (mainly German) intellectuals.

There is a large lesson in Kriegel's political story. What she offers, in the wake of Foucauldian analysis but with a renewed interest on older scholarship, is a critique of power and its relation to morality. The critique is presented in methodological as well as historical terms. She deplores not only attitudes toward power traceable to Roman and feudal—to "imperial" and "dominial"—ideas and practices but also the reductionist theories of economists and sociologists claiming to find the hidden mechanisms of historical change, which are not only to be recorded, perhaps, but also manipulated. Such reductionism she regards as a return, in effect, to the Roman obsession with imperial will and to seignorial doctrine. It is not economics but politics and political ideology that shape the human condition, and she calls for a deeper understanding of the familiar social sphere defined by law and public institutions. "Anti-statism" is thus seen as a tradition beginning in societies grounded on master-slave relationships and ending in antipolitical (and so antihumanist) theories of social behavior and organization, such as those that underlay and contributed to the aspirations, events, and disillusionments of 1968.

In general the classical tradition of political theory comes off badly in this account. Roman law is denounced for its "absolutist" tendencies and its rhetoric and neglect of human rights, and Germanism for its romantic populism, which has encouraged and legitimized modern authoritarian government.[4] Political villainy suggests contamination by one or the other of these ideological viruses, which thrive in conditions created by antistatist attitudes. For Kriegel, the source of human liberty and the law that guards it is neither the classical city-state nor the Germanic forest; it is rather the "small, lost people [that] emerged from the wilderness over three thousand years ago" and the larger Judeo-Christian tradition that carried on the struggle against a slave mentality. Judaic law and derivative Christian morality and the individual rights they embody represent an alternative that the European state, at least in its ideal form, the "state under law," has sheltered and protected; and it is this shelter, so long in the making, that we must cling to and through which we must seek liberty and continue to build communities in a shrinking world and an approaching millennium.

There are of course other stories to be told on this level of political ideas and their supposed provenance in the Western experience. For one thing, the Romanist tradition is not as black as it is painted here (and in the denunciations of such German romantics as Heinrich Heine). Roman law in fact has another, kinder, and more constitutional face in keeping with the values Kriegel prizes, being the source not only of authoritarian and proprietary but also of libertarian and anti-absolutist formulas. Like the Bible, Roman law can be cited by the devil, but it can also offer aid and comfort to the forces of good and the champions of limited government.

Conversely, the English model of the state, especially the vaunted, immemorial tradition of common law, is not nearly so benign as represented here.[5] Based on another sort of Germanist myth, English constitutional government was tied to principles of private property and —in this sense giving things priority over persons—to restrictions on liberty and the severest criminal penalties for violations of property and possessory rights. But this argument, not pursued in this book, leads us back to another corner of history, and this time it is Marx who is waiting.

Germanism has been associated with its share of fallacies and offenses. The "German idea of freedom" was indeed based on a paradox—inner liberty being separated from outer, or political liberty, and civil society (and, by implication, law) from the state; and the Nazis took advantage of this unfortunate caesura.[6] Yet it should also be recalled that Kriegel's own ideal of the "state under the rule of law" (*état de droit*) is a German vision, too; for the German equivalent, the *Rechtstaat*, was the underlying vision of the Prussian code of 1795 and was specifically opposed to the idea of a state based on force (*Machtstaat* or *Polizeistaat*).[7] Germany did not take this road to the modern state, but Germans did envision it.

*The State and the Rule of Law* is conjectural history in the best sense, offering not only an iterpretation of political history but also a vision of future possibilities projected from this interpretation. The book aspires to revive an older wisdom, marking a turn toward historical understanding, political prudence, institutional accommodation and (to invoke Weber once again) an ethics not of ends but of responsibility. For French intellectuals, it suits the post-Marxist mood that has been intensified by the failures of Sovietologists and China watchers to detect the underlying forces of change, by declining confidence in the predictive and governing powers of social science, and by the general discrediting, since 1968, of the vocabulary of revolution ("The French Revolution is over," as Furet has famously pronounced). In the face of the free market, ideas of social control and social engineering—those monsters created by the dreams of the Jacobins—continue to haunt political ideology and political practice, but for many they have lost their attraction.

Yet, as this book reminds us, the state is the political reality that, for good or for ill, we possess. Anti-statist lines of argument appear both from below and from above—from groups both sub- and supernational—but the individual rights enjoyed in the West continue to be located, defended, and argued about within the framework of the state as it has devloped over six or seven centuries. Indeed anti-statism itself, in the company of naive or objectionable ideologies, including not only communism but also communitarianism, has arisen and flourished within this protective framework—as has the confusion of values that has so distorted historical scholarship and political understanding.

Is this the message for the millennium? Does this mark—again—the "end of ideology," the "exhaustion of utopia," as Daniel Bell argued more than a generation ago? Is it an old genealogy rehabilitated or a "new radicalism" seeking reconciliation with almost-forgotten historical roots?[8] Or is it the emergence of a new, or renewed, "myth of the state"? The question is whether it may not be too late to recover old political values in a time when, if we can believe Hannah Arendt, "authority, resting on a foundation in the past," is dead. Incalculable economic, social, nationalist, and internationalist forces continue to threaten the antique political structures and human rights produced by the Western historical process. Whether the state can be recalled to old values and restrictions is both a question for and a challenge to intellectuals in this (no longer just post-1968 but now) post-1989 world, a world in which we shall need all the wisdom we can find. And who—the ideological giants having departed—will be waiting around this corner?

*Donald R. Kelley*

# The State and the Rule of Law

# The Paradoxes of Anti-statism

Tʜᴇsᴇ ᴀʀᴇ hard times for the state. For those who have already reached their verdict, there is a single perpetrator of the troubles of our times, of the crimes and the camps. The guilty party is what Marx called the parasite that clogs all the pores of society, what Nietzsche dubbed the coldest of all cold monsters. The rumbling swells. It is said that the most extreme and rigid forms of power are the natural consequences of its ordinary and benign manifestations, that the socialism of concentration camps is an avatar of both Platonism and Nazism. Totalitarian society, we are told, is a society devoured by the state, and the liberal state, which appears different from the despotic one, is in essence the same. It seems we are all slouching toward the totalitarian state, the end-product of political entropy.

So as not to hasten the arrival of the beast by beckoning him, perhaps it would be prudent to demonstrate the paradoxical nature of this anti-statism. It has, to be sure, reconciled fraternal rivals: since May 1968, the challenge to the structures of authority in Western democracies has combined with the discovery of socialism's heinous massacres to forge a sweeping critique of socialism and capitalism, a unitary hostility to the state shared by liberals, libertarians, and Marxists.

In Western Europe, anti-statism is an innovation, the product of horizontal and doctrinal crisis, but also vertical and political crisis. The state is "doubly challenged, at the supranational level by multinational corporations . . . and at the local level by regionalist movements."[1] The great exhaustion of the state makes itself felt. "Down with the police state," the students shouted in May 1968, expressing an idea that has become the ideology even of those who govern us. The "ruling class" itself is tired of the state, tired of sharing with the middle classes the benefits of that which is rightfully its own. Is this the new industrial age, the age of multinationals whose irresistable rise is barely impeded by lilliputian states? A new moral universe of pluri-regionalisms that restrain the powerful central bureaucratic forces? It is as if the captains of industry and the Basque and Breton separatists were preparing the sacrifice of the state along with the smaller and middle-sized industries and the unenlightened nations.

Elsewhere, anti-statism is a tradition: the Communists rejected the dictatorship of the proletariat and rallied around the self-governing call to order, just as Lenin embraced sovietism. They preserved the Marxist-Leninist doctrine of the state as an apparatus in the service of the dominant class, an apparatus that must necessarily be destroyed and transported, as Engels announced, "to the museum of antiquities, to be exhibited next to the wheel and the bronze hatchet." As for the liberal state and human and civil rights, their defense has been left to the Soviet and Chinese dissidents, to Sakharov, Pluyusch, and Li Yizhe.

The first paradox is the following: the consequences one anticipated in the East from the withering away of the state were precisely the inverse of those expected in the West. Rooted in liberal theory, many Westerners hoped to overcome authoritarian socialism. To live without a state, to return to society what the state has taken from it, would be the means to attack the totalitarian regime. This program reflected the equivocal success of the French "new philosophy," which relied not only on the proximity of elections and the translation of Solzhenitsyn's masterpiece (rendered by André Glucksmann in the wild-eyed language of the leftist generation) but also on its claim to have discovered, in the excesses of the state, the secret etiology of what Bernard-Henry Lévy called "barbarism."

For others, for the orthodox Communists, the anti-statist tendency was precisely the starting point for their totalitarian regimes. In this spirit one distinguished between the *theory* of the withering away of the state, proclaimed by Marx in *The Civil War in France* and restated by Lenin on the eve of the October Revolution in *The State and Revolution*, and the *practice* of its formidable reinforcement by which it appeared to instantiate the Nietzschean prophecy: "Socialism is despotism's younger brother; it will triumph to calls for 'as much of the state as possible.'" A grand opportunity to demonstrate the distance between dream and reality, hell and utopia!

It remains nevertheless to understand how the undauntedly anti-statist position could in some circumstances result in the construction of Leviathans whose cruelty imprisoned and poisoned their societies. It remains to be explained by what infernal mechanism the doctrine of "the withering away of the state" yielded, not only in the Soviet Union and in China but also in Cuba and Vietnam, a formidable reinforcement of power. Anti-statism has also imposed a negative and univocal philosophy of power, propounded today by writers whose anti-Hegelianism does not hinder their borrowing, without the nuances observed by Hegel himself, the thought that power is *mastery*. This is an old idea. In the *Gorgias*, Socrates debates it with Callicles, refusing "with reasons of iron and of diamonds" to reduce the public relations of free citizens to the private relations of master and slave.

Here is the second paradox. This doctrine of power uncritically accepts German romantic political philosophy, which imposed itself in Europe, via Fichte and Nietzsche, only in the nineteenth century. The doctrine has nothing to say about another tradition in political philosophy, that of the early moderns, which helped give birth to societies based on the rule of law in Western Europe. This early modern political philosophy had a greater sense of history than its nineteenth-century sibling, despite the latter's claim to supremacy in this respect. From the sixteenth century on, in Machiavelli and in Bodin, and in such ideologically opposed authors in the eighteenth century as Moreau and Mably, one finds analyses of historical and geographical diversity of states according to their subjection to law. One finds a stark opposition between despotic domination (the most celebrated characterization of which is in Montesquieu's *Spirit of the Laws*) and legitimate power, which never consists of the right of the strongest. At the moment when the states of Western Europe, forming and reforming their legal codes, were developing a process of juridification of their societies, their political theorists, in denouncing despotism (and prior to despotism, feudal regimes), were rejecting all unilateral conceptions of politics. They distinguished states according to their indifference or subjection to the law.

All this was reversed in the nineteenth century. Such authors as Marx and Nietzsche invoked a homogeneous conception of the state. If they disagreed about its origin—for Nietzsche, it was in war and forceful blows, the "blond beast of prey"; for Marx, it was the economic division of society between owners and producers—they agreed on the immutable identity of the state. The genesis of the state was treated as a unique event, on the one hand producing society, on the other hand domesticating society and turning it against the state itself. The state came to be viewed as an inert but complex mechanism dedicated to social reproduction; its motions are all reactive, parasitic on the active forces of society. Like a parasite, it bleeds its host, sucking life from the social organism. Tacitly or expressly, these univocal theories of the state reduced all the faces of power to the menacing sneer of despotism. Whence the volley of insults: liberalism is but a facade for oppression; socialism is despotism's younger brother. This idea of the state as despot, a heritage of the nineteenth century, based on an identification of the totalitarian state with the state itself, makes its reappearance today at the expense of the early modern idea of the state.

These two paradoxes merit some scrutiny. Behind the anti-statist opprobrium lies an assumption of the unity of the state. Behind the identification of all forms of the state, we may discern a German romantic doctrine (given its canonical form by Marx) to the effect that there is no such thing as a history of the state, for the state is mere superstructure to be cleared away by socialism. But is the state some "one thing"? Are the most extreme and oppressive forms of power the quintessence of the state? What if, on the contrary, there were a number of states, a genealogy of their diverse structures—what if there were, in sum, a *history* of the state?

As for the second paradox, we are entitled to some suspicion of this modern—all too modern—idea that all power is equal, that in all contexts, politics is force, domination, and servitude, *imperium* and *dominium*. Governing is, in the end, a matter of regulating conflicts. A half-century of socialism should have been sufficient to teach us that no transparent or reconciled society is within our grasp. The visions of a utopia just around the corner, happiness in twenty years, have all borne rotten fruit. In democratic states, as in all states, the conflicts that the "dictatorship of the proletariat" sought to cover over, the "cultural revolutions" unleashed, and the various coups d'état kept reenacting—these conflicts have displayed remarkable staying power. How should conflicts be resolved? Who should decide their outcome? To reply that "force" decides is insufficient, for even if relations of force are "all there is," it remains to determine what kind of relation obtains—ritual, regulatory, military, or juridical. Are reasons of state perhaps not always bad reasons? Could it be, as the ancients thought, that there are some exercises of power that are less bad than others? And that finding out which those are is the task of the prince?

These two problematic identities—of the state and of power—are our subject matter in this book. We will examine them by reflecting on two critical junctures in the history of the state: the emergence of the sovereign states of Western Europe at the beginning of the modern era and the later formation of the German nation-state.

．　．　．　．　．

These questions regarding the state came to my attention through two related experiences, one of anxiety and one of suspicion. The central sociopolitical experience for Frenchmen of my generation was the Algerian War and the student uprisings of May 1968. The enigma of the totalitarian sphinx posed itself sharply to us then; whereas for some the enigma was a harmless riddle, for others, like me, the enigma produced anxiety. For most of us who wanted to change the world when we were twenty, the gulag was not invoked merely to rationalize a retreat from idealism into bourgeois life. For the less self-reflecting among us, those who sought to drive intellectual ideals from the battlefield of public opinion, the discovery of the gulag provided the occasion for harried, bombastic books and a pretext for instant conversions. For most of us, however, the gulag represented evil, endemic but mysterious. To understand its genealogy, we thought, might permit us to glimpse *a contrario* the genealogy of liberal democracy. To seek such an understanding was a task we had not assumed on our own but were, so to speak, assigned. Will we be able to carry it out? Renan observed that the great generations are those who realize in part the ideals of their youth.

To this anxiety was added, in the course of my research on historians and power in the seventeenth and eighteenth centuries, a suspicion. My prejudices gradually but ineluctably gave way to a conviction that the classical state did not function in ways that a despotic state did. The former did not control its intellectuals nor transform them into mercenaries. On the contrary, it established research institutions, thereby running the enormous risks of critique and opposition, and subjecting its power, de facto, to law. I noticed that the academies of the age of Louis XIV were nothing like those of the Soviets. This aroused my suspicion against lumping together all forms of the state. In the archives of the Bibliothèque Nationale, I was compelled to surrender the maxims I held most dear, those which, in keeping with the spirit of the time, viewed the state with the utmost contempt. The "State" was always capitalized, as if to reinforce its transcendent evil.

According to the prevailing view, a single strand of indefensible domination wound its way from the Platonic utopia to the absolutist state to the Stalinist nightmare. The excesses of the state were the roots of the totalitarian malaise. "Society," by contrast, was fetishized: the antidote to the expanding malignant tumor of the state was the fortification of healthy social tissue, which would do battle with, and ultimately sap, the strength of the state. The labor of those intellectuals who sought to reconcile socialism with liberty was devoted to the formation of a coalition between the individual and society, who together would overthrow the state. This enterprise, of course, provided a whole generation of intellectuals with ample material on which to bestow their labor.

This was the point at which suspicion and anxiety joined. Was anti-statism the best characterization of this tendency? Perhaps the mystery of the socialist drift in the general direction of concentration camps was to be unraveled by trying to understand the differences among political arrangements, rather than by the notion of anti-statism. Perhaps the type of state that had fostered the development of liberal democracy had its own particular role to play. Perhaps, then, the time had come for the restoration of a historical perspective on the question of the state.

The present book seeks to exploit such a historical perspective, to reflect on historical questions, and to press historical knowledge into service. It makes no claim, however, to be a history book. Its aim is to assemble, in a spirit of speculation, reflections toward a history of the state, rather than to provide such a history. Even this minimal project, along with the typology of the state that we permit ourselves to propose, is useful only to the extent that it permits us to reopen a discussion that unilateral anti-statism has closed off prematurely. This vulgar anti-statism, which has provided more darkness than light, has also, of course, spawned a number of colossal states itself.

For those who retain socialist hopes, the drift toward the gulag displayed by all forms of communism imposes a bitter but imperative need for a critique of Marxist politics. The critique cannot be as simple as the signing of a death certificate (Marx is dead) nor as cool as a denial (there is no Marxist political doctrine). For the corpse seems to wriggle its fingers now and then; the Marxist doctrine that politics has no reality of its own has itself had quite "real" effects in the real world. For those, too, who believe that one must first put one's own house in order, we must also examine characteristics of our society—the decline of rights, the growth of regulation at the expense of law, the weakening of the juridical—if we believe that politics is not for the prince alone and that those in power must always be watched.

# PART ONE

# The State and the Rule of Law

He that will not give just occasion, to think that all Government
in the World is the product only of Force and Violence, and that
Men live together by no other rules but that of Beasts, where
the strongest carries it, and so lay a Foundation for perpetual
Disorder and Mischief, Tumult, Sedition and Rebellion . . . must
of necessity find out another rise of Government, another Original of
Political Power, and another way of designing and knowing the
Persons that have it. . . .

—LOCKE

# CHAPTER I

# Problems for a History of the State

WHAT IS a state under the rule of law? A number of lawyers would respond without hesitation that it is a state in which there is a body of laws, in which there is a constitution. Such a definition, generous to the point of irresolution, is geared to the new type of state that historians usually call the nation-state, which emerged in Western Europe in the seventeenth and eighteenth centuries, notably in France, England, and Holland. There are two reasons for this terminological development.

First, there was a desire to appropriate the early modern legal tradition, the source of the idea of the rule of law. When the French Revolution declared in 1791 that there is no authority in France superior to the law, it did not invent the rule of law but rather inscribed itself at the end of a long process, which began at the end of the Middle Ages. As the state came into its own, it took more precise forms, grew more complex and more extensive, appropriated and rejected various elements of Roman law, put customs and mores into writing, and collated and reformed various codes. In the course of this long and gradual process, law became part of the fabric of society and gave legitimacy to the state. Second, there arose a need to penetrate the mystery of those forms of the state that had fostered the development of liberal democracy, a need that historians sought to satisfy by approaching the question of the state from a historical perspective. The terrain of the historian, it was agreed, included the most abstract forms of spirituality and the most concrete details of material life, so why exclude the state from that terrain?

Before attempting a history of the state under the rule of law, the problems endemic to the project must be set out. They are, in the first instance, general problems for political history. Political history has a bad conscience, because a part of it has, in the past half-century, essentially collapsed. While economic history and the history of class struggles have thrived, the history of political facts and events has fallen into disrepute and oblivion. The phenomenon dates from the moment when historians, in response to the efforts of sociology to oust history from the crowded domain of the human sciences, began to focus on social morphology, and to do so by studying economic and social history at the expense of political history. Emmanuel Le Roy Ladurie explains the process quite clearly: "present-day historiography, with its preference for the quantifiable, the statistical and the structural, has been obliged to suppress in order to survive, which is a pity. In the last few decades it has virtually condemned to death the narrative history of events and the individual biography."[1] In 1934, the historian Louis André wrote that

> the administrative history of seventeenth-century France is no more advanced than the economic history of the same period. Perhaps even less. The great importance of the topic, which no one has ever denied, stands in marked contrast to the utter neglect in which it has been left to languish.[2]

The observation retains a certain validity today. The defects of economic history have been made good, most notably by the Annales school. The history of political institutions, by contrast, suffers from massive neglect. There are important exceptions—in France, Michel Foucault, Annie Kriegel, Alain Besançon, François Furet, Pierre Chaunu—whose work on institutions, revolutionary parties, intellectual societies, and administrations has held off the complete demise of political history. But their lessons have not always been heeded, and the history of political institutions must continually fight uphill battles against hostile attitudes. What we may call the devaluation of ideology views ideology as inconstant, vaporous, evanescent. It holds the words of a theory as of less account than the deeds of labor. This is why Augustin Cochin's inspired interpretation of philosophical societies was so neglected. Furet rediscovered it and showed that Cochin's originality consisted in his penetrating to the heart of the mystery of the French Revolution, its political and cultural dynamic.[3] This rediscovery paves the way for a reevaluation of the phenomenon of ideology, which in turn furnishes those who have been studying revolutionary parties with more solid foundations. As a result, the history of ideologies—including the history of religions—can once again become a decisive element of political history. In contrast to these signs of revival in political history, no similar renewal has taken place in the history of the state.[4] The field has fallen so fallow that it does not even recognize as its own or give deserved attention to such historians (again, in France) as Michel Antoine, Bertrand Gilles, Robert Estivals, Daniel Roche, and Étienne Thuau. Their studies of institutions, ideologies, statistics, and early modern politics could serve as stepping-stones for the assault on the problem of the state.

The general problems of political history are exacerbated by the special problems of the history of the state, which have to do with the devaluation of law and institutions. Here the history of the state must confront head-on the presuppositions of modern political sociology. Like layers of earth that sink into sediment but do not disappear, political history burrowed its way underground but never suffocated completely. Fallen into disrepute among historians, it resurfaced in the hands of certain sociologists. Sociology, however, is a new discipline. In looking at history, its practitioners were naturally attracted to those predecessors who shared their interests. Hence Montesquieu and Tocqueville dominate political history as it is practiced by sociologists. One could do worse, of course. Neither Montesquieu nor Tocqueville was content to describe political societies; they sought to understand them, by means of paradigms and typologies. Tocqueville, for instance, was one of the inventors of the methodology of what Weber would dub the ideal-type: "I admit that I saw in America more than America; it was the shape of democracy itself which I sought, its inclinations, character, prejudices, and passions."[5] He also initiated speculative conceptual history, freely mixing "history proper with philosophy of history."

Yet the reliance on Montesquieu and Tocqueville has had its costs, not least the neglect of legal and institutional history in favor of social history. The brilliance of Montesquieu and Tocqueville has obscured the histories of jurisprudence and of institutions by Rodolphe Dareste, Adolphe Chéruel, Ernest Glasson, Émile Chenon, Olivier-Martin, the successors of Guizot, Taine, and Boutmy. These names have vanished into obscurity. Even the grand historians, the masters of total history, such as Charles Langlois, Ernest Lavisse, and Charles Seignobos, have fared better than the specialists in institutional history. A rich historical heritage has thus been allowed to sink into an abyss of silence and oblivion.

The second drawback of the dominance of Montesquieu and Tocqueville has been the loss of the early modern terminology. The concerns of Montesquieu and Tocqueville are entirely late modern. They are, indeed, our own: society versus the state, despotism versus democracy. Montesquieu's attack on despotism casts in geographical terms an antinomy that jurists had previously viewed as a historical problem and one that posed no challenge to social hierarchies. Tocqueville focused on the question of democracy, a question of little import in early modern political and legal theory. Neither took up the problem of the state in its relation to law, for they neglected the problem of the state as such. Differences among political regimes are viewed through the optic of social change and described in terms foreign to the classics of (pre)liberalism and democracy.

So long as law and institutions, the very source of differentiation among states, are neglected, there can be no history of the state. Instead, there is only a history of societies, precisely Marx's hope. That is why, absent elementary knowledge of legal and constitutional realities, it is so easy today to combine an analysis of the state under Louis XIV with that under Stalin; it is assumed that there is a difference in degree but not in kind, whence the great fear of the state as a massive wildcat, immobile, immutable, and cruel.

For these reasons, I have sought to return to the early modern thinkers, to self-consciously put aside the concerns of contemporary political sociology in order to revisit the problems that the early modern theorists hoped to solve. The legal historians came to occupy an important role in this effort; their interests, ideas, and even language direct our attention to the early modern legal theorists. This explains the somewhat "archaic" cast of my bibliography. With a few important exceptions, the history of the state has been neglected for some fifty years. This is by no means catastrophic. After the French Revolution, a similar period of neglect set in, to be set right around 1830, when Guizot, Mignet, and Thierry took up the mantle where their predecessors had left it before the French Revolution. Their example can serve as a model for our enterprise.

In the first place, then, our subject matter is the early modern doctrines of the rule of law. Our method will be a parallel reading of the jurists and the natural-law philosophers. Normally these two groups are studied separately—the jurists by historians and lawyers, the natural-law philosophers and their social-contract doctrines by the philosophers. As a result, certain differences have gone unnoticed. The early theorists were of course a disparate group. Their professional status was quite different, the jurists having state employment, pensions, and publication rights from princes, the philosophers maintaining the independence that their doctrines themselves called for. The views of these theorists diverged widely, from the absolutism of Hobbes to the liberalism of Locke, from the monarchism of Bodin to the republicanism of Rousseau. Finally, the theories in question stretch over a highly differentiated historical period, more than three centuries, to be precise.

I shall have little to say about those phenomena that a sociohistorical inquiry, or a history of the changing conditions of clerics or state intellectuals, might explain. My hope is rather to uncover some of the prescience and originality of the jurists, who in many respects blazed a trail for the philosophers to follow. I hope to raise some doubts about the alleged utopianism of the philosophy of natural law and to exploit this philosophy for the light it can shed, retrospectively, on the intentions of the jurists who made it possible. I hope, in sum, to reinscribe the history of political theory in the history of the state.

A parallel reading of the jurists and the natural-law philosophers permits us to chart the development of a consensus, at least a negative consensus, that amounts to a new political theory reducible to three essential components: a doctrine of power, a doctrine of individual rights, and a political morality of law. This theory, in turn, amounts to something like an "ideal-type" of the state under the rule of law. We shall begin by reconstructing this theory and this ideal-type.

# CHAPTER II

# Sovereign Power

The Prince is not superior to the laws.

—DUPLESSIS-MORNAY

THE EARLY modern doctrine of power can be summed up in a word: sovereignty. Amid the most strident of the civil wars against Henry III, Jean Bodin articulated the doctrine, "A commonwealth [or republic] may be defined as the rightly ordered government of a number of families, and of those things which are their common concern, by a sovereign power."[1] A century later, it was restated dramatically by Charles Loyseau: "Sovereignty is the defining moment and culmination of power, the moment when the State must come into being."[2] The concepts of legitimate power and of beneficent power are present in these early definitions. Supreme power, as Bodin defined it, is also, as Loyseau emphasized, *the very essence of the state:* "Sovereignty is the form which gives being to the state; it is inseparable from the state; without it, the state vanishes."

## Is Sovereignty an Evil?

Sovereign power does not have a very good reputation. It is often confused with absolutism. "The two concepts of sovereignty and absolutism were forged together on the same anvil," wrote Jacques Maritain.[3] Then as now, the doctrine of sovereignty served as a focal point for anti-statist charges; it appeared to represent an aggrandizement of the institution of the state and a valorization of power, an interruption in the process of the withering away of the medieval state and of the devaluation of power that early modern political philosophy had initiated. For a long time, the ancients and the Christians had fared well. The Greeks scrutinized the most intimate features of the political pathology and cataloged in detail the destruction wrought by untempered power in the polis; their sages, fed up with the princes, vilified capricious authority and the unregulated tyrant. The theologians justified obedience to secular power by appealing to the teaching of St. Paul that "there is no authority except from God, and those that exist have been instituted by God. Therefore he who resists the authorities resists what God has appointed" (Rom. 13:1–2). After Augustine, they were careful to shadow the political bodies with mystical ones and to subject imperial power to the church, which wielded the celestial sword of justice over the inclined head of imperial power.[4] But according to one view of the matter, this duality collapsed. The state reemerged, toppling the tradition that had successfully accused it of degeneracy, promised to transcend it, and drowned it in a philosophy of suspicion.

Some hold that the political theory of sovereignty that emerged in modern Europe is the statist ideology itself. Not content with emancipating the state, it dared to legitimate and sanctify those forms of power that should be constrained and suspected at all times. This entitles us to lay the blame on the ideology of sovereignty for opening the door to the various despotic developments of the state, for granting access to the police state, the prison state. There is, in short, a slippery slope from the sovereign state to the totalitarian state.[5] The state is force, politics is subjugation; the nation-state is already despotic, for the essence of unchallenged power is tyrannical.

Is it here, then, in the doctrine of sovereign power, that we can discern the already-monstrous embryo of the modern omnipotent state, which will receive its definitive incarnation in nineteenth-century German philosophy? Does the doctrine of sovereignty contain within itself the monist conception of the state, the justification of absolute power? Does it set us on a slippery slope toward the despotic state? Is the ideology of sovereignty—defender of the autonomy, secularity, and legitimacy of the political authorities—merely the ideology of naked power? In short, does Leviathan pave the way for Callicles?

There are two types of objection to this view of sovereignty. The first is extrinsic. The theory of sovereignty, as a matter of historical fact, developed in the thirteenth century in France and England and is in no way linked to the absolutist period. Contrary to the suggestion of the German jurists Meyer and Rehm, it was not essentially French, either in origin or in application.[6] In the form of a theory that articulates a conception (the idea of legitimacy) and an institution (the state), a principle ("benevolent power") and its application (the use of authority), the doctrine of sovereignty was a European, or at least a Western European, phenomenon.[7] In one form or another, it appears among the statists (Machiavelli, Bodin, Hobbes), the theologians (Luther, Calvin, Suárez, Mariana), and the "liberals" (Locke, Burlamaqui, Barbeyrac). Its definition and implications are different in different theorists' hands. For some, sovereignty is theft, justified by the strength that makes it possible; it is absolute in the hands of a monarch, and well on its way to victory along with a new order of things. For others, it is a force for social cohesiveness, the result of some universal law of gravitation governing political bodies (since the notion of a civil society was not yet in vogue). Sovereignty comes from the people and belongs to the people, or to its representatives, and it must be constantly "tracked," as if it were a projectile whose trajectory one sought to register. What everyone in this period admits, though, is that the idea of sovereignty is an idea of rational and legitimate power.

The second type of objection is intrinsic. The same early modern authors who introduced the theory of sovereignty and forged the basic doctrines of the modern state also denounced as tyrannical the despotisms and feudal lordships that they considered the antithesis of sovereign power. It will be objected, though, that the ruse of "reason of state" corrupted their best intentions. But before reaching a verdict, we should inquire into their arguments. The early modern jurists defined sovereign power at first by contrasting it with feudalism rather than with despotism. Nevertheless, in order to understand their aims, it is useful to begin with Montesquieu and, as we shall see, with his shortcomings.

### Sovereign Power Is Not Despotic

"I have had new ideas; new words have had to be found or new meanings given to old ones," wrote Montesquieu.[8] This is no truer for any other word than "despot." Our author unwillingly misleads us here, for he simultaneously recovers and redirects the great tradition of the critique of despotism to be found in Machiavelli, Bodin, Loyseau, Hobbes, and Rousseau. Faithful to its predecessors, Montesquieu's famous definition seems to crystallize all the characteristics of both tyranny and feudalism: "In despotic government, one alone, without law and without rule, draws everything along by his will and his caprices."[9] And later: "the principle of despotic government [is] . . . FEAR."[10]

Despotism exhibits political asthenia and juridical anemia, an absence of deliberation; power is all, politics is absent; commandments are absolute, laws are worthless; implacable oppression and inept administration are the order of the day.[11] Extreme simplicity and massive confusion share the same space. There is no law, no counsel, no politics.[12] The categories of public and private are conflated, and the political fades into the domestic. Palace intrigues and family quarrels take the place of public hearings and collective debates: "Everything comes down to reconciling political and civil government with domestic government, the officers of the state with those of the seraglio."[13] Absolute power, although concentrated in the

hands of the despot, is afflicted by a strange malady: it flows uncontrolla-
bly. Like water from a punctured vase it seeps out inexorably, rendering
the despotic body bloodless: it "passes entirely into the hands of the one to
whom it is entrusted. The vizir is the despot himself, and each individual
officer is the vizir."[14] This characterization of the descending appropriation of despotic power, "from one petty tyrant to another," echoes Montesquieu's friend La Boétie.[15] A government not stabilized by limits is vol-
atile; domination not circumscribed by laws is evanescent. Monarchy, by
contrast, in which "power is applied less immediately," contained as it is
by the concrete force of institutions, retains what it delegates—as if one
truly possesses only that which one has consented to share: the monarch
"distributes his authority in such a way that he never gives a part without
retaining a greater part."[16]

To this point, apart from the quality of his formulation, Montesquieu
has said nothing especially original. Statists and natural-law philosophers
had already brought charges of iniquity against despotism, and Bodin,
Loyseau, and Moreau, as well as Diderot, Rousseau, and Mably had all
sought words adequate to its condemnation. Yet they tended to treat despotism as merely a new term to designate tyranny and the substitution of
arbitrary will for law, a form of government in which terror replaced justice, a regime in which fear took the place of legitimacy. Montesquieu even
says that religion has a place in despotism, albeit only in the form of a
"fear added to fear." If despotism, in sum, was no more than a state without law, then Montesquieu's analysis would have nothing to add to that of
his predecessors. But such is not the case.

For the author of *The Spirit of the Laws*, despotism does not constitute
an addition to the famous Aristotelian triad of good political regimes
(monarchy, aristocracy, republic), nor does it merely reproduce in a new
category the pathology that Aristotle dispersed among the degenerate political forms (tyranny, oligarchy, democracy). Far from lending a new title
to newly reborn tyranny, or persistent feudalism, far from falling within
the traditional taxonomy of past and present regimes, despotism is a type
of government that is essentially foreign for Montesquieu. It is the "other"
state, geographically distant from Europe, socially cut off from Western
civilization. Paul Vernières has made this point graphically: "Montesquieu replaced the tripartition founded on numerical categories [one,
two, three types of regime] with a new spatiotemporal tripartition: present, past, and *distant*."[17] He finds the roots of despotism in Persia, Turkey,
and China, uprooting it from our own genealogy in order to deport it to
Oriental civilization. There follows on this eradication an emigration of
images of absolute power, which until the resurgence of totalitarian states
in the early twentieth century will be associated with exoticism and xeno-
phobia. The consul and the gonfalonier, the marquis and the count, the

duke and the prince, the king and the estate holder, monarch and emperor no longer evoke images of total domination and unregulated power. Those images, under the influence of Montesquieu, attach to foreign titles: sultan, caliph, emir, sheik, pasha, vizir, bey, aga, nabob, rajah, shah, maharajah. As Anquetil-Duperron writes, Montesquieu "fixed our ideas on the nature of despotism," but he did not invent the concept.[18]

At the end of the seventeenth century, the tendency was to compare the evolution of French absolutism with despotic evolution. An explosive pamphlet entitled *The Sighs of France Enslaved* (1681–89) made just that argument, and Pierre Bayle entitles chapters 64 and 65 of his 1784 *Reply to the Questions of a Provincial* "On Despotism," a trait that Fénelon had attributed to Louis XIV. In these polemics, the traditional juristic critique of a regime in which subjects are treated as goods gives way to a simple incrimination of the absence of liberty; the indifference toward servitude, likewise, contrasts with the extreme sensitivity to tyranny.[19] Initiated by the "clan of dukes" grouped around Saint-Simon toward the end of Louis XIV's reign and under the regency, the attack against despotism was disseminated by such "intellectuals" as Boulainvilliers. In reality, antidespotism was for a long time essentially aristocratic.

By designating despotism as an impending danger rather than one that had been overcome, Montesquieu reshuffled the cards, mainly for the benefit of those who were not watching carefully enough. If we let ourselves forget that he was participating in the general effort of the feudal philosophy to deny the defects of feudalism and to disassociate the critique of despotism from the critique of feudal domination, we may indeed be fooled. The critique of the despotic state is in fact a diversion, a masking of the feudal helmet under the veils of the seraglio.

Prior to Montesquieu, indeed, statists and natural-right theorists had demonstrated the parallels between Oriental despotism and Western feudalism. They had identified the recent past as the dividing line and vilified the inferno from which we had emerged rather than the satanic future that threatened. In meting out the derisive titles of tyrant and despot, the jurists had sought to discredit a more formidable enemy than the Turk or Persian, a more familiar foe than the Oriental tyrant; they sought to bring dishonor on feudal power. We might never have lost sight of this if the early modern critique of feudalism had not been obscured in the nineteenth century by the blinding light of feudalism's armor. Marx participates in this enterprise. In keeping with the conventional wisdom of his day, he exalted the "heavenly ecstasies of religious fervour," and "indefeasible chartered freedoms" of the Middle Ages, soon to be drowned in the bourgeoisie's "icy water of egotistical calculation."[20] The compelling historical work of Bloch, Elias, Duby, Le Goff, and Le Roy Ladurie has shown us the role of plunder in feudal life, the insecurity that prevailed, and the burdens laid on the peasant laborer by the generalized state of war characteristic of feudal anarchy. These realities fail to excite in us the nostalgia for "patriarchal, idyllic relations" that gripped Marx.

## Sovereign Power Is Not Feudal

For the jurists, feudalism was the antithesis of the sovereign state, just as the suzerain was the opposite of the sovereign: "suzerainty: a word as strange as its referent is absurd," writes Loyseau.[21] His critique may seem disconcerting, for before becoming sovereign princes, the kings of France, lords of their realms, "universal and above all," had by no means disdained the perquisites of suzerainty.

In the course of its development, the French monarchy was astute enough to take advantage of medieval principles and the support lent it by feudal structures. Mandated by God, traditional royalty represented the interests of the realm as a whole, *utilitas totius regni,* and was responsible for defending the kingdom against external enemies, *tuitio regni.* To this end, the king had the right to levy troops and to call the barons together, and his justice was sovereign. Monarchs sought also to transform feudal ties into means of governing and to remedy the administrative difficulties that arose in the wake of the Carolingian wars. They tried to multiply their vassals and to impose feudal obligations on the great lords. But that was not all. The arsenal of power was the site of a battle between sovereignty and suzerainty. At least in the French state, right up to the Revolution, a dual structure of power prevailed: the monarchs invoked their power as suzerain when that was convenient, and their authority as sovereign if a situation dictated that. It is this composite character of the French monarchy that distinguishes it from the British Crown and that lies at the heart of the many misconceived debates between historians over which of these two faces of the monarchy was its true one. Earlier historians were sensitive to this difficulty. Dareste de La Chavanne, for example, explains that

> the royals were no longer content with the patrimonial rights of suzerainty. They wanted to join to it the political rights of sovereignty. . . . All the kings were simultaneously sovereigns and suzerains. As suzerains, they presided over feudal structures; as sovereigns, they combated these very structures.[22]

What the jurists defend is sovereignty, or at least its ideal and essence. The partisans of royal power do not hesitate to attack feudalism when it suits their purposes. From Jean Bodin to Jacob-Nicolas Moreau, with the partisans of the doctrine of popular sovereignty in tow, the attack on feudalism is the common thread.

The critique of sovereignty revolves around two themes, themes that the jurists, far from inventing, borrow from the aristocracy, and which stigmatize feudal lords as conquerors and masters. Sixteenth-century legal theorists took as their task not so much the comparison among historical representations of feudalism as an engagement with the models of power contesting each other in their age. The lack of historical foundation for their conception is of little import here, since their achievements as historians interest us less than their political reflections. Sovereign power, in their view, was the antithesis of feudal power. In what respect? In the sense that it was neither *imperium* nor *dominium*. It was not an *imperium*, because it was not based on military power, and it was not a *dominium*, because it did not institute a relation of subjection, in the manner of the relation between a master and a slave.

The *imperium* was the totality of civil and military powers possessed first by the Roman kings, then under the republic by the consuls and (during their tenure) the dictators, and finally by the Roman emperors. Their powers included the right to command the army, the right to wage war and make peace (*jus belli ac pacis*), and the right of life and death (*jus vitae necisque*). In itemizing the attributes of the *imperium*, one will have itemized the royal powers. But the *imperium* is also the empire, the Roman conception of power that the Germanic Holy Roman Empire would seek to resuscitate, beginning with Otto. The early modern jurists sought to distinguish sharply between sovereign power and imperial power, so as to show that the sovereign state is not a creature of war but rather of peace, and that it prefers the pacific negotiation of rights to the clamor of arms.

This explains the return, signaled by Machiavelli, of a conception of justice based on the peaceful operations of law, and of a political philosophy that admires above all the Roman republic. The history of Rome, and the passage from republic to empire, becomes the crossroads of all political comparisons. The *majestas* is rediscovered, and the title of "prince," immortalized by Machiavelli, unseats that of "lord."

Still, the theory of sovereignty was by no means always anti-imperialist. By the end of the Middle Ages, the extension and acceptance of Roman law had been assured throughout Western Europe by the work of Francesco Accursius in the thirteenth century and the constitution of the *Corpus Iuris Canonici* in the fourteenth. At this point, the royalist jurists did their utmost to co-opt the notion of *imperium* for the monarchs. The kings were subject to the papacy and the Germanic Holy Roman Empire, a subjection of the temporal to the spiritual modeled on that of vassal to suzerain. Any proclamation of royal sovereignty, especially when cast as *suprema potestas* or absolute sovereignty, had the appearance of a declaration of independence. After the rescue of imperial dignity by Otto in 962, the *imperium* was the main legal argument on which the German emperors stood. The apologists of the Holy Empire, most notably the four counselors of Frederick Barbarossa, sought to give Roman law the status of *lex generalis*. They invoked the formulas of Roman absolutism and adopted the nomenclature of the regalia in order to portray the emperor as master of the world and of the living law. In order to contest these claims, the kings of France and England deployed two expedients. The first of these was the relegation of Roman law to the status of foreign agent, that is, an agent of Germanicity. In France, its sphere of application was limited to the Midi, where it persisted *consensus populi et ex permissione regis*. The teaching of Roman law was suppressed by the decree *Super Specula*, which Philip II extracted from the pope in 1219, and the renewal of the ban by Philip IV in 1312 remained in effect until 1673. The second stratagem of the monarchs was the appeal to texts on sovereignty. "What pleases the Prince is law," one finds in an anonymous book, originating in Orleans, entitled *Jostice et plet;* "What he wishes to do should be upheld as law," Beaumanoir writes in his book, *Les Coutumes de Beauvoisis;* "for the King has no sovereign among temporal things," we are told by *Les Établissements de Saint Louis*.[23] The British kings, too, laid claim to the imperial title.[24] At this stage, use of the notion of *imperium* was largely defensive and polemical. It is in the reign of Philip IV that the jurists put their cards on the table in deploying the formula that holds that "the King of France is emperor in his kingdom."

This formula envisaged the king as the equal rather than the vassal of the Holy Roman Emperor. Sovereignty, in this sense, was a late arrival relative to royalty and monarchy, and its triumph, as the German jurist Georg Jellinek rightly emphasized, was by no means foreordained. The doctrine, as well as respect of it, evolved slowly, in the course of the battle against the powers of the church, the empire, and the seignories, all of whom threatened the fragile inroads made by the state.[25] In the meantime, the enemy had changed. The external rivals give way to internal adversaries, and the doctrines of sovereignty were erected polemically against feudalism. Bodin proclaims, with a certain amount of arrogance, that "a definition of sovereignty is needed because no jurist and no political philosopher has yet provided one."[26] Henceforth feudalism is the primary opponent of the sovereign state.

The jurists believed that feudal power militarized politics and individualized justice. Its critique required an attack on two principles. First, that power is essentially force. Feudal power is always acquired "at the end of a gun" or, as Duplessis-Mornay puts it, "at the end of a sword, a shield, and a standard."[27] Bodin distinguishes between the functions of royal and feudal monarchies:

> Royal, or legitimate, monarchy is that monarchy in which the subjects obey the laws of the monarch, and the monarch obeys the laws of nature. . . . Feudal monarchy is that monarchy in which the prince is made lord of goods and persons by the right of arms and of effective war.[28]

Loyseau reinforces the point: "Feudal monarchy is always introduced by force alone, either by internal usurpation or by foreign conquest."[29] J. N. Moreau, on the eve of the Revolution, denounces just this feature of feudalism:

> The same era that sees our kings stripped of their authority witnesses the annihilation or, if you prefer, the suspension of all political legislation. There is no cooperation in governance between the monarch and the vassals. They are at war with each other.[30]

These views necessitate a careful division of powers between feudal lords and sovereigns. The realm of feudalism corresponds spatially and temporally to the realm of conquest: the great civilizations of the past (Assyria, Asia, ancient Persia), colonial empires of the present and future.[31] Bodin perceptively designates the colonies of Charles V in Peru as feudal. He points to the surviving domains of his day, residues and "offshoots," such as "the remaining signs of feudal monarchy in Germany."[32] And Loyseau catalogs the Oriental feudal regimes, Turkey, Muscovy, Ethiopia, which Montesquieu will call cases of controlled despotism. The world-historical and prehistorical perspective on the feudal regime clues us in to Montesquieu's subterfuge, his substitution of despotism for feudalism as his target. For Montesquieu, despotism is an Oriental threat hanging over our own liberty-loving aristocracies. For the jurists, feudalism is a past political regime that everywhere overflows feudal borders. (This is not to say that the jurists idealize the feudal regime; on the contrary, they identified it with the feudal.) Brought to power either by conquest or by plunder, feudalism is regarded with contempt, because it reduces law to force, and justice to victory in war. One hears premonitions of Rousseau when Loyseau writes that:

> rational justification of feudal law is made even more difficult by domains' having been established by means of chaos, by force and usurpation; it has proved impossible to bring order to this chaos, to transform this force into law, to impose reason on this usurpation.[33]

More than a century before Rousseau, then, the claim that "might does not make right, and that one *is* only obligated to obey legitimate powers" takes its place in political discourse.[34]

The second principle on which early modernity would focus its attack assimilates justice to combat and order to equilibrium in a battle. The statists support the monarchical project of attaining a monopoly on justice and on punishment, which involves eliminating both the private feudal wars and the ecclesiastical tribunals. When Charles Dumoulin chronicles the advance of regal power, he adopts an openly Gallic and antipapal posture in the dispute between *sacerdotium* and *regnum* and defends lay

justice.[35] Earlier, Claude de Seyssel, who betrays a number of Machiavel-
lian sentiments, nevertheless confidently affirms the supremacy of public
justice over force. The former, he writes, is

> the true pillar of royal authority, for by means of justice, the prince is obeyed
> everywhere similarly. If he relied on force, he would need to have an army
> posted through-out the regime. Yet even then, violence is less powerful than
> justice, for people naturally resist force, but willingly obey the ministers of
> justice.[36]

The point is not embroidered with narrative or reportage. In reading the
early modern jurists, one encounters none of the indignant accounts of the
abuses committed by "feudal justice" and the havoc wrought by private
wars.[37] Nor do they explain the historical process by which modern justice
establishes itself, substituting its motto *pax et justitia* for the Saxon motto
*bellum et justitia* and securing a statist monopoly on violence and a juridification of social conflict.[38] From reading the early modern jurists, one
would never suspect the role of the church, by dint of its evocation of
divine peace, nor that of the security and order imposed by the kings, nor
the economic conditions—all the factors that ultimately conspired to drive
out the private wars that constituted medieval justice. These writers are
not seeking reasons for bitterness about the past but rather the principles
that would pave the way for the present and future. Among these principles, the object of universal admiration, is that by which justice was made
the business of the state. "The lords of France (who have converted minis-
tries into domains) have usurped the duties of justice."[39] Those duties,
according to Loyseau, belong irrevocably to the state and are inseparable
from the public authorities. Feudalism is war, *jus vitae necisque*, conscrip-
tion of human life; sovereign power is peace, security, and prohibition of
the taking of human life. It substitutes law for force and order for death.
It consists of a powerful constraint on the Roman *patriae potestas*, on the
right to determine who shall live and who shall die. It pacifies society,
guarantees individual security, and makes life its chief aim. It is the product of a negotiation of rights rather than an expiation of arms.

This is not the era of "biopolitics," of therapeutic technologies, demo-
graphic regulation, and pedagogical and penal discipline, the nineteenth-
century development chronicled by Foucault.[40] But a symbolic politics of
life has emerged. Feudalism was war; now the sovereign state promises
peace.

*Dominium* is subjugation, appropriation by a master of a human being
as if he or she were a thing. The jurists take care to disqualify mastery as
a definition of power; they reject the feudal relation of dependence and
criticize servitude generally. Vassalage, villenage, and servitude are direct
relationships and confer power over a human body. "Oppressed" as we

are by the abstract, mediated, impersonal social relations of our own day,
we can easily forget how concrete, how direct, how "human, all too
human" were the feudal "relations of dependence."[41] Likewise, when we
object to the merely "formal" liberties that in modern states guarantee the
rights of man and citizen, we are careful not to mention the real chains
that fastened faith and life. Feudal domination was direct; it vassalized the
individual, naturalized men, and privatized politics. This raised three
questions to which statists sought to reply in the negative:

*Must subjects be treated as slaves?* Feudalism "governs its subjects as
the father of a family does his slaves," writes Bodin.[42] Likewise Loyseau:
"Feudal monarchy runs directly counter to nature, which has made us all
free. . . . Private seignory may be used at one's discretion and as one
wishes; but public seignory concerns those things that belong to other people, people who are free." Two doctrines—that of property and that of the
appropriation by each individual of himself—rule out domination as a
definition of politics. The relation between governed and governing is understood here as a compromise; only later, with the natural-law philosophers, will the model shift to that of a contract. But the compromise model
suffices to eliminate a series of traditional references: master and servant,
commander and soldier, father and son. Most importantly, the classical
model of the social relation as that between freeman and slave is decisively
broken with. Henceforth, the sovereign who abstains from taking the life
or property of his subjects is no longer acting as master. The jurists invoke
Christian principles in order to align feudalism with Greek slavery. Nietzsche is not without justification in viewing the modern state as "a compromise with the slaves."

*Must human beings be treated as things?* Should the relations between
human beings in society be modeled on the relations between humanity
and nature? The medieval view defended social microcosms by appeal to
physical macrocosms and viewed human beings as a form of nature
among other forms of nature. The jurists, by contrast, view the possessions
and life of each individual, *imperium in imperio,* as the unbreachable limit
of political dependence. Bodin defines these individual rights in terms of
"natural liberty and the natural right to property."[43] This nominalist view
privileges subjectivity and interprets the political animal as the product of
a culture that is opposed to nature. Modern mechanics transformed the
definition of nature by replacing Aristotle's hierarchical and qualitative
cosmos, a world in which the laws of nature are inequality and difference,
with an infinite universe, quantitative and homogeneous in all directions,
the laws of which are equality and isotropy. This change will permit the
natural-law philosophers to invoke nature itself as an argument against
domination. Within the *res publica* (*res natura* or not), the individual
himself is no longer a thing of which one can become master and proprie-

tor. The techniques of governing a *res cogitans* cannot be derived from the rules for possession of a *res extensa*. Moral beings, writes Pufendorf, are not things like physical beings; "they only possess each other by means of institutions."[44]

*Do political relationships derive from property relationships?* In a definition that would obsess the historiography of the nineteenth century, Loyseau calls feudalism "power by means of property." This deep truth leads to a fundamental objection against feudalism: it confuses public relationships among individuals with the private relationship between a human being and a thing, treating persons as goods. Jacob-Nicolas Moreau, the royal historiographer, one of the last in this tradition of jurists, summarized on the eve of the Revolution the fundamental vice of feudal government, the confusion of property with power:

> The power of government is thus transformed into the power of property; this disorder is the greatest scourge to be visited upon humanity. . . . Everything that public authority had possessed seems to be a dependency and an attribute of property, and its revenues become the products of feudalism.

This leads to two conflicting agenda in the attack on feudalism: first, to undo the amalgamation of power and property and, second, to secure the autonomy of both the governance of human beings and the possession of things. The stubborn obstinacy with which the jurists pursue this point of view is striking. Loyseau begins by affirming the specificity of public offices relative to property:

> Power is common to feudal lordships and to public offices, but property distinguishes lordships from public offices; the power of the latter derives from the functioning of the office or the exercise of authority, whereas that of the former derives from a property right.

The major premise of this line of reasoning is its claim that public offices belong neither to lords nor to a prince, nor even to the state, for they *are* the state itself. The middle term of the argument is that one cannot possess power as property. The prince does not own his office; it is not his property:

> *Princeps* in Latin and *prince* in French designate, properly speaking and originally, the premier chief, the premier officer of the state who has the premier authority to command and sovereign power, but not in the form of property. . . . He is charged with administration and, like any officer, must carry out the tasks with which he is charged.[45]

Consistently in light of his other views, Loyseau thus rejects the patrimoniality of offices.[46] Moreau will go even further: only an office, he holds, possesses authority, and only a magistracy holds power. Land and property, always private, are bereft of power.[47]

If there is a fundamental difference between early modern political and legal theory, on the one hand, and nineteenth-century social philosophy on the other, it is that the former seeks to dissociate power from property, and the latter ties politics firmly to economics. "The spirit of the laws," writes Simon-Nicolas Linguet, "is property." Marx registers perfectly this monumental shift, which its authors try awkwardly to dissemble. The only real relations are property relations. Marx cites Linguet in order to develop his own conception of the relationship between law and politics, on the one hand, and economics on the other; he devotes an entire chapter to him in *The Theory of Surplus Value*. The distance between Linguet and the early modern theorists is enormous:

> The laws are geared to the securing of property. And since one can take much more from those who have much than from those who have nothing, the laws are of course a means for protecting the rich from the poor. . . . Therein lies their true spirit; it may or may not be a shortcoming, but it is inseparable from their existence.[48]

This rejection of the doctrine of the independence and transcendence of politics, a doctrine dear to the early modern political theorists, is the point of departure for later "social" theory. The notion of the "power of property," of the spirit of the laws as the spirit of property, has in the wake of Marx been applied to all forms of society; the jurists had applied it only to feudalism. It is no exaggeration to say that social theory exercises a return to the seignorial doctrine; having shed its commitment to the independence of the legal and political realm, it winds up holding that the social is all there is. Swimming against the current, Moreau defended the traditional view throughout the 1780s. Public law is not, he insisted, an emanation from private law, and political relations do not derive from property.[49] For the early modern writers, the individual is not a slave, a thing, or property in any sense, but rather a subject, a person, a locus of liberty. The monarchy and the state profess to enlarge precisely what feudalism sought to annihilate. The hour of the declaration of the rights of man has not yet arrived, nor has the call to class emancipation been sounded. Yet the doctrine of power limited by individual rights has already made itself heard. Feudalism was servitude; the sovereign state heralds enfranchisement.

Only after its expression by the jurists do the natural-law philosophers and advocates of popular sovereignty take up these two principles: that sovereign power confers no right over human lives and that human beings cannot be property. Locke maintains that political society is neither conjugal nor parental, nor "dominial" (if the neologism can be permitted). Indeed political society exists only where men have agreed, in order to preserve their "lives, liberty, and property." Property most of all. Locke privileges property, "the great and chief end . . . of Men's uniting into Commonwealths, and putting themselves under Government," to the same extent that Hobbes privileges security to substitute public justice and law for private justice and war.[50] The notion of political power as a property right is discarded at the same time as its prime duty is made the protection of individuals' private property. The despotic power of the feudal lords is to be exercised only on those who are stripped of all property as a result of some irremediable "defect."[51]

The firm distinction between private and public domains undermines the patrimonial doctrine of power that assimilates sovereignty to a monarch's possessions. As a result, a debate over the origin and limits of sovereignty is opened up. Relying on the public nature of sovereign power, Loyseau argues that offices do not belong either to the magistrates who fill them, to the lords, or to the state; rather, they *are* the state. Later, Barbeyrac, Diderot, and Rousseau will place patrimonial monarchy in the category of despotism and defend the popular origin of inalienable and indivisible sovereignty.

Does sovereign power remain a form of mastery? Rousseau says no: "A free people obeys but does not serve; it has leaders but no masters; it obeys laws but it obeys only laws."[52] This explains the semantic reorientation of the term *dominium*. For the Romans, it designates ownership of property and is grounded in actual possession rather than law.[53] Hobbes, for instance, writes of the mastery of slaves or infants, but whereas the Latin would mark the singularity of animals by *potestas dominica* or *patria potestas*, Hobbes rejects the Latin terms out of hand. The definition of *dominium* as property-power and power-property was accepted by the early modern writers at the expense of feudalism. Feudal individualism had drawn up a list of rights as an extension of the power to subjugate and appropriate. The early modern political doctrine, by contrast, proclaims that politics is not servitude, nor is its foundation property.

To say that power is not feudal dominion was no trifling matter, especially given the fact that day and night one prayed to the Lord of all things. Indeed, the prince refrained steadfastly from challenging God, from secularizing faith. He recognized the hierarchy that placed below him a visible limit to the individual rights of his subjects, and above him an invisible barrier to divine transcendence. The kings of France, no matter how absolutist their tendencies, never crowned themselves in the way that the emperor did, the way that held such fascination for the German nationalists: sacred, anointed by the Lord God, and subjected to a higher transcendence. Royalty was feudal dominion for a long time; sovereignty would never take the form of suzerainty. Modern sovereign power defined itself by opposition to domination based on either force or mastery. To those who reproach it for being imperial or dominating, one can simply reply that five centuries ago, the jurists threw the imperial and dominial doctrine of power out of court.

## So What Is Sovereignty?

In the course of depicting the splendors of coronation, André Duchesne shows how the mortality of kings is outweighed by the immortality of the crown, how the petrification and degeneration that takes place underneath the robes and scepter is of little account. The sovereign, it seems, is not the same as sovereignty.[54] Sovereignty articulates a threefold conception of the state: external independence, internal coherence, and supremacy of the law. Let us review them in order.

*External independence.* Sovereignty is the principle of autonomy with respect to foreign powers. "The king has no sovereign among temporal things," as *Les Établissements de Saint Louis* would have it. The final emancipation from the pope was proclaimed as early as 1324 by Marsilius of Padua in his *Defensor pacis* and later in his *Defensor minor,* as well as by William of Ockham in his *Breviloquium.* Here the realm of politics confronted the realm of theology in order to defend the temporal rule of kings and to recast in moral terms the secular aims of the state. The lay aspirations reached their zenith in Grotius's bold claim, much admired by the natural-law philosophers, that "everything we have just said [about the organization of the state] would hold true in one way or another even if one granted—what one cannot grant without committing a horrible crime—that God did not exist, or that he exists but takes no interest in human affairs." Liberty is demanded, liberty from the empire and from those states that understand sovereignty as the "internal milieu," in the sense in which the physiologists use the term, a sense utterly different from the *imperium romanum.* Hitherto, the world had been a fallow land, open for occupation to the extent that, lacking time or troops, the Roman legions had not yet reached it. Sovereign states tend their own garden incessantly and expand only in order to better exclude the outside world. A new, "intensive political culture" takes the place of the extensive militarization of the ancient and Germanic worlds. Was this but a pause before the "civilization" of Africa and the dismemberment of China, which the Western nation-states would undertake in the nineteenth and twentieth centuries? Not quite. Among the intermittent chaos of invasions and the brutality of battle, a logic of plurality prevails: there are many states. *The*

Holy Roman Empire, Rome, Christianity are no longer the animating forces. The world of balances of power has begun. One aspires to be first, but *nec pluribus impar*, as Louis XIV put it. It is no longer possible to be the lone possessor of the world. The dream of Charles V, which permeated the Spain of Philip II, met its end at the hands of the English fleet. The absoluteness of sovereignty does not compromise the multiplicity of nation-states. Pufendorf and the Salamanca school reinvent the *jus gentium* in order to regulate relations among states.

*Internal coherence.* In a sense, the European wars were continuations either of the old feudal ambitions of expanding the fief, stretching the bounds of one's possessions, evicting the occupant; or of the ancient drive to annex and colonize. But in another sense, they differed markedly. They consisted of territorialization, manipulation of internal geography—work, as it were, behind closed doors. Machiavelli and Claude de Seyssel catalog the means available for naturalizing conquests and obscuring the hardships of annexation. Methodically, slowly, not without a certain amount of sadism, the states adopting the rule of law set about cutting back the brush of the old topographies in order to make their territories administrable. They seek to "officialize" society; the legal, economic, and military systems are used to harmonize and parcel out the territory. This enormous feat of legal and political cultivation levels the soil, compiles cadastres, and remakes maps. Rare survivals of feudal geopolitics today, such as Monaco and Andorra, are like wild shoots or weeds that the planters of the new fields overlooked. As a result of peripheral autonomy, political society must be defined outward from the center with an umbilical cord connecting the subject to the king, the citizen to the republic. The republic is "rightly ordered" and endowed with "sovereign power," says Bodin.[55] The idea is not only that the family, as Aristotle noted, is the primary social unit, but to bring together society and the state, community and sovereignty, within a single body politic. Instead of separating *Gesellschaft* (society) from *Gemeinschaft* (community), as the German romantics did, Bodin makes one derive from the other. Sovereignty is public authority, and internal cohesion is the basis both of the republic and of emancipation from external powers.[56] Loyseau, too, places great emphasis on the internalness of sovereignty and adopts Bodin's vocabulary of *suprema potestas*.[57] Sovereignty is the power of a body closed in on itself, an interior life that fosters and maintains a consensus; it never openly challenges community, even if its definition remains uncertain when it meets with a hierarchical society that maintains a division of orders. For Thomists, it is an institution, a consortium in which individual good is included in the common good. For Hobbesians, it is an obligation, a *vinculum*, a contract, less an internalized institutional relation than an explicit contractual relation.[58] The very nature of a social contract is an object of debate: a pact of submission, as Pufendorf conceives it, or of association, as Rousseau insists. But beyond the plurality of definitions, the forging of a political-civil unity, of the body politic, freed from relations of intersubjective dependence, is the persistent theme.

*Supremacy of the law*. There remains the definition of sovereignty as an absolute. It is an equivocal definition, to be sure, one which first arose in the midst of the civil war between Protestants and the Catholic League, while Henry III was in grave danger. Bodin, the doctrine's author, writes of an "absolute and perpetual power in a republic that the Latins called *majestatem*"; a similar view is taken by other expositors, Loyseau, Hobbes, and Domat.[59] "Sovereignty," writes Bodin, "is not limited either in power, or in function, or in length of time."[60] Absolute authority, absolute weight, absolute duration, such is the supremacy of sovereignty. Does this amount to a profanation, this transfer of supremacy previously reserved to God? Perhaps not. Is it a preeminence of the sovereign over sovereignty, or of authority over the law? In fact, it is neither of these. Nor is it supremacy of the sovereign, for even the most fervent defenders of monarchy affirm the indifference of the principle of sovereignty with respect to the different types of regime, namely, monarchy, aristocracy, and democracy.[61]

For most of the jurists, the doctrine of sovereignty is closely linked with the exaltation of the monarchy: "monarchy is the most universal, most ancient, most natural, and most efficient of regimes."[62] Yet they never confuse their thesis about the power *of* the state with their view about the highest power *in* the state, to adopt the felicitous formula of Jellinek. Sovereign power, though absolute, is always limited. In the absence of limitation, sovereignty would be no different from feudal dominion. The limitations stem from the law in its three incarnations, divine, natural, and fundamental.[63] The absolute sovereign, Domat explains, has not only rights but also duties. With respect to divine law, his duty is to conform law to justice.[64] With respect to natural law, he must respect the personal rights of his subjects, their liberty and property. The citizen of a Bodinian republic is neither a slave nor a subject, but a "free subject" who participates in political society, and who "has a right to life and limb and to association, and certain other privileges" as well as "access to all or certain offices and benefits from which foreigners are excluded," and the right to will his property as he sees fit, and so forth.[65] Among fundamental laws, finally, the laws of the crown, the Salic law, inheritance, and inalienability of royal domains are those most often alluded to.[66] On this issue, the "liberal" theorists of the natural-law school, Pufendorf, Grotius, Barbeyrac, Burlamaqui, and others, are not the innovators they are sometimes taken to be.[67] When Jurieu writes that "one must distinguish carefully between two things that many people confuse, namely, absolute power and power without limits, as if they were one and the same thing," he is walking through a door already open.[68] The most zealous partisans—and most servile subjects—of royalty made precisely the same distinction.

Consider Bossuet, the ardent, pitiless adversary of Fénelon, who had courageously censured monarchical despotism. Bossuet also forcefully opposes arbitrary or absolute government.[69] Even if the only guarantee he imagines to check the will of the prince is submission to divine law, he takes great pains to distinguish between arbitrary government, propelled by caprices and whims, and absolute monarchy, which is ruled by law. Consider Massillon, who, in a sermon for Palm Sunday, informs kings that they "do not command slaves, [they] command a free and bellicose nation, as jealous of its liberty as of its faith."[70] It is not the sovereign, then, but law that should govern peoples. The priests who consecrate absolutism and elevate the authority of kings above human power do not fail to contain the magnificence of the kings below the higher splendor of God. They confer on spiritual power the means of control that the nobility and the parliamentarians sought to reserve to "intermediate bodies." All conspire to establish the supremacy of laws over kings. Hence the king, even if he is "above the laws," is never "lord of the laws," as Duplessis-Mornay puts it. The doctrine of sovereignty exploits the burgeoning growth of the legislative function. Citing Pindar, Bodin observes that when "the prince obeys the laws of nature, and the people the civil laws," "the law is king," and that tyranny is the regime in which the laws are disregarded.[71]

The doctrine of sovereignty that establishes the supremacy of the state and the legitimacy of this supremacy does not defend power without limits but rather a self-determined power that recognizes no restraints other than the law that it gives itself. It countenances no subjection which emanates from beyond its borders but constrains and restrains itself by the instauration of a legal order on which it depends. "Sovereignty has the exclusive capacity to determine itself and to restrain itself from the perspective of the law" (Jellinek). Kant's notion of individual morality as self-legislation by a good will is modeled on the politico-legal notion of sovereign power.

The omnipotence of the state is, then, quite intentional. It concerns law and the constitution of authority subject to law. The limitation of the state by law is more durable than any particular limitation of sovereignty, and the former begins with the notion of individual rights.

# CHAPTER III

# Human Rights

According to natural law, everyone is born free. As a result of certain traditions and customs which have been honored for a long time, and occasionally as a result of misconduct by their predecessors, many of our common people have fallen into a condition of servitude. In consideration of this fact and other conditions which displease us, we note that our kingdom has been called and named the realm of freemen (that is, Franks), and we seek to bring the reality into conformity with the name and to improve the condition of the people.

—Louis X, "The Quarreller"

Not all rights are alienable.

—Hobbes

Individual rights, or human rights as they are called today, are less recent acquisitions than we tend to think. Faced with Amnesty International's battery of accusations in the form of numbered, itemized, quantified documents depicting the daily attacks on individual rights by states—entombment in dungeons without rhyme or reason, condemnations without trial, tortures conducted patiently and systematically—we are driven to attach ourselves to a Robinson Crusoe myth. According to this myth, there arose, at the beginning of the eighteenth century, a new island, this absolute beginning called the individualist doctrine of human rights. Pure, smooth, round, healthy, and naked, this doctrine was like the noble savage, the Huron, the Iroquois, the Caribbean. In the dark megalopolis, suffocated by noise and smog, it is still comforting to imagine this new doctrine conferring on each of us our own code of laws. We are tired of immense collectivities, the eternal winters of the modern state; we long for "small," immediate, and private liberty. The state of nature fascinates and entices us. We imagine human rights as a text wielded defiantly by a single individual against all comers, an immense and singular banner constituting an entire parade by itself.

In reality, though, there can be found among the early modern French and English theorists a doctrine of individual rights that is neither liberal nor democratic in the modern sense, a doctrine that can be extracted neither from the narrowly individualist premises dear to liberals nor from the populist demands so highly valued by democrats. This doctrine is neither "civil" nor "social" but rather arises from a resolutely "statist" perspective, which places a premium on defining the relationship between, and the limits of, the rights of authorities and the rights of individuals. The doctrine of individual rights was not born with the eighteenth-century declarations of rights, the most famous of which are the French and American, nor was it coextensive with the development of civil liberties that took place largely in the nineteenth century. It was neither capitalistic nor linked to the movement that magnified the claims of society against the state. Nor, on the other hand, do its roots lie in the ancient political democracies that recognized the rights of a minority of free males.

Three conditions are necessary for a doctrine of human rights. First, human beings as such must be recognized as having value. Second, this recognition must be given legal expression. Finally, this legal status must be guaranteed by political authorities. The idea of the human being is biblical. The Old Testament provides us with a conception of human persons as possessing inalienable value by virtue of their being created by God and joined to him in a covenant; their collective destiny, sealed by the law, has transcendent meaning. The New Testament adds the further notion of an individual's having inalienable value since his salvation, through redemption, is an individual matter. These notions of the human being are not to be found among ancient writers, whose world consisted of Greeks and Romans on the one hand, barbarians on the other; citizens and free men on the one hand, servants and slaves on the other. For this reason, the doctrine of humanity was at first a purely theological doctrine, defined in part by Augustinianism and institutionalized by Gregory VII when he imposed on the penitent of Canossa the doctrine of the separation of spiritual and temporal powers, affirming that no authority could appropriate a human being. Next, in the thirteenth century, the Franciscan nominalists blazed the *via moderna*, which proclaimed the existence of individual and subjective rights. Duns Scotus, the *"doctor subtilis,"* mistrusted the natural order and valorized the willing individual. William of Ockham, the *"venerabilis inceptor,"* companion of Marsilius of Padua at the court of Louis of Bavaria, introduced a notion of subjective rights that broke with Roman law as well as with Thomist legal theory.[1] Finally, the jurists of the French and English states under the rule of law brought the idea of inalienable individual rights into the framework of early modern political right. Why, one might ask, did the gap between the theological conception of humanity and the politico-legal realm take so long to bridge? Why 1788 and 1789, the Bill of Rights and the fall of the Bastille? Why was it only in the eighteenth century that the declarations of the rights of man rang out clearly and loudly?

### Human Liberty and Civil Liberty

In the doctrine of human rights, there are two distinct aspects, human liberty and civil liberty, which we may call *status libertatis* and *status civitatis*. *Status libertatis* has to do with liberty and personal security, the right of each person to his own body, the right to life. *Status civitatis* pertains to citizenship, to civil liberties, and to political rights.[2]

Since the eighteenth century, liberal theorists have accustomed us to confining human rights to liberties, to *status civitatis*—freedom of opinion, assembly, association, property, and so on—and to neglecting personal security and liberty. Civil liberties are, to be sure, more modern; they imply a share in, and oversight of, government by the citizens and are hence closely tied to the rise of democracy. Yet, paradoxical as it may seem, these liberties have their roots in private contracts among peers, in feudal relations of dependence, and in privileges. Their origin, as Boulainvilliers, Montesquieu, and Tocqueville recognized, was essentially aristocratic.

The concept of a subjective right simply cannot be found in Roman law.[3] By confining the legal status of autonomous subjects to male heads of families and by exacerbating the alienation of slaves, women, and children, the Roman jurists generalized what modern law has made a rare entitity: lack of legal power. They also narrowed the juridification of individual liberties. Although Rome was effective in protecting certain liberties and civil realities—proper marriages, the family, and (to a lesser extent) the liberties of inheritance law—it did not guarantee individual security, the right to act as one sees fit, freedom of conscience, of assembly, of association, and so forth.[4]

Whence come these civil liberties? Recall what Montesquieu says of representative government: "This beautiful system was found in the woods." The author of *The Spirit of the Laws* subscribed to a Germanic origin of liberty and was convinced that monarchies remained free to the extent that they conserved the spirit of the German founders. He glorified the peoples of the North, "these brave nations who sallied forth from their own lands in order to destroy tyrants and slaves."[5] He shared with the (pre)liberal theorists of the eighteenth century the idea that the barbarian warriors, violent of spirit but never oppressive in practice, had brought the energetic principle of independence to the Gauls, who had been softened by a decadent despotism.[6] He thought that liberty emanated from feudal grants of rights and privileges, that its etymology was its essence, an element of the private law of the Franks, those architects of the feudal regime. The majority of the "Germanist" historians likewise counted the liberal idea among the positive contributions that the German tribes had exported throughout Europe and that generated the aristocratic oligarchies.[7] Marc Bloch's work supported this interpretation. He showed that feudalism could not be reduced to a unilateral hierarchy. To the extent that the suzerain pledged to protect his vassal, the relation of dependence, documented by oaths and itemizations of rights and duties, took the reciprocal form of a personal contract.[8]

At the heart of the feudal anarchy that succeeded the collapse of ancient civilization, faced with threats from both within and without, various groups spontanteously came together and fell into hierarchies. Gradually and laboriously, there emerged the idea of an organic ensemble of reciprocal services and duties, subject to the tacit clause in a contract to which the superior was party and that bound him at the same time as it obligated the inferior. The development of civil society may be rooted in this reciprocal contract between free persons, which New Testament principles contributed a great deal to strengthening. According to this line of thought, then, one should seek the origin of liberty and of the individual contract in those feudal privileges that were independent of royal power and the direct links of dependence. The greater or lesser liberality of the various European countries is seen as a function of the power of the aristocracy. France, where the role of the nobility was abolished, provides a negative counterpoint to the shining example of the German aristocratic entrenchment.

Despite the narcissistic wound it inflicts on democratic pretensions, this attempt to provide an aristocratic lineage for liberty barely merits discussion. To ascribe a feudal origin to individual liberty and its legal recognition is to mistake a part for the whole, the part being *independence* in contrast to *liberation, autonomy* in contrast to *emancipation, liberties* rather than *liberty*. Independence and autonomy are indeed inextricably linked to the existence of an independent realm and a protected enclave within a coercive setting, reduced as this enclave may be. Liberties, in the form of individual private rights, have the same origin as feudal liberties; they express personal privileges. Hence the indispensable role of aristocracies—oligarchies, elites, alternative centers of power—in the defense of liberties. It is no accident that the defense of freedom of conscience—for instance, by libertine intellectuals—was supported by the greatest feudal lords. In Czarist Russia, as in revolutionary France, the defeat of the aristocracy dealt a withering blow to liberty.

The feudal theorists, then, are right to say that the aristocracies invented liberties. But they did not discover America, imagine liberation and emancipation from slavery, the rule of law, or habeas corpus. The liberty of the serf came about without them and often despite their opposition. Christianity, which proclaimed the supreme dignity of the human being, contributed far more to the process by which slavery became indefensible. It was the kings who published edicts enfranchising the serfs in the royal domains, and it was the British idea of the rule of law that, still more precociously, guaranteed free disposition of one's own body, a shift that constitutes the origin of both liberty and property. Liberty is not exhausted by the right to make contracts; it begins with the protection of life secured by law. Consequently, subjective rights are directly linked to the conception of power that rejects slavery and dominion. They are inseparable from the new political arrangements and a new conception of rights as law.

Servitude lasted an awfully long time. On the eve of the French Revolution, there were still a hundred thousand serfs in France and slavery was being rapidly reinstituted. Two years after the death of Colbert, the "black code" was promulgated. Yet it was the state under the rule of law that, at least within its borders, undermined the rationale and utility of servitude while its jurists rejected its underlying principles. The demand for civil liberties, for which the heroes of the nineteenth century would give their lives, is absent from the agenda of the early modern jurists. Yet they obstinately and patiently established the foundations for personal security and liberty, those fundamental rights that enabled us to emancipate ourselves from the state of war and servitude, and which we today take for granted. It is worth imagining, however, what it might have meant to a nation of peasants, villeins, and serfs to have received a statute of liberty by which the sovereign state recognized each person's free possession of his own body and the right to dispose of it as he saw fit. Confined as it was to the relation between the central power and its subjects, this event, rather than destroying the feudal relationship, merely supplemented it with a new civil relationship that came to compete with it, undermine it, and in the end destroy it.

The right to liberty was the first of all human rights; but its affirmation by the jurists as a *right* comes quite late. They were quite aware, of course, of the unseemly existence of servitude, and they even attempted on occasion to regulate it. But they treated it as a dispensation from natural law, a survival of feudalism, a relic of the past. True law, they knew, consisted of freedom. "According to natural law, all are free, but freedom can be corrupting," wrote Beaumanoir in the thirteenth century.[9] Recall the words of Louis X, which serve as an epigraph for this chapter, and which were originally addressed to agents charged with liberating a number of prisoners: "According to natural law, everyone is born free."[10] Modern natural law has a different conception of nature from that of the ancients, for whom slavery existed "by nature."[11] Yet again, Antoine Loysel lays great emphasis on the difference between the remnants of servitude in early modern Europe and classical slavery: "there remain serfs in France who are by no means free persons; yet nor are they slaves."[12] Likewise, Guy Coquille: "The conditions of servitude that exist in France are quite different from those prevalent among the Romans, who trafficked in bondservants as they did in beasts."[13] The differences have not only to do with the recognition of some right that was extended to serfs and that contrasted so vividly with the civic nonexistence of slaves. More importantly, the origins of the two statuses were different. Enslavement resulted from war and military defeat, whereas servitude was a product of colonization and economic undertakings.

Under the Old Regime, then, the sovereign recognized the right of every free subject to dispose of his own body as he saw fit and to his own life, but this right never transcended the narrow sphere of political relations, nor did it impugn directly the feudal relations in the domain of the sovereign.[14] Yet the status of liberty was not merely affirmed as a vague principle but theorized by those jurists considered resolutely absolutist, such as Bodin and Loyseau. Its most jarring incarnation is to be found in Hobbes. The doctrine of individual rights as it appears in the work of the absolutist theorists has a special claim on our attention, as it presents a limit case. Prima facie, no one should be less disposed to protect individual rights from the abuses of authority than they. If they defend these rights, it suggests that within the states where the rule of law prevailed, even the most zealous champions of monarchy were unwilling to sacrifice individuals to the omnipotence of the state.

A somewhat technical discussion of the Hobbesian argument is in order here. A number of revisionist commentators have in recent years brought attention to the important place of individual rights in Hobbes's doctrine.[15] The great Michel Villey goes so far as to view the author of *Leviathan* as the true founder of the modern doctrine of subjective rights, a doctrine of which the Franciscan nominalists of the thirteenth and fourteenth centuries were the precursors. To be sure, in several passages scattered through his political works, Hobbes defines a right as an attribute of individuals.[16] Foreshadowing Spinoza, he views rights as consisting of three parts, the individual, his desire for self-preservation, and his "powers" or abilities.[17]

Such a definition, which ties rights to individuals and to their *libertas*, breaks decisively with Aristotelianism and with ancient natural law, which conceived of rights and law as *relations* of equity within a natural political society, or as a legalized expression of the most just distribution according to the order of things. Hobbes, by contrast, thinks of rights as the attributes of an individual, a manifestation of his potentialities in the state of nature. In lieu of a realist and objective theory of law, we are confronted with a subjectivist and naturalist view. Law is the natural power of an individual. For feudal jurisprudence, which had defined law and the feudal relationships of dependence by reference to powers, *aptitudo, facultas*, and *libertas*, this aspect of Hobbes's analysis represents no radical innovation.

But Hobbes does not stop there, any more than he stops at the nominalism in which he was reared. For Hobbes, at the heart of natural attributes lies the desire for personal security and for the preservation of individual life, a concern that had little hold on the Franciscans. "Every man," he writes, "may preserve his own life and limbs, with all the power he hath."[18] Rights and law, then, are a manifestation of power, a sign of aggressivity turned on the outside world. But they also reflect an appropriation of one's self, an appropriation directed inward, the expression of a desire to persevere in one's being, to preserve one's life and guarantee one's security. This desire for personal security, this affirmation of subjective rights, is the principal condition of, and motivation for, the social contract. The civil edifice and the contract by which it is born flow from reciprocal surrender of individual rights to the sovereign, from the desire of each individual to gain the personal security he lacked in the state of nature. The contract in turn establishes civil law, then political law, but also family law and hereditary law; gradually, law in its entirety is built up from subjective rights. At the starting point of the Hobbesian system, individual liberty and subjective rights, sacrosanct and inviolable, occupy center stage. If at its termination point the Hobbesian system bears little resemblance to the Hegelian, it is important to remember that at its starting point it is quite similar.

This does not mean we should ignore the end point. The modalities of the contract that Hobbes imagines require a radical alienation of subjective rights. This fact instigated sharp rejoinders from more liberal thinkers even within Hobbes's lifetime. Once the moment of contract has passed, Hobbes dismisses all disobedience to the sovereign as illegitimate. The antimonarchists had sought to justify disobedience on a wide scale, up to and including regicide, such as in the case of Charles I. (*Leviathan* first appeared in 1651, three years after the execution of Charles I.) Hobbes throws down the gauntlet to Coke, whose defense of parliamentary supremacy to the sovereign was widely accepted. For Hobbes, the alienation of rights to the sovereign was inescapable, as a result of the mechanistic model to which the contract conformed: the union of individuals eventuates in the unity of the state, and the contract gives birth to a full-fledged civil person.[19] Political identity does not belong to individual citizens considered separately; it is an attribute of the body politic as a whole. The political mechanism illustrates this striking loss of individual identity quite clearly: inside Leviathan, the grand machine, each individual is a mere part of a larger whole. The sovereign has confiscated, for himself, all subjectivity. In the polity imagined by Hobbes, then, we find none of the individual civil liberties of Locke's *Second Treatise* and the solemn declarations of rights of the eighteenth century. Hobbes neither defines a *status civitatis* nor allocates a role to civil society. He appears to have sounded the death knell of individual rights and to have initiated absolutism's inescapable degeneration into despotism.

Yet this appearance is not the reality of Hobbes. However severe the mechanistic alienation of subjective rights is, it is not, as Georges Lyon and Robert Derathé have shown, exhaustive. Hobbes is as explicit as one can be: "Not all rights are alienable."[20] Personal security is the end and object of all social transactions; hence it cannot be placed on the market.[21] To alienate one's safety would be an absurdity. The desire for self-preservation is the greatest human desire of all, and in the calculus of utility that governs all of human conduct, it can never be subordinated to any other desire. Surrender of the right to self-preservation would be a contradiction of the nature of the contract. Hobbes, the fervent partisan of royal authority, does not hesitate to justify the right of resistance when an individual's life is threatened.[22]

The right to personal security, then, has pride of place among all individual rights. It is the only one that is nonnegotiable. More importantly, it is the only *civil* right. In the state of nature, personal security is merely the object of a desire, an aspiration of the individual, but never a reality. *Homo homini lupus:* the anarchical and collective law of force poses a constant threat to each person's physical safety. In the civil state, by contrast, the sovereign's confiscation of all acts of war, his monopoly on the sword of justice, brings about individual security by means of the rule of law. The civil state confers reality on a right that remained virtual in the state of nature.

At the core of a political right, then, we find the right of a man and of a citizen in the modern sense of the term, a right that is both natural and civil. It will reappear in the corpus of British common law as recorded by Blackstone: "The absolute rights of every Englishman (which, taken in a political and extensive sense, are usually called their liberties) [are] . . . the right of personal security, the right of personal liberty, and the right of private property."[23] And the right of personal security, Blackstone adds, "consists in a person's legal and uninterrupted enjoyment of his life his limbs, his body, his health, and his reputation."[24] The same thought will also be found in the French declaration of 1789: "the end of all political association is the preservation of the natural and inalienable rights of man, namely, liberty, property, security, and resistance to oppression." Personal security, notably, is relegated to the third position here.

Bodin and Loyseau, like Hobbes, defend the individual right to personal security, but they supplement that right with a right to liberty. Recall Bodin's emphasis on the dual limitation of power: "natural liberty and subjects' ownership of goods." Loyseau, having explained that "lordship concerns those things that belong to others and those persons who are free," concludes that "this power must be used with reason and justice." For Hobbes, the right to personal security is the first, but also the last, of individual rights. The French jurists view personal security as a matter of emancipation, the rule of law as a matter of personal liberty, and the appropriation by each person of himself as an issue of property. Although they never postulate, as Hobbes the "modern" social-contract theorist did, an original equality among human beings, they are in fact more generous in their specification of individual rights.

A common point cuts across these differences: individual rights are not individualist, civil rights are not "civilist." In Hobbes, the right to personal security, which the contract guarantees by means of the rule of law, is the result of a relation between the authorities and the citizen, the consequence of a political theory of sovereignty. It depends on a certain anti-imperial organization of power. Not all states guarantee individual security, only those that refrain from exercising the right of life and death over their own citizens. Leviathan, the sovereign state, the state under the rule of law, is capable of terminating the wars within the body politic precisely because it does not make itself a conqueror or even military leader with respect to its own citizens; it takes the people's welfare as its objective.

The defense of citizens' rights, then, is linked to an anti-imperial conception of power, but it goes no further than that. For the French jurists, the personal security of free subjects, tied to the existence of a peaceful body politic and hence an anti-imperial use of power, is supplemented by an antidominial conception. At the point where Hobbes nearly permits "government by institution" and "dominions paternall and despoticall" to converge, the French prefer to draw a firm boundary.[25] The doctrine of individual rights, then, begins to echo the doctrine of sovereign power. The affirmation of a right to personal security guaranteed by the rule of law and to personal liberty touches directly on the question of power, since these rights cannot be secured absent a certain type of state, namely, the sovereign state or the state under the rule of law. Two conditions must be met if personal security and emancipation are to be achieved. First, the authorities must not have the right to mete out life and death to citizens; they must not wield the *jus vitae necisque* that the Roman emperor, and military leaders generally, relied on. In short, the state cannot be imperial; it must function in the mode of peace rather than of war. Second, power cannot amount to property. The relationship between sovereign and subject cannot be that between owner and object; thus the state cannot be dominial. Law rather than mastery or domination must be its foundation.

Human liberty and civil liberties are not identical, either logically or chronologically. Logically, because they are governed by different legal logics. Human liberty arises from the modern and antidominial conception of power, and it is tied to the notion of a social contract and to a conception of rights as law. Rights are guaranteed by the form of the state. By contrast, civil liberties, most clearly those declared in the eighteenth-century declarations of rights, are derived from the purely individualist notion of contract and from private law. Rights are only exhausted by the limits of the state. Nor are human liberty and civil liberties chronologically identical. Emancipation opened up careers to civil liberties and to individual autonomy, because emancipation was the first conquest of free subjects.[26] It amounted to the right to preserve one's life, the right that Hobbes declared inalienable. By means of the juridical peace secured by the state under the rule of law, free subjects come to possess the same liberty that feudal lords exercised over their fiefs, the same independence the lords enjoyed in waging war. These forms of emancipation were orignally authorized by the doctrine of power in which sovereignty reaches its end point, by the idea of the personal security of individuals.

Human liberty, an individual right, is also a political right, by its nature opposed to slavery. For the first time in politics, theorists recognize a personal right to security and to liberty, to be possessed by the governed, the dominated, the subjects, and which imposes limitations on the governors, restrains domination, and places obligations on the prince. Political liberty is not yet the order of the day; inequalities, some forms of oppression, and a guild mentality survive. *Homo hierarchicus* has not been vanquished. But to say that not everything is changed is far from saying that nothing has.

The importance of the status of liberty has been underestimated in two main ways. First, because the persistence of relations between masters and servants, and supervisors and workers, has been mistaken as a continuation by other means of the relation between free men and slaves; second, because the winds of change that gradually eliminated servitude from Atlantic Europe and sowed its seeds from Prussia to the Urals have not been adequately accounted for.

### Masters and Servants

We should begin here by distancing ourselves from the view, eloquently advanced by Alexandre Matheron, that early modern political philosophy simply accepted as legitimate a certain residue of slave theory and servitude.[27] Our estimation of the early modern doctrines' complicity with, or hostility to, the feudal doctrine will depend on our agreement or disagreement with Matheron, as will our evaluation of Marx's theory of exploitation. Marx took the proletarian who alienated his work value as the strict and equivalent successor to the serf and the slave. This identification spurred him to deride the juridical liberties as merely "formal" devices for disguising economic subjugation.

The evidence for the claim that the early modern doctrine is unduly tolerant of servitude is, it must be admitted, more than circumstantial. Pierre Charron drew attention to the analogy between the "renting" of vagabonds and beggars, on the one hand, and the servitude of the same men's fathers. Grotius, who would later become a favorite among colonialists in need of a good conscience, unabashedly approved of slavery consequent upon military victory. As against Charron, one is entitled to reject the analogy between ancient slavery and modern servitude in part on the basis of Charron's own indignation about "the monstrous and shameful side of human nature," which permits "slavery and the power of seignors or masters over them." Charron holds, moreover, that Christianity, unable to abolish slavery with a single blow, had gradually but irresistibly undermined it.[28] Grotius, for his part, will come under withering attack by Locke, Rousseau, and others for his concession to the "right" of enslavement. The connection between the early modern jurists and slavery, then, does not result from a few infelicitous expressions, slips of the pen wrenched out of context by their critics. Yet Matheron highlights a more important point, the theory of alienation according to which, just as a citizen alienates his political liberty in the social contract, so a servant alienates his economic liberty in a contract for labor.[29] It is this theory that will give servitude a second life in political theory stretching from Hobbes to Rousseau.

Given that such an alienation is countenanced, it remains to be seen whether any limits are set to it, what its range of application is, and to what extent it is countenanced; only then can we judge whether endorsing it amounts to endorsing and legitimizing slavery. "Not all rights are alienable": this Hobbesian maxim is a veritable motto of the early modern theorists, who demand first and foremost individual security. The reasoning of Grotius and later of Pufendorf follows lines similar to that of Hobbes. Whenever the right to life is safeguarded by a master or a military commander, the security acquired establishes a contract and legitimates voluntary servitude.[30] Robert Derathé, in his study of Rousseau's engagement with these two jurists, emphasizes the modernity of this theory of voluntary servitude, nowhere to be found in Roman law: "For the Romans, slavery does not result from a contract; it is always an involuntary privation of liberty, a deprivation which one undergoes against one's will."[31] The Romans viewed slavery as a fact, not a right; a result of the state of war, not a function of the civil state. Yet Grotius and Pufendorf, following in Hobbes's footsteps, reduced individual rights to the right to survival, and the body politic to the guarantee of this right. This left them isolated in the tradition of early modern political and legal theory, since most authors had designated the *status libertatis* as the prime inalienable right. Later, the doctrine would be shared by Locke, Jurieu, and Montesquieu.[32] But even if the right to personal security is sufficient for the social contract, it cannot bring about emancipation. Order does not guarantee liberty.

Yet it is Grotius who articulates more clearly than anyone the distinction between possession of one's own body, which he views as inalienable, and liberty, or each person's capacity to determine his own action, which he permits us to barter away. In Cartesian fashion, the early modern jurists view man as a psychophysical substance. The new axiom of political philosophy is dualist. It prohibits one from putting a price on one's life, from allowing one's physical person to be confiscated, but it countenances the sale of liberties and of discretional authority. This represents a break with slave theory, which permits both. Slavery confers a right of life and death over an individual, the *jus vitae necisque* as a foundation for the appropriation of an individual's labor capacity. Rousseau brandishes this very principle in order to attack the juridical foundation of slavery: so long as there is no right of life and death—and Rousseau contends, logically, that there never is, since life is a subjective right—there is no slavery. The right of life and death and the right to enslave pursue each other in a vicious circle. Hence Rousseau's abrupt conclusion:

> It is therefore an inquitous exchange to make him buy his life, over which one has no right, at the cost of his freedom. By establishing the right of life and death on the right of slavery, and the right of slavery on the right of life and death, isn't it clear that one falls into a vicious circle?[33]

If the right of protecting one's own life and of assuring one's security is inalienable, the contract based on a threat of death is nugatory as a matter of law; between master and slave, a state of war never ceases to obtain. Alienation of liberty for a circumscribed period, which is what both domestic service and salaried labor amount to, are never confused by the early modern jurists with slavery. The servant is not a slave—indeed there is no equivalent in ancient political philosophy to the modern servant. Nor should we even confuse the modern salaried worker with the mercenaries whom Cicero distinguished from slaves. Salaries are peaceful retribution for work in a social context; mercenaries are compensated for the risks of military action, the disciplinary enlistment of men whose aim is the subjugation of other men. In the ancient world, as well as in the feudal world, the military participated indirectly in the system of production, since the army was largely, as it were, a recruiting tool, a machine for creating

slaves and acquiring further productive forces. By contrast, salaried workers are engaged in a project of economically driven transformations of
nature; thus their relation to the system of production is utterly direct.
Whereas the human relations of mercenaries are militarized, those of salaried workers are naturalized. Salaried workers mediate social relations by
juridical means, whereas the social relations of mercenary soldiers are immediate and brought about by war and domination. This is why domestic
and salaried workers are cut off from war, isolated from *imperium* as
much as from *dominium*.

On this crucial point, the early modern political doctrine, which precedes and, to be sure, legitimizes the conditions of salaried workers, is
fundamentally opposed to both domination and slavery. Not only do lives
and bodies not belong to the master; even the labor of the worker cannot
be appropriated. Only his labor power, an abstract principle, the spirit of
labor, a potential distinct from a will and liberty. The salaried worker
must be free to make a contract, and the early modern jurists discover the
reversibility of liberty and of alienation. If we must always return to the
original contract, all alienation is rooted in an original liberty, from which
an arbitrage may be exercised. Liberty, like rights and law, is in this sense
strictly formal. But life—the totality of powers that resists death—is also
an abstract principle. Early modern politics manipulates ideal entities but
preserves the body, whereas feudalism and the ancients preserved ideals
but put the body into play. The paradox of this situation is that the early
modern abstraction liberates the material productive forces of society, a
paradox similar to that discussed by the Greeks concerning causation by
mathematical ideal entities; the latter, despite their abstraction, were more
useful than empirical techniques of calculation. Safeguarded in its biolog-
ical security, the body becomes untouchable, a machine that, as François
Guéry and Didier Deleule have shown, is increasingly reduced to a locus of
productivity.[34] The idea of a salaried workforce links together wills, contracts for decisions, musters abstract forces; the body is made productive
because the principle of production is deracinated from it and invested in
a liberty that manipulates and disciplines it.

Here again, the early modern doctrine fatally undermines the feudal
and ancient structures that countenanced neither free will (there are only
wills to power) nor consensual alienation (subjection of individuals is per-
petrated on them). The theory of alienation invalidates rather than legitimates slavery, a fact made evident, as we will see later, by the further fact
that the renaissance of feudal philosophy in the work of Karl Ludwig von
Haller takes the form of a critique of the theory of alienation. How could
this have been so widely misunderstood? Perhaps because from a pro-
slavery point of view, feudalism conserves and provides nuance to the ancient view, rather than transforming it. If one is not careful, it is easy to

overlook the fact that the principal target of the antifeudal polemic of the early modern jurists is slavery. It is easy, that is, to forget what Rousseau taught us, that "these words *slavery* and *right*, are contradictory."[35]

### Eastern Europe, Western Europe

The evidence against lumping all absolutist states together is perhaps the progressive disappearance of slavery in Western Europe, as against its consolidation and expansion in Eastern Europe. France in the eighteenth century can very nearly be characterized by Antoine Loysel's sixteenth-century remarks: "All persons are free in this realm, and as soon as a slave has set foot in it and been baptised, he is emancipated." The progress of emancipation was irrepressible, and proceeded by means of both the rapid dissolution of one form of servitude and the chronic disintegration of the other.[36] As Pierre Chaunu has put it,

> the institution of the monarchy, an offspring by and large of the structures of the world itself, was able to keep Europe content and protect it from the havoc wreaked by the seignory prevalent in the East, which amounted to slavery and alienation of all liberty.[37]

One form of servitude was that of the Carolingian slaves, who were already better off in both economic and juridical terms than their ancient predecessors. They could not be sold or executed at any moment, like vulgar merchandise, nor were they completely deprived of their personality. They could marry and have a family, and men exercised paternal authority just as they also possessed goods, such as furniture and housing. Still quite permeated by slavery in the sixth century, according to Gregory of Tours, society underwent modifications in the seventh century. By the practice of "chasures," the *domini* ceded to slaves their holdings and identified them with the land they cultivated. As a result, the condition of the serf evolved imperceptibly from personal slavery to real service. But at the same time, duties proliferated while rights failed to keep pace. Taxation was prohibitive. The *chevage* tax was fixed at four deniers per year and served as an infamous badge of servility; a "gratuity tax" was earmarked for protection provided by the lord of the estate; the *mainmorte* was a tax on the humble patrimonies of serfs who died without direct heirs; and the *formariage* tax was imposed for marrying outside the fief. In the realm of civil rights, serfs were barred from the religious life and from service as judge or witness in public tribunals.

The transformation of the condition of the serfs was precipitated, at least in part, by increased hierarchization. Historians disagree about whether the process proceeded from bottom up or top down, from the demotion of the early settlers to the status of near serfs, or from the emancipation of lowly serfs. By the end of the eleventh century, though, the sharp boundaries between villeins and serfs had been markedly eroded. A new form of servitude arose at this point and tended away from personal service toward real service, and away from a basis in birth toward a foundation in the demands of the fields. It immediately came under pressure from three forces. First, the church was able to open the religious orders up to the serfs, first on its own lands, where it established refuges in which the servile condition was abolished. Some abbeys, such as Saint Denis in 1232 and Saint Geneviève in 1246 and 1248, practiced collective emancipations. Second, the kings were a powerful force of encouragement for the emancipation of certain communes. The first privilege of the inhabitant of a chartered city was his civil liberty. A serf who succeeded in fleeing obtained offical emancipation after a year and a day of clandestine existence in a free city. Urbanization provided an opportunity for the lowly and a risk for the lord, since it irreversibly upset the rules of the feudal system. Third and finally, the pioneer spirit and the great movement to cultivate new lands raised a valiant army of peasants. In order to support this reconquest of lands, certain lords created *hostises*, free holdings for those bold enough to cultivate them. The map of France is filled with names of liberty—Villeneuve ("new city"), Villefranche ("free city"), Bastide, Neuville ("new city"), Neuvic ("new vicarage"), Bourgneuf ("new city")—peopled originally by emancipated peasants, newly made proprietors of their own bodies. The institutions of servitude recoiled, faded, lost their luster. In the eleventh century, it disappeared from Normandy; in the twelfth, Poitou, Roussillon, the West, and the Midi left it behind; and in the thirteenth, it was eradicated in Touraine.[38] By the end of the thirteenth century, there were no serfs remaining in the region of Paris, nor in the Senonais. Throughout the twelfth, thirteenth, and fourteenth centuries, monarchs exercised collective emancipations. Louis VII and Philip Augustus freed the serfs of Orleans and its surroundings, Saint Louis liberated those of Villeneuve-le-Roi, and Philip the Fair obliterated the seneschalsies of Toulouse, the Agenais, and the Rouergue.[39] Thus in fourteenthcentury France, all city dwellers and the great majority of the rural population were free.

A residual servitude persisted, however. On the eve of the Revolution, there were approximately 150,000 people in a condition of servitude. On the night of August 4, 1789, the duc de La Rochefoucault-Liancourt successfully sponsored a bill abolishing all servitude, both real and personal, without indemnity. But by then, the servitude that had survived had much the aspect of a survival, indeed of a relic. This is clear from the customs books that began to appear in the sixteenth century, and which, with a few exceptions, make no mention of servitude at all.[40] Spurred by the Assemblies of Blois in 1576 and Paris in 1614 and by Voltaire's campaign in behalf of the serfs of the Abbey of Saint-Claude, Louis XVI, on August 8, 1776, abolished all forms of servitude on royal domains. He even expressed regret that the state of his finances prevented him from repossessing all the feudal holdings in the realm. Within his domain, he converted all such holdings into freeholdings.[41] These trends permitted the early modern jurists to speak of the "honorable liberty" or "common liberty" of the French. Olivier-Martin has amply documented the modes of expression of French liberty: in 1596, a bishop is known to have explained to Henry IV that the kings of France "prefer honorable liberty in their subjects to vile servitude." In 1607, an archbishop was heard expressing his desire to adopt "French liberty" in addressing the king. And in 1641, the prince-bishop of Grenoble defended the liberty of the Church of God in "the freest monarchy in the world."[42]

The disappearance of slavery in England was far more rapid than in France. To begin with, British serfdom hardly ever amounted to servitude. The term *vilanus*, which designated the British serf and dominated the vocabulary of serfdom, indicated a servitude based on real landholding rather than on personal subjection. Under Elizabeth, there were no more than ten thousand serfs remaining, and well before the Tudor dynasty, the majority of peasants had become free. In the seventeenth century, the words "serf" and "villein" vanish altogether from the vocabulary, the last case of villeinage dating to 1618.[43] Habeas corpus may be regarded as an extension into the realm of penal law of the limits imposed on central authority by the right of each citizen to the appropriation of his own body. Habeas corpus was a late arrival in France, where secret prisons and lettres de cachet survived until 1789; in England, by contrast, it was early seen as an implication of the idea of liberty espoused in the Magna Carta of 1215, and it was codified juridically by the Act of 1679.

During the same period, the *macula servitutis*, the stain of servitude, thrived with little abatement in Germany, Russia, and Eastern Europe generally. In the eighteenth century, the second form of servitude began to cast its shadow. To judge from the Russian example, it would appear that the state played an active and direct role.[44] Beginning in the second half of the fifteenth century, the burdens imposed by the fledgling Muscovite state, exercising its authority over a vast and sparsely populated territory, prompted widespread flight and vagabondage among the peasants. In response, the state mercilessly whittled down the right to leave one's manor. The code of 1494 prohibited farmers from leaving their master before the end of the fall harvest. These tendencies grew more pronounced in the seventeenth century and reached their apogee under the great Czars Peter the Great, Elizabeth, and Catherine II. Peter the Great extended the status of servitude to all escapees, emancipated slaves, fallen bourgeois, professional beggars and vagabonds, and to the previously free peasants of Novgorod and Arkhangelsk. Elizabeth went still further, authorizing lords to have recalcitrant serfs deported to Siberia, and Catherine established the right of selling peasants along with the land they work.

Those commentators who have taken an economic approach recognize this distinction between Eastern and Western Europe. Perry Anderson, for example, writes,

> The Absolutist State in the West was the redeployed political apparatus of a feudal class which had accepted the commutation of dues. It was a *compensation for the disappearance of serfdom.* . . . The Absolutist State in the East, by contrast, was the repressive machine of a feudal class that had just erased the traditional communal freedoms of the poor. It was a *device for the consolidation of serfdom.*[45]

But these writers fail to draw all the conclusions warranted by their findings, in particular the distinction between feudalism and aristocracy. The absolutist state that oversaw the abolition of servitude may indeed have remained an aristocratic state, but it was no longer a feudal state, a system of imperial and dominial power like that of the Eastern European states. Absolutism, or more precisely those elements of the modern state that are rooted in absolutism, may also be rooted in the seignorial system but not in the feudal system. The historians of taxation have sufficiently documented this division between East and West: in societies based on a closed agricultural economy, with a shortage of workers, the state tended to confine the peasant to the land he worked and to favor the progress of dominialization, for clear fiscal reasons. By contrast, the increasing power of the state in monetary economies had the opposite effect, contributing to the emancipation of the peasant.

Without the benefits of the rule of law that flourished in Western Europe during the Englightenment, Eastern Europe was also deprived of the concept *status libertatis*, a deprivation that would have profound effects on its future.


### Liberty


The idea of individual liberty was the grand innovation of the state under the rule of law, the foundation of the first body of law and politics that rejects slavery. In the ancient city, enfranchisement and emancipation were private affairs and events that occurred at the margins of society. The rule of law, by contrast, is embodied in general laws that modulate the exercise of power in the state. The guarantee of individual rights presupposes an anti-imperial and antidominial center of power committed to peace and respect for law. The first states under the rule of law gave neither power to the people nor political liberty to the citizen. They were neither democratic nor liberal. Yet by protecting each person's right to appropriate his or her own life, they liberated men from slavery. Where the rule of law prevailed, servitude vanished; where servitude thrived, empires imperceptibly decayed and took on the attributes of political obsolescence.

The status of liberty also reinforces the point that without a political guarantee of legal recourse, there are no individual rights but only pious professions of the value of human beings. Without the rule of law, there are no human rights. It is, indeed, only in those states committed to the rule of law that liberal democracy has taken root, for a people can choose its own destiny, enjoy political liberties and civil rights, only if it is composed of free human beings. The status of liberty explains why those states that today trample on individual liberties after having formally pledged their respect for them commit a crime more egregious than the mere destruction of civil liberties. They undermine the *status libertatis* and reinstantiate, by dint of their dominial exercise of power, the political conditions of slavery.

The doctrine of sovereign power and the guarantee of individual rights are linked by what the early modern jurists called the "body politic." The ways in which the body politic functioned and cohered was the core of the early modern jurists' theories. Later, regulation of the social world would be viewed through the economic prism of liberal theory, which detaches the social world from the state. The early modern jurists, for their part, analyzed the prospect of such regulation from the perspective of moral imperatives and sought to reconcile the civil and political spheres. Legal historians know that the first great tranformation wrought by modern political and legal theory was the doctrine of subjective rights; the second was the recognition of rights as elements of law. The new civil consensus was firmly anchored in the political morality of law.

# CHAPTER IV

# Law and Morality

We must find a form of government which puts law above man.

—ROUSSEAU

O<small>FTEN THE</small> indictment of the state is accompanied by an offensive against law itself. Critics remark on the imprint of the law on the arms of condemned prisoners headed for execution, as well as the proletariat en masse. Hatred for the state and for the law mutually reinforce each other. This is quite logical, since the modern state has indeed linked itself tightly with law, as Hegel was quite aware.[1] A rarity among the German philosophers, capable of resisting the romantic juggernaut, he extended Enlightenment political thought by explaining that there is no state without a public morality, without *Sittlichkeit,* an ethical life that modern sociology has only imperfectly translated as "values consensus." The principle of public morality is not love, which is proper to familial morality and to faith. It is law.[2] But is law merely subjection of the individual? The ethical life can exist only for a community of human beings—or, as Bodin put it, "free subjects." It is the "idea of freedom" by means of which individuals are enabled to affirm their particularity. The ethical order in which "a human being has rights in so far as he has duties" is utterly foreign to the slave.[3] The internal obligation of the law is but the reciprocation of a satisfied right.

The resurgence of law in the modern state draws sustenance from three ancient sources: Greek natural law, Roman civil law, and Jewish moral law. The role of the Scriptures is less often appreciated than that of the Greco-Roman tradition. Even Montesquieu renounces any debt to divine law and insists on detaching the "spirit" of the laws from theology. Yet there are important indications of the importance of the Old Testament in the formation of a civil morality based on law. First, the philological passions of the humanists were mediated by the Protestants, who translated, purified, and revived the Old Testament. These writers knew and used ancient Hebrew as much as they did ancient Greek. The German scholar Johannes Reuchlin (1455–1522) fought as assiduously for the establishment of academic chairs in Hebrew as he did for chairs in Greek. Richard Simon and Jean Mabillon, the seventeenth-century theologians who are the true founders of modern intellectual history, sustained erudite exchanges with talmudic scholars. For many of these figures, the "feeble" historicism of the Gospels paled beside the "robust" philosophy of history of the Old Testament. As Renan would later say, all the social sciences are stepchildren of philology. Second, Jews reentered the secular sphere with the immigration of Spinoza, an event that laid the foundations for eighteenth-century French philosophy, and which bore dividends immediately, their protestations to the contrary notwithstanding, in the work of Leibniz, Lessing, Jacobi, Fichte, and Schelling.[4]

Third, the link between morality and law was being forged ever more strongly and would culminate in Kant's *Critique of Practical Reason*. The tendency was toward the elaboration of a public morality decisively influenced by theological debates. This explains the paramount political importance of the theological discourse of the Renaissance and early modern period.[5] Protestants and Catholics, Lutherans and Calvinists, Arminians and Socinians, Jansenists and quietists: the disputes among these sects did not concern only the path to salvation, the sex of angels, and the nature of the city of God, but also the definition of justice, of the "human condition," and of the "new Jerusalem." We ought perhaps be more attentive to, and willing to recognize, the links between religion and politics. From the deep faith of a dissident like Solzhenitsyn to the role of Catholicism in Jean-Bertrand Aristide's politics to the careful division of credit given to Jews and Christians in the history of socialism: these and other examples should keep us on guard against neglecting the prolonged and permanent impact of religion on politics. But the impact is by no means univocal or direct. To reduce the modern state to a reincarnation of the Christian Church or the basic laws of the modern kingdom to canon law, or to excommunicate the state after having persuaded it to be appropriated by clericalism and to have confiscated violence and the sacred—these oversimplifications are no less mistaken than the neglect of religion's role in politics. The challenge is to analyze, for instance, the elective affinities among the diverse types of state and of church and to note that states tend to have the churches they deserve (and vice versa). Just as the word of God enters the human world only by the intermediary of a prophet, and just as grace must be mediated by the elect, so religion in general only passes into politics by means of a human go-between, namely morality.

The discovery of a political morality, a civic morality, a lay morality: such was the paramount aspiration of the three great "immoralists," Machiavelli, Spinoza, and Bayle. They sought a form of legitimation that would be freed from the tutelage of the church and of Catholic monarchs. Although they are often thought to have located that new form of legitimation in the right of the stronger, it was in fact morality that they sought. Spinoza was the virtuous atheist whom the Great Condé did his utmost to meet. Bayle showed that immorality abounds in Christianity and that virtue is not absent from paganism. But if no society can function adequately without a consensus, an idea of morality shared by the majority of citizens, then perhaps Freud and the anthropologists are right in holding that modern power has added nothing new to this picture. Morality is a system of obligation that imposes duties, ideals that affect behavior on the model of a military strategy commanding disciplined divisions: such ideal entities cannot be improvised. The genealogy of morals is an old story in which ancient sediments accrue atop archaic debris. The state, then, has invented nothing but merely gathered up the remains, that is, the Scriptures.

In the matter of morals, as Nietzsche rightly held, the Greco-Roman heritage lost its early appeal, and it was Judeo-Christianity that became the moral tutor of the West. Rome remained its law professor, and Greece its science instructor. Consequently, early modern political morality had a choice between two systems: the morality of law, based on the Old Testament; and the morality of faith, rooted in the Gospels. The good fortune of Western Europe was to choose both alternatives, to develop a canon that could privatize religion completely in the manner of the Reformation or respect the autonomy of the church in the manner of France, but which escaped the political secularization of faith that would later wreak havoc on nineteenth-century Eastern Europe. The collective political ethos lent its values to a morality of laws, leaving only subjective rights to depend on a morality of faith. A morality of laws and a morality of faith each have their advantages and drawbacks, and they can, to be sure, come into conflict with each other: "In order for a sanctuary to be built, a sanctuary must be destroyed." The likelihood of conflict—between Jews and Christians, Protestants and Catholics—is often underestimated, in the absence of a proper history and geography of religions. Since the Renaissance, though, all of Western faith, that of the Reformation and that of the Counter-Reformation, has rested on a combination of the Scriptures.[6] In Eastern Europe, by contrast, the Old Testament was largely abandoned.[7] To evaluate a moral system is to determine the nature of the sacrifice of values one must make in order to adopt it; as there are no benefits without costs, no savings without sacrifice, so there are no moralities without a price, and a moralist must balance the accounts. In a sense, the morality of laws is diametrically opposed to the morality of faith. "The just man seeks truth and justice without the commands of the law," says the Old Testament; "Man is justified by faith without the works of the law," writes Paul.

## *The Morality of Law and the Morality of Faith*

Jewish morality appears to its detractors as an archaic morality, an alarming and strange ideal, conveyed by a strange people who acquired their identity only by means of the severe imposition of the law. It was the fate of the Hebrews, a small nomadic Caucasian-Semitic clan squeezed between the great Assyrian and Egyptian Empires, to survive in an unprecedented and unimaginable fashion. For the great civilizations, conquest was the means of territorialization, which in turn enabled them to establish a beachhead as nations and civil states; victorious strength was the mark of the masters. The Jews took a quite different path to securing their future: the law. The inscribed tablets, vessels of the law, itemized the values accepted by all and for all, liberated the Jews from slavery, endowed them with a national identity, and recaptured their lost homeland. Only after receiving the tablets of the law does Moses lead his people toward the promised land of Canaan. It was for having respected them that the collectivity, however dispersed, survived. The law, in sum, transcends territory and defeat and the ephemeral lives of individuals; it assures, so long as it is safeguarded and transmitted, the perpetuation of an identity. Let liberty perish, let the earth itself vanish, let the temple be reduced to a single arid wall; thousands upon thousands may die, yet the nation, so long as it continues to exalt justice and its values, survives so long as there remains a single just member. When one has shed territorial particularism, the true flesh and blood of the country is revealed to be the abstract and obstinate repetition of the law, which sows in the soul the seeds uprooted from the soil by the wanderings of a people. The morality of laws secures national identity by means of transcendence.

The values announced by the Decalogue and expressly prescribed by the Book of Deuteronomy are the same *moralia* that Thomas Aquinas took as the principles of justice and natural law. This is a morality of justice and of judgment, of equality and of rites, of works and of the city, of what is written, and of the rejection of death ("thou shalt not murder"). It is a morality of peace and of the fathers, a morality in which justice is everyone's affair, compulsory for all, yet transcendent of each individual. The law is revealed and inscribed in durable lapidary form on tablets and in human practices; it is formalistic and literal. No one is above or outside of the law; neither Caesar nor any tribune is exempt from it. It prescribes justice for all and subjects all to the fear of justice. All are judges, and all may be called before the law. Each is called on to give to each his due, to honor the rules of sharing and distribution, to distinguish good from evil, to anoint the just and to punish the unjust. The morality of law is the exaltation of collective justice.

In time, though, the law grew stale, a thorn in the side of the unjust.

Repeated transgressions sometimes went unpunished, and as a result sin and evil flourished. Excessive formality tended to stifle the life of the law, and there is always an individual who tries to breathe life into the collective asphyxiation, a rebel who has good grounds for rebelling. The Essenes and the Dead Sea masters of truth, in the period leading up to Christ's day, hoisted the banner of the spirit against that of the letter of the laws, faith against law. Although the battle was waged not in the name of abolishing the law but rather of more truly complying with it, the defenders of faith were driven to the view that sinners are justified by faith and not by the works of the law. The morality of faith emerged, a morality of grace and salvation, of hierarchy and sacrament, of the asceticism from eros, of the Word, of the Son rather than the Father. This was a morality in which salvation, a concern of every man, is withdrawn from the city because it requires the unique redemption and crucifixion of an individual. Salvation calls for free and transcendent grace, for the preaching of faith, for the living bread of the Word inscribed on tablets of flesh, its vitality and its spirituality. Each must have faith in the distribution of grace, circumcised and uncircumcised, and each must render unto Caesar that which is Caesar's. Faith is for the elect in the desert of individuality; all are called, but few are chosen. "Judge not lest you be judged; forgive those who have offended you; love your neighbor as yourself." The sacrifice demanded by the morality of faith is to treat one's life as a means and one's death as an end, to accept death in this world in order to ascend to another realm. "He who loves his life will lose it, and he who despises his life in this world will retain it for eternity." "For it is the spirit which enlivens the flesh, and the flesh is as nothing." The morality of faith is the proclamation of individual redemption.

Between these two different ways of imagining and experiencing transcendence, the way of collective justice and the way of individual grace, early modern political morality opts for the former and in this way avoids identifying the state with Christ. The modern state repudiated the project of saving society and of bringing about "emancipation"; it left to the individual and to the church the task of salvation and concerned itself with justice alone. The mortal god, as Hobbes put it, never sought to displace the immortal; Leviathan refrained from becoming Behemoth. These aspects of the modern state were not adopted suddenly. The triumph of the political morality of law was the culmination of a protracted plurisecular struggle marked by the overturning of a double obstacle: modern political philosophy had to shed both medieval antilegalism in the form of political Augustinianism, on the one hand, and classical natural law together with Roman civil law, on the other.

Political Augustinianism is little more than a prolix confession of the absence of a philosophy of law. Myth portrays the Middle Ages as characterized by the devastation of Attila, the indifference of the Merovingians, and the prayers of saints, a disordered and troubled world in which faith had entirely displaced law. This myth neglects the continuing influence of Roman law and the development of Saxon law, both within the framework of canon law. The *jus novum* emerging from the *jus antiquum* revives the idea of law.[8] Modern civil law is as much the product of the interaction among these elements as it is of early modern political thought. With those qualifications, it remains true that between the High Middle Ages and the precocious early Renaissance, between Augustinianism and Thomism, a rupture of some consequence took place, a caesura that separates mistrust of the law from its exaltation, neglect of justice from its active pursuit, disinterest in justice in this world from an effort to promote it.

This indifference to law is most clearly expressed by the example of Augustine himself, the greatest of the church fathers, who disdained history as an unimportant manifestation of arbitrariness. It is true that he advocated obedience to the secular laws "until such time as iniquity shall pass away and all human damnation shall be annihilated when God acts through us all." Yet, like Paul, he viewed faith as the true law, and he rejected the ideas of earthly justice and natural law.[9] In accents that betray his Manichaean education, Augustine flatly denounces the placing of any hope in the justice of human beings.

Thomas Aquinas is able to defeat Augustinianism by reaching back to Aristotle. In the *Summa Theologiae,* he recognizes that there is no peculiarly Christian legal doctrine but sets himself the task of breaking with the tradition of indifference toward human justice, and of formulating a secular legal doctrine with the help of the Aristotelian idea of natural law. Trusting to "reason and its capacity to know the temporal order by means of observation," Aquinas blazes a trail later to be followed by Hobbes, Pufendorf, and Wolff: the trail of a lay legal order based on reason.[10] This project represents a decisive break with the tradition of Gratian, who around 1140 had placed his formulation of canon law unstintingly under divine patronage.

Early modern political theory fails, however, to remain utterly faithful to the Thomist legacy. Most of the modern authors understand law as a corpus of written commands that derive either from human nature, reason, and the inalienable rights of individuals, or from a voluntary decision by a sovereign, monarch, aristocrat, or people. Even the great early modern jurists are "natural-law" theorists only in a sense of natural law quite different from that of Aquinas. The second great step taken by modernity, then, is the repudiation of natural law as it had been reformulated by Aquinas. For better or for worse, modern political philosophy sheds both the classical conception of law and the Roman idea of a legal code.

The orginality of modern political right and of the modern state under the rule of law lies in their distance from Roman law. In the twelfth century, recourse was had to the Roman models. This recourse was necessary so long as one was combating legal nihilism, desperately trying to replace military disorder with legal order, seeking to win acceptance of the legitimacy of the principle of law. Once the principle had been established, though, societies were ready to proceed to its application, to go from form to substance, to establish modern political right as a rule for the governance of free men and women, for the legal emancipation of the serfs, and for the securing of subjective rights. For these projects, the tools of Rome, and of the ancients generally, were inadequate. Most of the contract theorists expressly repudiate the ideas of law as a quest for the just, and of justice among human beings as a reflection of the order of things. They view law as the application of civil statutes and in this sense are deaf to natural law in its strict sense.

The concept of natural law is exceedingly complex, a concept that contains a cluster of ideas. First among these ideas is the equal intelligibility of civil law and the order of nature. The early moderns tend to accept this idea. It defends, at a minimum, the rationality (or more precisely the amenability to rationalization) of the legal order. As for the concept of nature at work in this idea, we have already seen that the early moderns had replaced Aristotelian hierarchies with mechanistic equality. This imposed on them a burden of explaining the passage from the egalitarian state of nature to a civil state in which hierarchies and inequality prevail. Their explanations, of which Marx would make great sport, are sufficiently within the spirit of natural law to merit designation, other things being equal, as natural-law theories.

But other things are not equal. A second component of any pure theory of natural law is that it treats legal relations among human beings as essentially similar to relations among things. The legal order is an order of things, because human beings are one ingredient of nature among others. This idea is emphatically rejected by the early moderns. "Moral" beings are not physical beings, as Pufendorf put it, and the *jura* are not legal usages of things but rather human subjective rights. Juridification is a purely civil process. Roman jurisprudence was founded on private law; it was, as Jhering would put it, a "politics of force." In choosing another path, early modern political theory blazes an entirely new trail. This choice is in part compelled by its ambitions, for it seeks to codify aspects of social life hitherto considered off limits to the law. The most important of these new objects of law is power itself, which was treated by Roman law as a matter of fact, not of law.

## The Birth of Political Right

The prodigious blossoming of doctrines of power in the early modern period—Guicciardini and Machiavelli in Italy, Suárez and Vitoria in Spain,

Bodin in France, and Hobbes and Locke in England—may have resulted from the simple fact of the growth of the state. But it bespeaks also a transformation of the essence of politics. For if the classical Greco-Roman state had simply been enjoying a revival—if, that is, the process under way was merely a reconstitution of empires—then one might have expected a revival of interest in Roman law and in classical political theory. But modern political doctrine adopts entirely original objectives: it aims to discern not only the proper allocation of resources but also the amount and distribution of power itself. It seeks to juridify the political sphere. This explains the interpenetration of law and politics so characteristic of the age, a phenomenon that never ceases to surprise us, in spite of our best multidisciplinary intentions. Legal scholars stumble upon politics wherever they look in Bodin, Grotius, and Domat; and political scientists are confronted with legal problems they do not expect to encounter. The new object of law is politics, and politics is increasingly considered in legal terms. A doctrine of political law or political right is foreign both to Roman law and to political science today: Roman law does not think of law in terms of power, and our own political science is so taken with revolutions and grand movements in politics that it neglects the legal niceties of day-to-day governance and rarely conceives of power in terms of law.

The laws that regulate power, which have no precedent in Roman law, are equally absent from feudal law: the development of political right constitutes a simultaneous overturning of Roman law by feudal law and feudal law by Roman law. In order to provide foundations for their abstract nonterritorial laws of sovereignty, the early modern theorists pointed to the abstractness of Roman law. But to establish a link between politics and law, they turned to feudal law, the source of the translation (a radical innovation on Roman law) of power into law. These relations have been analyzed not only by Villey[11] but also by Fustel de Coulanges (1830–1889) and Henri Sée (1864–1936), members of the "dominial" school, which has fallen into disrepute.[12] For Sée and Fustel de Coulanges, the feudal system of domains had emerged from the Gallo-Roman villas, and hence from the classical world. More importantly, though, Sée and Fustel de Coulanges place great emphasis on the fusion realized by feudalism between property and power. The great landowners had become masters who governed, possessors of full jurisdictional rights over the workers on their land. They were responsible for the latter's acts, they collected taxes from them, imposed corvée labor on them, and in general presided over an entire economic and political conglomerate. This was precisely the "power in property" described by Loyseau, where power had become law and where law had been simultaneously politicized and privatized.

We need not enter into the debate between Germanists and Romanists in great detail. In the second half of the eighteenth century, the debate over the Germanic conquest that had dominated historical discussion gradually gave way to a discussion of the nature of feudalism, and this new topic remained a central concern of nineteenth-century historiography. The "Germanists" included Boulainvilliers, Montesquieu, Mlle. de Lezardière, Mably, and later Tocqueville. For them, the great migrations of the Germanic tribes effectuated a historical rupture. Feudalism, on this view, was a radical novelty. The chief "Romanists" were Jean-Baptiste Dubos, d'Argenson, Moreau, and later Fustel de Coulanges and Sée. This group viewed the decline of the Roman Empire as a gradual process, stretching into the Middle Ages. The great rupture in history is that between feudalism and modernity. The Germanists, then, highlighted the "legalization of the violent blow," where the Romanists saw a slow inflexion of classical political and legal practices.

The uniqueness of Fustel de Coulanges in this debate was his refusal to study feudalism from an *ad quem* perspective, returning instead to the viewpoint of the early modern jurists, who distinguished sharply between feudalism and monarchy. Rather than a usurpation of royal privilege, feudalism seemed to them to be a pathological development of the link between power and property.

Be that as it may, the renewed discussion generated by Esmein's publications reveals how both viewpoints appreciated and accounted for the changes that took place. The Romanists saw a residue of the ancient political order beneath the surface of serfdom, and the Germanists saw a transformation in relations among men. With the holdings of domains and the rights of masters, feudalism fashioned a novel combination of power and property that blurred the distinction between private and civil rights by extending Roman law's juridical sphere in two unfortunate ways. Whereas in Roman law men had rights over possessions and power relations among men were facts of life rather than rights, feudal law encompassed the rights of masters over men as well as civil rights based on property ownership.

Modern political right, then, corrected feudalism in two decisive respects. It separated property and sovereignty by turning the domain into a territory. Kings and states became sovereign over subjects residing in a given place but no longer belonging to a domain. Feudalism also placed masters under the rule of law and so freed the law from the masters. The doctrinarians of sovereignty and the defenders of the state under rule of law kept the link between power and law forged by feudalism, but they inverted their relationship. Instead of trying to balance laws with powers, they subjected power to law and in so doing civilized the law.

No legal model existed for the massive inversion that took place. Roman law had never individualized rights, and feudal law had never imagined the social contract, an agreement by a collectivity subjecting order to law and security to liberation. The unique challenge to which modern politics rose was to leave slavery and to promulgate a body of law that guaranteed liberty, to find a way of coupling law with liberation. This road did not lead to Rome. What no classical legal doctrine could supply would be provided by a text of a distinctly nonlegal nature, the Bible.

Confronted with the obstinate, repeated, ubiquitous biblical allusions throughout early modern political and legal philosophy, we tend to dismiss them as remains of another day, obligatory bows to tradition, precautions, acts of prudence. Thus, apart from rare exceptions, such as the recent work of Jean-Pierre Duprat, modern scholars have neglected a full half of Hobbes's *Leviathan*, books 3 and 4, devoted to buttressing the social contract and emancipation arguments with the text of the Old Testament. Hotman, Bodin, and Grotius carry out similar exercises, scouring the biblical texts for support and scaffolding. Liberation by means of law, law as liberation, is a prevailing metaphor. Having found no legal model that would guarantee the collecive emancipation of the slaves by means of law, the moderns unearth an analogy in the covenant between God and Abraham and in the emancipation of the Jews from Egypt. What the early moderns draw from the Scriptures is not so much a religion as a political ideal, a theologico-political authority. They take the metaphor of the promised land, promised as part of a covenant, the covenant by which the Jewish people were emancipated from slavery and founded a nation. "The Kingdome of God," writes Hobbes, "is properly his Civill Soveraignty over a peculiar people by pact."[13] It is only at a very high price that we ignore or dismiss the biblical archaeology that lies at the heart of early modern political right.

During the same period, the respect accorded Roman law was in steady decline in both France and England. The Bible is consistently preferred to it and to feudal law as an authority for the liberation of men and the juridification of politics. The early modern jurists never vacillate between Roman law and national law: "It is treason to pose Roman law against the ordinance of one's prince," writes Bodin.[14] Most of the French jurisconsults (Guy Coquille, Étienne Pasquier, and others) side with Charles Dumoulin, who held that one should have recourse to Roman law only for its reasoning but never as a matter of common law: *non ratione imperii sed rationis imperio*.[15] "In France, where custom dominates, Roman civil law is not the common law; it lacks the force of law and is useful only for reasoning about law. Our customs are our true civil law."[16]

Loysel and Dumoulin also celebrate the merits of national customs and deride the faults of Roman law; it is the philosophers who turn decisively to Scripture. In the course of its vilification, to be sure, Roman jurisprudence underwent a good deal of distortion. On the pretext of cutting away the medieval embellishments, the moderns carried their attack to the *Pan-*

*dects* and the *Digest*, though their reconstruction of classical law was beset with problems analogous to those that distorted the portrait of the Roman republic in political theory. In time, the most audacious legal syntheses, such as those of Domat, abandoned the tripartite structure—persons, things, actions—of the *Institutes* of Gaius, in favor of a rationalist and individualist approach that reduces law to rights.[17]

The fixation on customary law, which bore the imprint of feudal archaisms, was doubtless a force for the rejection of Roman law. But it was not the sole force. Classical law was found wanting in a variety of ways. It had no social-contract doctrine, no idea of an exchange and equilibrium between power-wielding institutions and individuals, no doctrine of the relation between law and order, or between liberation and security. Hence the resistance of the moderns to Roman law may have resulted less from its objectivism (although the moderns were subjectivists) than from its tendency to envision things where the moderns saw human beings. Roman law arose in a slave-holding society that appropriated to itself collectively the lives of those individuals reduced to slavery and hence could not recognize the individual liberty to appropriate one's own life. Here lies the gulf separating the *status libertatis* of the Roman citizen who is not a slave but the father of a free family from the legally assured security of an emancipated member of society. The ubiquity of the Old Testament in the writings of the early moderns, then, is not so much a sediment of the past as an instrument for resisting Roman jurisprudence, precisely at a time when modern revisionism of Roman jurisprudence was coming to a head.

Does the use of the Scriptures constitute an intrusion of religion into politics? Yes and no. In the absence of a juridical model, the use made of Scripture was finely tuned to grant entry only to its moral teachings and to filter out its institutional structure. The moral teaching thus granted entry was the morality of law. At first, relations between the liberated individual and sovereign authorities were not completely juridified. The morality of law was interposed only so far as to establish a mutual consensual obligation between citizen and sovereign, arising from the social contract, to subject themselves each to one another and to comply with the law. This obligation remained less demanding on the prince than on the citizen, and, at the margins of juridical indeterminacy, the despotic tendencies of power endured. Nevertheless, the juridical sphere had enjoyed a significant expansion: collective law had been extended to areas where only fragmentary rights had been acknowledged; a general system had taken the place of piecemeal rules with limited application; political right, in sum, had emerged to overtake civil law. Modern politics had embarked on its path to democracy, but not the oligarchic democracy, or oligodemocracy, of the ancients, which rested on a foundation of slavery. Modern democracy was to take the form of macrodemocracy.

*Rights as Law*

There is only one way to bring about the juridification of politics: by distinguishing between rights and law and by establishing the supremacy of law in the operations of a government. The definitions of law vary from one author to another: "*the* law," for Hobbes and Rousseau; "the laws," for Locke. For some, law is original and recurrent, whereas for Voltaire, "laws are made after the fact, in the same way that one caulks a ship after it has sprung leaks."[18] Yet one thought unites such disparate doctrines, the idea that the law is the obligation of a body politic in its entirety to submit itself and subject itself to juridification. By contrast, a right can be a particular person's or class's advantage, a privilege; a law, modeled on the covenant with God, imposes on every individual an obligation to the collectivity as a whole. Hobbes, the theorist of the modern state *in statu nascendi*, expresses it most clearly of all:

> The names *lex*, and *jus*, that is to say, law and right, are often confounded; and yet scarce are there any two words of more contrary signification. For right is that liberty which law leaveth us; and laws those restraints by which we agree mutually to abridge one another's liberty. Law and right therefore are no less different than restraint and liberty, which are contrary.[19]

By what *right*, then, is the *law* made and enforced? By the right of contract exercised by a collectivity and by the right of the weak. Hobbes distinguishes further between a charter and a law; the former is a gift, a concession (*dedi, concessi:* I have given, I have granted) dependent on the sovereign's goodwill, whereas the latter is a command (*jubeo, injungo:* I command and enjoin), which arises from the necessary obligation of the civil order. The one is particular, the other universal—hence the requirement that civil laws be written and known, in the absence of which they are merely natural laws.[20] Rousseau, too, emphasizes the general and universal character of law. It is not enough for him that a law be "the will of a superior," as it was for Pufendorf. It is necessary but not sufficient that it be promulgated or written. Its form as well as its object, like its content, must be general: "What is a law? It is a solemn public declaration of the general will on a matter affecting the common interest."[21] The distinctive characteristic of a law, for Rousseau, is this twofold generality, of the will that ordains the law and of the object that it affects.[22] As a result of the law's transcendent character, the legislative function and its supremacy take their place within the state, its administration and finances as well as its system of justice. The justification of the importance imparted to law lies in the blossoming of legislative power: "It is not through laws that the state subsists, it is through the legislative power," he writes, and Locke adds, "the Legislative . . . [is] the Supream Power in every Common-wealth."[23]

Yet Locke explains that the legislature holds no power over citizens' lives, nor arbitrary power in general nor a power over property.[24] The limitations imposed on the law by subjective rights constitute a fundamental dimension of the modern juridical consciousness. They originated in the thought of St. Francis, and they point the way to a transcendence that has little to do with that of faith. The law cannot call for one's life; it seeks no martyrs or sacrifices and places no positive value on death. It is the expression not of an arbitrary will but of a legislative intention—a general will, in Rousseau's lexicon. It does not begin with a clean slate, as God does, for the law does not compete with God. Finally, since it is not a power over property, since it is limited by human rights, it is not an agent of servitude.

The elevation of law, then, is the form taken, in the state under the rule of law, by the transcendence of a politics that organizes a social environment without assuming the prestige and commitment of faith. This is not something to complain about: the alternative, the hitching of the fate of politics to faith, has tended to eventuate in barbarism, totalitarianism, and despotism. In the modern state under the rule of law, the legislative function is limited to the accomplishment of justice, leaving to each individual the problem of his own salvation. A politics of law draws sustenance from, but distinguishes itself from, individual faith. The supremacy of law corresponds to a corrective extension of the sphere of law: politics becomes an object of law, and political rights are juridified, just as individual rights are. The deviation from Roman law is clear: no longer is the division of things law's sole object but rather constraints on power and limitations on human uses of things and of other human beings. Law is no longer the coin of a politics of strength, and force and power are no longer to be regarded as brute facts. They are all henceforth subjected to law, while law itself becomes a power, a force. The state adopts the rule of law. To make politics an object of law is impossible without the subjection of power itself to the law, the juridification of proprietors as well as of property, of the powerful as well as of power.

# CHAPTER V

# Toward a History of the French State

A NEW reality calls for a new word. The institution of the state is no exception to this principle. In the fifteenth century, Claude de Seyssell and Machiavelli used the word "state" in its modern meaning to signify the power to command men and, by extension, as government or regime. At first, the term *status* was a genitive, as in *Status Rei Publicae, Imperii, Regni, Regis.*[1] Earlier, one had spoken of *Res Publica, Corona, Regnum,* when the state still lay dormant in the depths of kingdoms. But in England and Bohemia at the end of the Middle Ages, the crown itself became an abstract notion that by its prestige erased the particularities of the *rex.* A new vocabulary was in the making wherein one can observe the people growing, becoming emancipated, and taking root in an institution, the political system of the state.

"In the beginning was the state under rule of law," as Georges de Lagarde put it in *La Naissance de l'esprit laïque au déclin du Moyen Age.*[2] In a chapter that attempts to define the nature of a state, entitled "Qu'est-ce que l'Estat?" Lagarde brings out the disturbing fact that the statute according to which the legal condition of a community, an association, or more often a city is defined, is a departure from the old contract of the fief. That contract, which was based on the layout of lands, engaged individuals, bonded persons for their lifetime, and stipulated a personal and transitory dependence. The state, however, based on the condition of persons, organizes a community, enlists several generations, and binds the functioning of an institution in enduring knots. Binding regulations "all in all fix the juridical statute of a community."[3] This statute thus defines the *estat* of a group, the body of its rights, which were originally exempted and privileged in the medieval sense, as well as its common laws and community principles in the modern sense. The *estat* is a statute of juridical and public right. According to Lagarde, it took at least

> two centuries to constitute in this way alongside the feudal lordships and the ecclesiastical immunities these countless disparate judicial circles within which people wishing to escape the feudal regime recast the status of their collective liberty.[4]

Little by little the various social groups, the bourgeoisie, the nobility, and the clergy each in its turn acquired statutes. Lagarde sees in this the origin of the different *estats* that made up the Estates-General. The import of these observations, extended by a critical discussion of the traditional interpretations of E. Lousse and O. Hintze, is to assign a specific historical origin, distinct from the feudal charter, to the social-contract theory that the natural-rights philosophers formulated at a later date. These observations led Lagarde to put forth the hypothesis that the state, the *estat*, by reason of its collective and communitarian juridical dimension, does not derive from the private contract. Lagarde, moreover, later emphasizes the anti-individualist character of corporatist statutes. His detailed analysis delineates the genealogies: the social contract, the *estat* under rule of law, is not a private charter. As for how these *estats* are connected to the state, the link might be found in the mechanism by which territorial princes multiplied and assembled the *estats* with the intention of reinforcing and facilitating the exercise of their own power. It might be sought in the mechanism of associative government—that is, with a juridical and institutional inquiry as the starting point.

## The Limits of an Economic Perspective

The merits of an approach to the history of states dissociated from economic preoccupations comes to light when one assesses the limitations of the British historian Perry Anderson's recent inquiry into the absolutist state.[5] Anderson's interesting and vigorous work has some fine points. Engels's assertion that "the absolute monarchy of the seventeenth and eighteenth centuries . . . held the balance between the nobility and the class of burghers" rallied a whole generation of historians behind Boris Porchnev, who was convinced that with the state history had reached its lowest point.[6] To counter this position, Anderson strives to give renewed significance to political history on its own terms. Reshuffling the accepted divisions into space and time, Anderson sees the history of the absolutist state developing over four centuries on European soil. To show how this is so, he provides an overview of Spain, France, England, Italy, Sweden, Prussia, Poland, Austria, and Russia, along with a comparison of Japan and Russia, from the fifteenth to the eighteenth centuries. Given such a vast field, there could be no question of doing original research on each state, and consequently Anderson's study is essentially a thoughtful synthesis of existing scholarship. This approach has led him to present the absolutist state as a feudal state organized to serve the dominant feudal class through centralized revenue collections. Such a state, Anderson maintains, is militaristic, mercantile, and patrimonial.[7]

Anderson's interpretation takes into account a number of facts: the unified civilization that presided over Europe's emerging industrial societies from the Atlantic to the Urals; the permanent state of virtual armed conflict that marked the period; the persistence of aristocracies and the proliferation of court societies. Anderson concludes that the absolutist state is an extension of feudalism and that capitalism emerges out of feudalism. Moreover, this view has the added advantage of shedding light on the industrial development of Japan, one of the few Asian countries to have a feudal system similar to Europe's. Anderson's problematic in this way takes up the view of the nineteenth-century German historians who attributed Europe's evolution to Germany's feudalism. Despite these strong points, however, the weaknesses in Anderson's account are perhaps more serious because it neglects to take into account other aspects that are just as significant as the ones on which he concentrates. In its indifference regarding the specific elements in the forms of states, Anderson's approach tends to put all states together in one category. France and England are set alongside Spain, Western states alongside Eastern states. Some forms of states thereby become reified and others are eclipsed. Such is precisely the case with England, as Anderson admits readily: "England experienced a peculiarly contracted variant of Absolutist rule, in every sense."[8] This is tantamount to admitting that his proposed interpretation does not apply in this instance.

The problem with Anderson's approach is its use of the concept of the feudal state to discuss states that aim at abolishing servitude, separating power from property, and gradually developing ways of settling civil suits by recourse to law rather than war.[9] On the basis of the evidence, the concept of an absolutist feudal state is hardly suited to a state under the rule of law. Anderson's economistic approach is preoccupied with surplus value and class struggle, but it is blind to the juridico-insitutional forms that engendered a new state organization at an early date in England and later on and only in part in France. In Western Europe, the characteristics of the merchant, military, and patrimonial feudal state were challenged, shaken, and often destroyed by those of the state ruled by law: sovereignty opposed suzerainty, the inalienability of crown possessions opposed their patrimoniality, and so on. What escapes Anderson's purview is precisely the state under the rule of law, which burst the seams of feudalism with its novel codifications and institutions.

Institutional historians had observed the inadequacy of a purely economic explanation. Chéruel has given an example that, although quite particular, is nonetheless very enlightening, because it reveals the specific nature of statist intervention: the differentiated evolution of the Italian and French bourgeois communes that proliferated in the Renaissance. As the classical terrain of municipal freedoms, Italy presented both the brilliant spectacle of Pisa, Genoa, Venice, and Florence, and also the painful image of their unceasing rivalry. Similar divisions threatened the French communes. Since the thirteenth and fourteenth centuries, Paris and Rouen had quarreled sadly over the toll revenues for navigating the Seine, never hesitating to block free movement and hinder commerce along the river.[10] In Italy there was no state; in France the state imposed itself. While beyond the Alps quarrels raged, Charles VII rose above the petty municipal rivalries to impose free movement along the Seine and bring an end to private combat among the communes.

It would be just as vain to pretend that economics explains everything or nothing. If economic and political doctrines rival each other foolishly, economic history and political history get along together. The study of juridico-institutional forms that presided over the birth of the state under the rule of law may be of value in this matter. We seek here only to prepare the ground and to raise a few questions, first with regard to a favored example of comparative history (France versus England) and then about the difficulties surrounding state control of law in France.

### France and England

The comparison of the French and English regimes is a standard exercise in political science. There are some commonly accepted explanations as to how England achieved national unity, the idea of the state, unified taxation and law, and free juridical institutions when other nations had no premonitions about such things. England was blessed with the development of civil society, an active aristocracy, and a weak state, whereas France was cursed with a lifeless social body, a humiliated nobility, and the rigid demands of public authorities. France had a strong and centralized state, coupled with a subservient civil society that nurtured popular reaction and a thirst for equality. England, by contrast, had a relaxed and decentralized government, an aristocracy unrivaled for its longevity and zealous for liberties. An old feudal land with king and lords celebrating the outdated rituals, England was paradoxically ahead of its time.

A reasonable approximation of this view arose in France, thanks to the efforts of Montesquieu and Voltaire in countering despotism. Montesquieu, who transformed his park at La Brède into an English garden, asserted in his *Notes sur l'Angleterre* that "England is the freest country in the world."[11] In his *Lettres philosophiques*, his letters on the English, Voltaire affirmed that "the civil wars of Rome ended in slavery, and those of the English in liberty. The English are the only people on earth who have been able to prescribe limits to the power of kings by resisting them."[12] A confirmed Germanist—he writes of "the barbarians who came from the shores of the Baltic, and settled in the rest of Europe, (bringing) with them the form of government called States or Parliament, about which so much is made and which are so little understood"—Voltaire propagated a mythical account of England's history, which unleashed Anglomania throughout Europe.[13]

The French were not alone responsible for this view of England, however. The myths about English political history owe a great deal to the British themselves, especially to Bolingbroke, Shaftesbury, and, somewhat later, Hume and Coke.[14] In the wake of the Glorious Revolution, these men drew the perfect picture of the evolution of the British realm. Their views were no less cogent than the those of the nineteenth-century French historians who were hypnotized by the Revolution. Both viewpoints were accommodations to the preoccupations of the time. The French historians became nearsighted from focusing on their recent revolution, and their English counterparts fixed their sights on the narrow perspective of their current history. This generally resulted in severing the period of the Conquest from England's history.

It was Lord Chief Justice Coke, against whose arguments Hobbes did battle, who popularized the idea of a Norman yoke. According to this view, before 1066 the Anglo-Saxons would have lived as free and equal citizens of a state with a representative system. The defense of parliamentary liberties would not entail any claim to new freedoms but was rather a return to ancient liberties.[15] English scholars avidly set themselves to interpreting the articles of the Magna Carta and so prepared the way for eighteenth-century French historiography, which was likewise taken up with discovering the founding freedoms in the March and May assemblies. The eighteenth-century English ideologues' historical interpretation reveals the limitations of conjectural evidence by omitting to take into account the period that followed the Conquest and by extolling the great contractual moments of English history as the expression of an incorruptible nature. Anyone who looks at the events of 1789–1793 without reservations will just as easily accept the idea that the Revolution was a total break with the ancien régime. The observation has no chance of being nuanced unless one is willing to take a few steps back. In reaction to this interpretation, later historians of English constitutional law, among them Stubbs and Freeman, took a more detached view and saw in William the Conqueror's expedition and its aftermath something quite different from youthful wrongdoing or hidden vice.[16]

The extent to which this reinsertion of an era that had been arbitrarily expelled from history changed how the English political regime and the France-England comparison were viewed can be gathered from reading *Le Développement de la constitution et de la société politique en Angleterre*, by Émile Boutmy, the founder of the École des sciences politiques. Boutmy's book, published in 1887, is a keen and subtle synthesis of what is known about the period immediately following the Conquest and at the same time a profound reflection on political history. His book opens the way for a rethinking of the comparative evolution of the French and English states and of the genesis of modern government on new grounds and in the distinctive terms of the liberal tradition. Boutmy's interpretation, along with similar interpretations of other historians of English political law—notably Glasson's—is of some value to our discussion.

## Émile Boutmy's Interpretation

According to Boutmy, English history can be summed up in three paradoxes:

> The extreme intensity of royal power at a time when barbarism still prevailed gave England a parliament that represented a homogeneous country and was the instrument of a free government. The precocious concentration of high feudal lords into an aristocratic political body gave the nation equality before the law and taxation and preserved it from the abusive privileges of a blood nobility. The rapid development of centralization personified in the circuit judges gave the country an administration by the country itself and consolidated self-government.[17]

Boutmy observed the seeds of a strong state and a movement toward centralization where conventional thinking had maintained the opposite.

Modern political England took shape between the eleventh and fourteenth centuries, when the country's territory, government, and law were unified. This was an astonishing advance by comparison with France. By the early twelfth century, when the kingdom of the Capetians was but a speck in the mosaic of fiefdoms, the English realm had already taken shape as a homogeneous entity. France achieved geographic unity and national identity only seven hundred years later, and then only through a cataclysm. In Great Britain, according to Boutmy, the egoism and narrowness of provincial mentalities disappeared at an early date. Yet this did not prevent the development of English civil society and the establishment of local government. When England, under the Plantagenets, entered upon the stage of European history, it was already ruled by "one law only, only one custom." In France, on the one hand, the state in the seventeenth century was still weak and besieged beneath the appearances of arbitrary power and prestigious royalty. The defensive and military character of political superintendents and officers revealed how much the state had clung to the siege mentality of bygone feudal anarchy. In England, on the other hand, the power of the monarchy knew from the start how to subjugate the entire people to its juridical and fiscal yoke. Within their unified kingdom, the English monarchs imposed their will by contrast with their

French counterparts. When Henry II and Philip Augustus joined hands to organize a crusade, they both instituted a "Saladin tithe," but the king of France had to give up any hope of collecting it, whereas the king of England, disregarding all complaints, succeeded in having the tax levied.[18] As late as the eighteenth century, Linguet could still compare French law to a tattered beggar's coat that had been mended again and again, but English high justice had moved ahead and unified national law by 1200.

Boutmy's placing the rise of the English state in the Middle Ages upset the terms of its comparison with France. Boutmy, however, did not rest content with a purely synchronic analysis of the differences between the two regimes, but attempted to assess on a diachronic plane how the two countries' institutional formations were related. This promising perspective allowed him to examine how much the English and the French states differed. More than that, he was able to see what England might have in common with France, but about which England was more nimble, more developed and forward-looking.

## Royalty's Strength and Feudalism's Weakness

On the continent, a weak monarchy made feudalism strong. In Britain, a vigorous monarchy sapped feudalism of its strength. That vigor was there from the beginning if one takes the Conquest as a starting point. The English monarchs did not follow the Carolingian practice of vassalage and land grants that dismembered, dispersed, and finally dissolved sovereignty under the tutelage of the feudal manors. On the other hand, in England, it was feudalism that broke up. The English monarchy at an early date put into practice the adage that later became the watchword of French royal politics: "Divide and rule." In all respects—in land ownership, politics, the military, as well as in society—feudalism broke down. Once the English king became the sole proprietor of the land, rather than distribute large domains, he granted to each of his barons territories located in different parts of the land.[19] As lords of scattered properties, these leading vassals were no longer sovereigns or dispensers of justice and so they could not assume the attributes of royal authority. There was nothing on English soil to compare with the threat posed by great fiefs, such as Aquitaine or Burgundy, that could become competing kingdoms in France. English feudalism, which Boutmy referred to as *féodalité parcellaire*, came about through the delegation of land at the will and under the control of a powerful monarch intent on implementing policies favorable to his own interests.

Feudalism in England also suffered a political breakdown. With the exception of the Counts Palatine of Chester and Durham, vested with regal rights by virtue of their charge to fight for the kingdom against the Gauls and the Scots, the great barons were not granted the same powers as the great feudal lords on the continent. In England there was no distinction between lands of obedience and nonobedience at the feudal lord's discretion. The English monarchs carefully reserved to themselves the prerogative of distributing power and property to another. Boutmy cites how King Stephen, for example, created counts without lands, who drew pensions from the royal treasury. The English lords were thus a mixed institution, midway between archaic Norman solidarity and modern court society. It was still dominated by personal bonds and already taken up with the system of princely freedoms at the time French feudalism had become a territorial hierarchy made up of independent and all-powerful dynasts.[20] The barons lost all administrative power in the counties, where the crown was represented by viscounts who were royal functionaries in no way dependent on the counts. From 1170 onward, sheriffs were chosen from among the officers of justice. With the establishment of circuit judges in 1176, the administrative structure was complete. The entire administration served at the pleasure of the monarchy. "In all matters," Boutmy says, "the king rebuked his viscounts, removed them, dismissed them as a body and individually."[21]

The breakdown of feudalism also weakened the military. The British monarchs were the first to deprive feudalism of a military monopoly by raising a royal army superior to the feudal troops. In France a permanent army was not established until Charles VII gathered a specialized and national band of fighting men that enabled him to demilitarize society.[22]

Lastly, feudalism underwent a social division. The English aristocracy did not become a caste, full of anger and arrogance as was the case in France, where titles, ranks, lineage, precedence, and family woes—legitimacy, adultery, bastardy—obsessed the aristocracy. The British dignitaries, whose wigs, robes, and ermines others foolishly laugh off, were never hypnotized by honors to the point of wanting to give each man a sort of cane and hat that would allow his worth and place in the social structure to be recognized instantly, according to the duc de Saint-Simon's fantastic project that continued to draw foreign attention long after the French Revolution. Things happened differently in England, because the Norman baronage broke down rapidly, without leaving behind a rigid division into high and low aristocracy.

The high aristocracy of the lords, dedicated to the professional exercise of power delegated by the king, gradually came to constitute a kind of statist technostructure of high rank. Since it was defined by its function, the peerage, and linked to an indivisible office that was strictly hereditary by primogeniture, the high nobility, instead of making up as in France an order of privileged families, constituted instead a restricted group of individuals with functions. In France the blood nobility and the exemptions connected with name grew in the proliferation of younger branches, but in England the higher aristocracy was limited to high-level political personnel and required new creations in order to prevent its extinction. The lower aristocracy as well, the knights preoccupied with the land, did not form a caste along the lines of the French squires. Instead, they quietly changed into a high rural class, the gentry, which was more congenial than hostile to the penetration of the agricultural middle class, the yeomanry.

Tocqueville was struck by the nobility's openness, flexibility, and professional character:

> I have always been surprised that a fact so strikingly peculiar to England, and which is the only true key to the peculiarities of her laws, her spirit, and her history, should have obtained so little notice among philosophers and statesmen. . . . The contrast between England and the rest of Europe arose, indeed, less from her Parliament, her liberty, her freedom of the press, and her jury system, than from another and more important peculiarity. England was the only country where castes had been not altered, but thoroughly abolished.[23]

Tocqueville wrote of the sad situation caused by the antagonism between classes in France, where privilege linked to blood rather than office lost its legitimacy and dignity, provoked the resentment of all whom it excluded, and became a costly and scandalous obstacle to social communication. In return, public offices tended to turn into privileges that set apart individuals, who then deserted their public mission to indulge in private gain and self-interest. Everything in life became ritualized and compartmentalized. Everywhere narrow-mindedness set in and people put on blinders, to the detriment of the body social.

In France, the nobility, which turned its sights toward a past weighed down with magnificence, remained for a long time a faction that fomented trouble and hampered the workings of a modern political order. But in England the aristocracy, freed of any backward glances at an early stage, entered into the agencies of royal administration without any hesitation, looked to the people for support, and became statist and patriotic. In England the territorial baronage disappeared at an early date and feudalism was overcome in short order. This defeat cleared the way for the establishment of a state under the rule of law.

## Juridical Unification

The mythic account of English history is preoccupied with interpreting the juridical system of common law. As a result of a confusion between its function in jurisprudence and its origins, common law has been said to originate on the local level. Nothing, however, is further from the truth. Common law has a royal origin. The falsification of the history of common law begins with Coke in the seventeenth century and continues in the tenacious assertions of Blackstone, the classical champion of parliamentary freedoms, whose great ambition was to demonstrate that, unlike the continent, England had prevented the development of absolute royal power. Blackstone presented England's national law as an outgrowth of the country and explained that common law was a sort of *corpus juris* that developed spontaneously through the accumulation of customs practiced in accord with natural justice. This became the official interpretation of English juridical science and can be found as is in Blackstone, who had no qualms in writing that the legal customs that make up the common law of England "are contained in the records of the several courts of justice, in books of reports and judicial decisions, and in the treatises of learned sages of the profession, preserved and handed down to us from the times of highest antiquity."[24]

William Stubbs emphasized how English law was spared by the scourge of the imperialist idea and the oppressive union with Italy and so developed apart from the absolutist tendencies of Roman law, but it also emerged from the concerted efforts of a small number of legislators.[25] It was the product of the curia regis and the casuistic developments wrought by a vigorously centralized administration of justice that was strictly subject to royal authority. In its origins, English law was much less customary than was continental law. The rise of common law and its procedures through the use of documents in good and due form that ordered subjects of the crown to appear before a judge under penalty for contempt of writ, is closely connected to the institution of movable judges. Common law was unified by circuit judges dispatched by the monarch to settle local suits that disrupted the body social and threatened the king's peace. Contrary to what might be thought, royal circuit justice was not erratic and improvising, and movement from place to place was not an occasion for hesitation or recantations. As Boutmy made clear, the English judges were the apostles of statist unification.

It is important to note that in England centralization was achieved through law. England was and remained a state under the rule of law. Historians of English law, such as Holdsworth and Allen, rightly observe that the developments of political society and of law were not separate processes. On the contrary, a judge was a man of the state; by the same token he is a judge. This state of affairs was rooted in the formation of a state under the rule of law in England, where sovereignty was established and developed through the workings of the law. The crown was the source of law, the fountain of justice, because the power of law itself bestowed authority on the sovereign. As the English legist Bracton asserted, long before the French legists, "the law maketh the king." The judge played a major role in English society, perhaps because he was from the beginning a buttress of the state, and the law has remained an indisputable authority, perhaps also because an offense against the law was an offense against a society composed of members who were all subject to the law but who also held the power to judge whoever disobeyed or transgressed the law.

France took a very different route. Whereas England was a "pure" state under the rule of law, France only approximated such a state. There centralization took place at a later date and more slowly, through the administrative channels of royal commissioners and superintendents of finances working against the judges, personnel who became an intermediary body resisting central authority. England, on the other hand, achieved centralization at an early date, through judges acting as the agents of royal authority, but judges had no authority in France compared to the functionaries and tax collectors. The official compilation of customaries in France did not really begin until the fifteenth century, after the ordinance of Montils les Tours in 1454, but in England the process began in the eleventh century, under the impetus of William the Conqueror. England was five centuries ahead of France!

The great jurists of the twelfth and thirteenth centuries, Ranulf de Glanvill and Henry de Bracton, were the true founders of English juridical science and of modern public law, as distinct from Roman law.[26] In *De Legibus et Consuetudinibus Angliae,* Bracton underscored the superiority of modern law. Roman law privileged royal interest, returned a freedman back to slavery for ingratitude, did not allow a woman to plead for another person or bear witness to a will, prohibited a son from acquiring property without the consent of the paterfamilias. English law, on the other hand, protected the national interest, forbade the return to slavery of freedmen, allowed women to plead, and permitted sons freely to acquire property. Bracton also extolled the English judiciary tradition's jury system and public hearings.[27] Britain's modernity is further attested in the early disappearance of servitude and the promulgation of habeas corpus.[28]

Boutmy's study of the English monarchy's beginnings challenged accepted ideas. Was the English state weak? The strongest of states imposed territorial and administrative unity by relying on the support of judges rather than tax collectors. Was the English aristocracy all-powerful? The greatest of the feudal lords forged a political technostructure, and the rest of them merged the landowners at an early date, thereby preventing the profusion of privileges for a blood nobility and promoting equality before the law and taxation. Was England a decentralized society? The rapid development of centralized government brought about by the circuit judges shaped the country's juridical unity. In its beginnings England was no less statist than France but was more diligent, more impetuous, and more radical in the way it went about forging a state under the rule of law.

## The Dialectic of Centralization and Decentralization

Even if one accepts this analysis of the administrative monarchy that preceded the Magna Carta, one still needs to understand how the situation turned around to allow for the rise of Parliament and local administration and for the checking of royal power. Although Boutmy's account of the evolution of the English regime remains incomplete, it nevertheless contains great strengths. The revolt of the barons that gave birth to the Magna Carta in 1215, he maintains, should be seen as the logical consequence of the absolute character of royal authority. Faced with a resolute power as consolidated as it could be, the great feudal lords of England had no hope of evading that power, resisting it, or becoming independent of it. Since it was impossible for them to escape the king's grasp, they had no other recourse than to conceive of some form of association with the king that would give them some participation in the exercise of power. Once sovereignty had become a firmly rooted institution, it could then be appropriated collectively.

Boutmy argued in much the same way to explain the establishment of justices of the peace, self-government, and local administration. At the origin of these institutions was the circuit judges' reactivation of an old Saxon institution, the county court, to which Edward II granted official status in 1361. According to Boutmy, centralization in England gave rise to decentralization. Justices of the peace were appointed by the crown, at first from the knighthood, then soon afterward from among all the landowners. Their mission was to supervise the maintenance of order, to reprimand infractions of the law, and to oversee the parish constables. This astonishing system became the object of all Europe's envy of the British Isles, where prominent countrymen born of the gentry and the yeomanry accomplished without payment the essential tasks of an immense undertaking, which everywhere else was entrusted to a central bureaucracy. Boutmy emphasized the strong antifeudal character of the justices of the peace, whose jurisdiction was more collegial than personal and revocable rather than hereditary. They held office by virtue of royal commissioning and not by concessions exacted from the crown. Justice was meted by gentlemen and commoners alike doing public service as jurors rather than by the private activity of jurisconsults in the hire of feudal lords.[29] Every landowner had the opportunity to be judged, but property was no longer the basis for exercising the right to justice. The creation of a lower house, conceived in 1295 and established in 1341, is for Boutmy a testimony to the prominent place the knights held among the justices of the peace and the important services they rendered to the state.

Beyond altering the conventional terms of the France-England comparison, Boutmy's study revamped the formulation of the classic problem in political science regarding the genesis of modern government as formulated by Montesquieu, precisely with regard to the English constitution, in *The Spirit of the Laws:*

> In each state there are three sorts of powers: legislative power, executive over the things depending on the right of nations, and executive power over the things depending on civil right. . . . When legislative power is united with executive power in a single person or in a single body of the magistracy, there is no liberty. . . . Nor is there liberty if the power of judging is not separate from legislative power and from executive power. . . . All would be lost if the same man or the same body, either of nobles, or of the people, exercised these three powers.[30]

In this passage Montesquieu developed his famous thesis that the separation or division of powers is the hallmark and condition of free government, of which England is the embodiment. The separation of powers was from Montesquieu onward taken to be the essence of modern representative government.

Boutmy's historical reflections bring to light an altogether different interpretation, according to which a division of functions would not be a condition or principle, but rather a consequence or result of, the English constitution. Boutmy uncovered a neglected genesis of modern government starting from a reflection on the mechanism of *association* rather than *representation*. Where the liberals explored the division into legislative, judicial, and executive functions, Boutmy emphasized the juridical unity that subordinated all other attributions to its rule. Where the democrats conceived of the representative assembly as a delegation of the popular will from the bottom upward, through agencies that represent and execute it, Boutmy sought to examine how the royal will functioned from above downward, through institutions that carry it out. Where one might expect a minute description of *representative government*, starting with society, to interpret the state, Boutmy revealed the traces of *associative government*, through which the state under the rule of law has shaped society.

In this Boutmy was more faithful to historical reality than the "Germanist" historians, who were quick to impose on reality the myth of a founding parliament. The doctrine of the separation of the executive and judiciary makes it impossible to distinguish the diverse powers within the king's council and difficult to attempt an interpretation of the English constitutional order. Élie Halévy has equally well underscored the amalgamation of judiciary and legislative powers in England at the beginning of the nineteenth century. Under the British constitution judges could exercise legislative functions and legislators judiciary functions. Halévy concludes that

> once again we are compelled to correct Montesquieu's interpretation of the British Constitution. His two definitions of that Constitution—a Constitution based on the division of powers, a mixed Constitution—are not equivalent, and the latter is the more accurate. The British Government was not a Government in which all the powers were clearly distinguished. It was rather a Government in which all the constituent parts were confused, and all the powers mutually encroached.[31]

Other historians of law and the state had earlier observed that the sovereigns, to increase their power, had built up the mechanisms that were destined to incorporate the taxpayers. Charles Petit-Dutaillis remarked that article 14 of the Magna Carta, regarding the granting of aid by the common council of the realm, did not meet with the wishes of the barons. The latter, who preferred individual consent to taxation, must have shown no inclination at all for the principle of a collective consent that made it possible for the majority to bind those opposed but not present. Article 14 of the Magna Carta, Petit-Dutaillis noted, may have originated with the king himself.[32] Historians of French institutions see a similar remarkable advance of royal authority in Louis VII's decree of 1155, which secured a ten-year peace throughout the realm in the wake of the council held at Soissons. In order to widen the sphere of his ordinance's application and have the barons observe it, the king called on the barons themselves to join him compelling them to join with him in formulating the decree.[33] Later, in England, the most energetic monarchs, Edward I and Edward III, took the greatest strides in instituting representation. The mechanism of *associative government* is difficult to grasp from the starting point of the French experience of monarchs stubbornly resisting the demands of parliaments for a share in legislative power. Such requests for a share in power seem to have been rejected again and again. Despite this, however, it should not be forgotten that deliberation, counsel, and justice were understood to be duties before they were asserted as rights.

To all these paradoxes that complicate the comparison of the French and English evolutions, one more could be added as a kind of postscript. The illusory image of England as aristocratic and civil, *semper eadem,* was elaborated and diffused on the continent, with the help of civilist thinkers, in the eighteenth century, at the very time when the traditional balances of forces that ordered England's juridico-political system were being shaken.

An open and liberal aristocracy at that time was becoming an oligarchic tyranny, while the middle class was breaking up. The patrimonial basis of feudal land ownership abolished under Tudor laws surfaced again through changes in inheritance laws that made it impossible to transfer two-thirds of the English and Scottish terrain. Protected by fiscal and civil immunities, the aristocratic oligarchy in parliament crushed the autonomy of local authorities. Boutmy describes how

> the country magistrates were not under any authority from above them, since the legislation had a vested interest in maintaining confidence in their integrity and the state was powerless. The magistrates also met with no limit to their power beneath them, since communal authority had disintegrated and the parishes were strictly subject to their tutelage.[34]

The restoration of feudal lordship had economic consequences as well, since it was the oligarchy that provided the impetus for the emergence of English industry between 1750 and 1780.[35]

The liberal and democratic constitution that marked the English state under the rule of law fell on hard times in the eighteenth century. A more traditional order would return, Boutmy explains, from 1830 onward. But it was at this very time that Voltaire and Monstesquieu, and afterwards Marx, believed they had found the key to England's history. Is it any wonder that they did not find any state under the rule of law?

We should be careful as to what to conclude from this. Although Émile Boutmy's book raises more questions than it answers, its chief merit is to render suspect accepted ideas and partisan interpretations. It does not hesitate to delve deep into England's remote past in order to challenge anachronisms, and it presents a more balanced comparison of France and England. Boutmy's book makes an important contribution to the history of the state under rule of law, because it examines English liberalism from the perspective of the state rather than society alone.

### Difficulties with State Regulation of Law in France

Contrary to what Marx thought, modern politics revealed its essence to the bare bones in France more than in any other country. The French state was only an approximation of a state under the rule of law in its pure form. France's earlier political legacy prevented her from achieving the same maturity that England attained. Even in the revolutions of the eighteenth and nineteenth centuries, French politics was a hybrid of modern notions of sovereignty and feudal forms of suzerainty.

Tocqueville analyzed the complex structure of French politics by distinguishing between two types of centralization, governmental and administrative, and observing that France, although fully engaging in the latter type, was unsuccessful in the former. His words bear quoting at length:

> There are . . . two very distinct types of centralization, which need to be well understood. Certain interests, such as the enactment of general laws and the nation's relations with foreigners, are common to all parts of the nation. There are other interests of special concern to certain parts of the nation, such, for instance as local enterprises. To concentrate all the former in the same place or under the same directing power is to establish what I call government centralization. To concentrate control of the latter in the same way is to establish what I call administrative centralization. . . .
>
> For my part, I cannot conceive that a nation can live, much less prosper, without a high degree of centralization of government. But I think that administrative centralization only serves to enervate the peoples that submit to it, because it constantly tends to diminish their civic spirit.[36]

Tocqueville further observes that there are two ways of decentralizing power in a nation. The first is "to weaken the very basis of power by depriving society of the right or capacity to defend itself in certain circumstances." The second way avoids these ill consequences "by dividing the use of its powers among several hands."[37] If Tocqueville is correct, France followed the first way by centralizing its adminstration rather than its government. State unification was achieved through public function, to the detriment of law.

Centralized government in France suffered from the slow process of juridical unification that did not take place until the Napoleonic civil code. The sphere of private law suffered the most from these delays. Legal historians have noted how feudalism's survival in the family and in property regulation entailed a host of consequences: the vast expansion of the system of medieval rents, the regulation of inheritance based on property, abuses in the benefits flowing from the right of primogeniture, the requirement that younger sons renounce all claims to family patrimony, and the virtual civil death of anyone entering a monastery. As Glasson says, "feudalism lost all of its political force, but it retained all its vigor in civil law."[38]

On the other hand, remarkable progress took place in public law. The French monarchy made a smooth transition from the private patrimonial law of the Merovingian monarchy, where the kingdom Clovis had conquered belonged to him personally, to the idea of a public law.[39] The modern doctrine of sovereignty was in some fashion already embodied in the *fundamental laws*, the "law of the realm," as the edict of July 1588 called it, or *customary constitution*.

As Olivier-Martin has explained very well, this "law of the realm" remained imperfect with regard to its influence in the civil sphere. In the face of ancient authorities and age-old traditions, the king could not take away old prerogatives in the name of an abstract conception of sovereignty. Thus, the monarchy argued for policies according to which kings would always have the right to interfere and to act after seeking counsel.[40]

The "law of the realm" was somewhat more consequential in the political domain. The monarchy met with two obstacles from without, the society of order and the society of the body that prevented it from achieving genuine governmental centralization. From within, however, the modern doctrine of sovereign power weakened the monarchy to the point of transfiguring it. Once power was no longer either *imperium* or *dominium*, the monarchy also ceased to be a *patrimonium*. The threat contained in the doctrines of Bodin and Loyseau was carried out in the fundamental laws that regulated sovereign power in matters of dynastic heredity, the concept of legitimacy, the unavailability of the crown, and the inalienability of dominion. The customary constitution was progressively elaborated over several centuries by royal legists, such as Jean de Terre-Vermeille, Claude de Seyssel, Charles de Grassailles, Jean Ferrault, Du Tillet, Guy Coquille, and others.[41] It objectivized legal proceedings, relativized the role of the monarch, and diminished familial power. In a word, it destroyed the state's patrimonial character.

The theory of legitimacy, which, as Guy Coquille put it, made "France a monarchy tempered by laws," is of interest to our inquiry, because it reveals the opposing natures of absolutism and arbitrariness.[42] The idea of the supremacy of law over kings was a commonplace of classical juridical practice, as Declareuil shows from statements made by traditional opponents who concur on this one point.[43] It legitimized the monarchy in the measure that it made the monarchy subject to laws that the kings themselves could neither abrogate nor modify. This triumph of the law over the monarchy was notably manifest in the so-called statutory theory of the devolution of the crown that established laws of succession that were in the interest of the state rather than the king. Since the time of Jean de Terre-Vermeille, the king did not succeed his predecessor as his heir, son, or next of kin, but solely because he was expressly designated by law beforehand. Bodin stated clearly that "the kingdom is not conferred by paternal succession but rather by virtue of the law of the kingdom."[44] That statute lay at the origin of the cry, "The king is dead! Long live the king!" and the maxim that "in France kings do not die."

The theory of legitimacy entailed several important consequences. Abdication was forbidden, the order of succession could not be altered, the king could renounce the throne for himself or his descendants, and there could be no regency in the legal sense. No matter how young the king was, he remained head of state and another could govern only in his name and by delegation. Royal consecration became essentially an act of piety with

no juridical significance. Furthermore, as Declareuil observed, the inalienability of the crown's dominion was a corollary of the unavailability of the
crown, since the king could no more dispose of what depended on the
crown than of the crown itself.[45] The maintenance of sovereignty required
the unity and indivisibility of the territory subject to it and made dominion
over the land a fiscal necessity. The fundamental law prohibiting the
transfer and limitation of dominion was developed from the fourteenth
century onward through a series of ordinances revoking property transfers
and usurpations, and received its definitive formulation in the edict of
Moulins in 1566. The requirement that the personal property of monarchs
be annexed to the crown became official with Henry IV. The king of
Navarre, heir to the House of Albret and also the sovereign of Béarn, invoked the interests of his sister in refusing to unite his patrimonial possessions to the French crown. Under pressure from the Parlement of Paris, he
finally acceded by his edict of July 1607, in the preamble to which he noted
that "our predecessors dedicated and consecrated themselves to the public
from whom they wanted to have nothing distinct or separate."[46] Histori-
cally the tendency was not that the dominion won the state, but that the
state won the dominion. Instead of the state's becoming a patrimony, the
royal patrimony was turned into a state.

French historians of constitutional law in the ancien régime, such as
Chéruel, Glasson, Chenon, and more recently Declareuil and Olivier-Martin, all point out that the patrimonial state was constituted by challenging
public law. Perry Anderson, however, seems to know nothing of this when
he writes that "the state was conceived as the patrimony of the monarch,
and therefore the title-deeds to it could be gained by a union of persons."[47]
Such a flagrant error makes it easy to equate the states of Western Europe
with those of the East. At the same time it also brings out the importance
of the judicial theme that permeates the history of the state. By failing to
grasp it, Anderson can go a long way and yet fail to grasp what really
happened. As Moreau pointed out in 1775, by the end of the ancien régime,
the state was not judicial and no longer patrimonial:

> The kings bind themselves by the laws they prescribe to their people. They
> are the image of God himself, who, as absolute master of the laws of motion
> which it was in his power to prescribe to nature in the mechanism of the
> universe, nonetheless invariably conforms to these laws and leaves his work
> to them.[48]

The achievement of centralized government through the unification of
power by the king was to a great extent successful within the state. On the
other hand, centralized government met with resistance from civil society,
which did not become unified by right or law but through administrative
and financial means.

### The Late Development of Civil Law and
### Centralized Administration

Linguet provides a harsh account of French civil law on the eve of the
Revolution, in the following terms:

> Like grenadiers armed with rattles, like a thirty-year-old wearing the outfits
> of a four-year-old or a man late in life making a single suit of clothes out of
> everything he had worn in his lifetime. . . . You can see all our authorities
> holding on to the outfits of their early years, which they readjust and sew
> together as best they can. . . . This is the bizarre patchwork of disgusting rags
> they shamelessly call treatises of jurisprudence.[49]

It was not that legists and monarchs were unwilling to modernize or unify
or even to codify the law. The legists themselves were at the origins of the
unofficial compilations of customaries in which bailiffs played a major
role. Originally these men were simply royal officers charged with admin-
istering justice and enforcing civilian and military obligations due the sovereign. In the course of time, however, through the jurisprudence of royal
cases and appeals to the default of law, they came to judge all kinds of
important matters and to defend accused parties of their bailiwick before
courts of parliament.[50] In the measure that they demanded that parliament grant them a part in jurisprudence, they played a fundamental role
in the shaping of customary law and in drawing up customaries.[51] Pierre
de Fontaine, bailiff of Vermandois, around 1251 compiled his *Conseil à un
ami* for the instruction of Philip the Bold and around 1280 Beaumanoir
drew up the landmark *Coutumier de Beauvoisis*. Customaries proliferated
in the thirteenth century, and by the fourteenth they were found in every
province, along with procedural handbooks known as *styles*.[52]

The king's ordinance of Montils les Tours in 1454 called for compilations to be made in every district. "Thus," as Montesquieu later observed,
"our customs assumed three characteristics: they were written down, they
were more general, and they received the stamp of royal authority."[53] The
project received significant impetus from Charles VIII and continued
under Louis XII and Francis I to the time of Henry IV. The finest jurisconsults were recruited for this work, among them Charles Dumoulin,
who commented the *Coutume de Paris;* Bertrand d'Argentré, the *Coutume
de Bretagne;* and Guy Coquille, the *Coutume de Navarre*. At the same
time, major ordinances, many of which dealt with private right, were also
modernized and codified. The Ordinance of Blois in 1579 called for the
codification of existing ordinances and inspired a number of new projects: the *Code Henri III*, an encyclopedic compilation of ordinances published in 1580; the *Code Michau*, edited by Michel de Marillac in 1629;

and the *Code Louis*, produced by Louis XIV's administration. None of these was ever promulgated, however. The first two met with the jealous hostility of parliaments and never took effect. The third remained a dead letter even if elements of codification were included in the ordinances of 1667 and 1670 that reorganized and unified the codes of civil and penal processes throughout France. Daguesseau, who denounced "the great inconveniences of diversity in jurisprudence," framed the three great ordinances regarding settlements, inheritances, and substitutions, of 1731, 1735, and 1747, respectively, but even he failed to bring about the desired codification.[54]

Between the thirteenth and eighteenth centuries, some efforts were made in France to collate and reform law codes along the lines of the juridication processes found in states under the rule of law. These efforts were not very successful with regard to civil law. Despite noble intentions, French civil law on the eve of the Revolution remained conservative and diffuse. Endless delays and fruitless discussions hindered the resolve of jurists, such as Dumoulin, Coquille, Loysel, Pothiers, Loyseau, Domat, and others, to unify the law. The codification project was all too easily reduced to mere publication. In 1274, Bourdot de Richebourg published a collection of customs arranged in no particular order. The mandate of the Estates-General of Blois in 1579 calling for the codification of major ordinances did not produce any results until the Académie des inscriptions et belles-lettres began publishing the *Recueil des Ordonnances des Rois de France* in 1723. France had to wait until Napoleon to produce a modern and homogeneous civil code.

What obstacles prevented the drawing up of a civil code? First of all, the feudal system weighed heavily on civil society. Local idiosyncracies, the resistance of privileged layers of society, and the fragmented character of the kingdom all conspired to delay juridical unification.[55] Some provinces, such as Brittany, obtained privileges that established reciprocally binding contracts between themselves and the realm. The country also suffered from the division between regions ruled by custom and those ruled by written law. The great judiciary bodies were jealous of their privileges and frequently opposed the unification of private law with all their might. In the juridical sphere, civil society was much more backward and divided than the state.

There were also difficulties over the independent status of the legislative function. Like Montesquieu, we take the legislative function to be a simple matter, but in earlier times there was no common understanding as to what law was or how it was formed. These questions were debated and fought over. The essence of the law was divine for the theologians, natural for the philosophers, civil according to the legists; and everyone, even while accepting competing viewpoints, considered all laws from his partic-

ular viewpoint. How were civil laws established? by royal will? once they
were sealed? through registration in the courts? In more modern terms,
were they established by principles of authority, legitimacy, or legality?
Circumstances dictated different answers, a sign that the legislative function arrived at autonomy and independence only at the end of a historical
process that was the same in France as it was in England.

Were laws made by royal will? Chenon observes that all the sixteenth-
century French legists asserted that legislative power belonged to the king.
The doctrine that royal intervention was the source of law, which Beaumanoir had formulated three centuries earlier, achieved its triumph in the
monarch's gradual confiscation of legislative power. The monarchy's
growing strength dispossessed the barons of the power they held to create
"establishments" or "assizes," as Geoffrey Plantagenet, the count of Brittany, had done in 1185 or Simon de Montfort in 1212. Under Louis XI, only
two or three feudal lords still legislated; by the time of Louis XIII, none did
any longer. Sovereignty absorbed legislation while the sovereign was assuming sovereignty unto himself. As Loyseau affirmed, "only the king can
make laws."[56] This was merely a theoretical definition, however. Unlike an
arbitrary system or a civilization without law, to use Aleksandr Zinoviev's
phrase, a juridical system's respect for a community's tradition in the civil
sphere is the opposite of the secret improvisation and clandestine decision
making found in despotic states. The state under the rule of law is under
obligation to articulate authority, legitimacy, and legality. When authority
is held to registering and publishing its acts, ordinances, and laws, it will
also be held to account and subject to challenge.

Legal discussions took different turns in England and in France. In
England the debate focused on sovereignty, and in France on legality. In
England, the early linkage of the three principles of authority, legitimacy,
and legality facilitated the development of an unchallenged and autonomous sphere for legitimacy in local justice and jurisprudence that introduced a tradition of rights in society. Consequently debate in England
centered on who held the legislative function and not on how law itself
functioned. In France, however, the longstanding separation of authority,
legitimacy, and legality opened up endless grounds for disputes every time
a law was to be registered and published.

On the one hand, the chancery's part in the process of making laws,
which involved registration, notification, addressing, and sealing, provided the chancellor with the occasion to demand some share in the king's
sovereignty. On the other hand, the legal forms of publication, which involved readings at public sessions of parliament and registration in the
clerk's office, gave public courts arguments for reservations or corrections
with which to reject or amend laws. Legitimacy in its very nature divided
the monarchs—who saw legitimacy as a matter of authority that was free

to neglect legal forms against the courts—and the courts, for whom legitimacy was attested to by legality, which set its sine qua non conditions. The debate was never resolved. By regulating power and arguing from judgment in equity, the parliaments constituted a sort of competing legislative process against the existing official legislation that the monarchy could not contend with. The outcome of Chancellor Maupeou's reform epitomized the many failures of the monarchy's attacks on the parliaments that set the stage for the Revolution. The division of authority and legality robbed legitimacy of a sphere of its own. Instead of being the object of *consensus*, as it was in England, civil law was the source of endless *dissensus* in France, where the debate over who held the legislative function took place before society was unified by law.

The parliaments were strong enough to hinder the juridical exercise of royal authority in juridical matters. French civil society posed an obstacle for a state under the rule of law to develop. But if the ethic of law remained weak, faith in the king was strong enough for the sovereign will to unify the country through the administration rather than by law. The state, which remained an alien body within a disparate society, clung to its archaic historical forms and engaged in a politics of siege mentality rooted in fear. From this came the gradual drift of centralized government toward centralized administration, from a state under the rule of law toward an administrative state.

## *The Administrative Drift*

The original work done in recent decades by such scholars as Michel Antoine, Pierre Chaunu, and Roland Mousnier has shed a great deal of light on the French state's drift toward an administrative state. Roland Mousnier has shown the part the state played in the gradual transformation of law-court officials from trustworthy agents of royal authority into privileged rebels who modeled their behavior on the nobility's.[57] While the English state remained a state ruled by justice, the French state was changing into a state ruled by office and beyond that into one ruled by finance. Mousnier provides unimpeachable evidence that the French state was at an early date a state under the rule of justice. Every royal decision, well into early modern times, was carried out as a legal ruling for which warrants and commissions were expedited. The king judged affairs of state in his council and derived all his powers from his role as sovereign justiciary. Likewise, his officers were judges who administered by decree. This phenomenon was widespread in Europe, where the modern idea of an a priori legislation did not yet exist.[58]

Pierre Chaunu dates the drift toward a finance state to the Renaissance,

when a monarchy centered on offices and finances replaced the judiciary
monarchy that had reached its height in the twelfth and thirteenth centuries. By the start of the sixteenth century, the greater part of France's
administrative corps of sixty thousand men was to be found in the finance
office. The increased needs of the tax system of the Valois-Angoulêmes
made the work of collecting taxes a top priority and gave finance officers
a place in the highest ranks of the realm.

In his pioneering work, *Le Conseil du roi sous Louis XV,* Michel Antoine
has shown that the year 1661 was an important turning point. By stripping
the chancery of its essential prerogatives, Louis XIV and Colbert accomplished a genuine revolution. Antoine emphasizes how

> [t]oo many historians, obsessed with the pitiable fate of Fouquet, have not
> grasped the full significance of what took place in 1661. If the person of the
> superintendent was subjected to persecution, the finance department, thanks
> to these spectacular measures, gained considerable power and influence.[59]

Once he was removed from the political council, the *conseil d'en haut,*
Chancellor Seguier ceased to be a minister of state, and the chancery, the
very symbol of the justice state, lost its functions along with its trappings.
By virtue of his prerogatives in expediting and sealing the royal acts, the
chancellor embodied the king's justice and stood at the head of the kingdom's entire magistracy. As the last of the crown's major officers, after the
constabulary and the admiralty had been eliminated, he was a survivor
from the time when the courts of justice, the power that settled suits, occu-
pied an important place within the kingdom. The decline of the chancery,
which had begun at the end of the Middle Ages, was sealed in 1661, and
from that point onward the responsibilities of the finance department increased greatly. By the late seventeenth century, the ordinary council of
finances established itself in independent realms and gradually took over
other services. Michel Antoine emphasizes the link between this increasing
financial control and the monarchy's military needs, since the resources
needed to wage war called for more and more efficient and centralized
collection agencies. As Antoine notes, the War of the Spanish Succession
went so far as to make a politics of public safety a matter of necessity.

This administrative drift, which made the intendant a key figure in the
state, was supported by a tax system that was anything but modern. The
ancien régime's tax system, as Clamageran pointed out over a century ago,
was greatly influenced by the feudal tax system.[60]

The feudal legacy was at work first of all in the system of prerogatives.
Clamageran pointed out that the establishment of a monopoly, such as the
salt monopoly that occasioned numerous conflicts, bore the character of a
dominial prerogative, because the state retained the exclusive right to sell
certain products that it declared to be dominial. In the measure that mo-

nopolized products were sold at a price higher than their real value, a monopoly is the equivalent of a tax on consumption. A parallel could easily be drawn between the ancient practice of attribution and modern contribution. The levying of taxes by attribution had its origins in the feudal system, in which taxation was a manifestation of power rooted in property. On the other hand, the levying of taxes by contribution was a privilege and a duty required of everyone, which implied the unity and consent of the body politic. It had a wider sphere of application and it was less coercive than attribution, since people subjected to public authority would likely regulate the services whose number, distribution, and remuneration were set by public authority. The power that required assent, which at a later date would entail the nation's voting on taxation, was by virtue of that requirement a public power.

The feudal system also had its legacy in the venality of taxation. By Clamageran's account, of the three characteristics of feudal taxation—its local apportionment, its customary aspect, and its venality—the most important was without doubt its venality. The office of tax collecting went to the highest bidder up to the time of the Revolution. Clamageran sees the venality of offices as the intrusion of fiscal dealings into the sphere of public positions. The payment for a tax collector's position was a kind of fee exacted by the privileged. Instead of imposing a fixed contribution on public offices, the offices were put up for sale.

The prerogatives and rents of the tax system of the ancien régime had their roots in an authoritarian and feudal conception of power as the object of appropriation and trade.[61] As it grew all-powerful within the state, the finance administration remained largely in the service of the privileged class. Fiscal history, like legal history, reveals the gap between intentions to modernize and their flawed actualization.

The monarchy succeeded in abolishing feudalism and feudal rights in the relation of sovereign and suzerain, but it failed to do so in the relation of suzerain and people. The lords were the great losers in the movement to centralize authority. In the twelfth century, they lost their privilege of arbitrarily imposing taxes on the urban middle class. In 1439, they were prohibited from levying the tallage (*taille*) to their benefit at the very moment the royal tallage was imposed on their farmers and tenants. Royal taxes were later imposed directly by the institution of the poll tax in 1695, of the tenth part in 1710, and the twentieth part in 1749. The egalitarian advance stopped there, however. Except for the abolition of the feudal tallage, the lords kept their rights and remained masters with regard to their subjects. The monarchy modernized the state, but it let civil society go its way. Rather than combat inequalities, the monarchy sanctioned them in its efforts to achieve a unified administrative power. The unity forged by the fiscal system seemed to be a great success, given that the prefect was in

many domains the intendant's heir. But it was bought at the high price of
the loss of civil initiative. Unification by law brought about decentralization, but unification by administration had centralizing consequences.
The transition to a finance state coincided with the placing of local communities under administrative tutelage and the formation of an administrative law that was an *imperium in imperio*.


## Princeps legibus solutus est

The decrees of 1681 and 1683 placed the sale of patrimonial properties,
municipal loans, and communal taxes under the authority of royal commissioners. Two important consequences came from these milestones in
the history of centralized administration. The first was to put an end to the
administrative and financial liberty of local communities, which had already lost their military and judicial independence. The state had its reasons for taking this step, since municipal management was subject to
abuses by local oligarchies that hampered the police, the highways, and
economic development. The second consequence was to establish the elements of administrative law characteristic of the French state through the
independence of the administrative jurisdiction. The monarchy often removed the serious fiscal crimes that were its particular concern from the
ordinary tribunals. The functionaries who dealt with these matters were
acting more and more like real judges. The *cours des aides*, the salt depot,
and the commerce court that judged fiscal affairs, the salt monopoly, and
customs duties, respectively, tended to become true jurisdictions.[62] The
same thing was happening with the great council. Under Richelieu and
Colbert, the administrative monarchy invested intendants with ever-in-
creasing powers of jurisdiction. The juridical initiatives of Colbert, who
guided the great reforms of Louis XIV's reign, were a striking illustration
of the subjugation of the right to control finances. Seguier was assigned to
preside over the magistrates' councils charged with drawing up the civil
ordinances of April 1667 and August 1669 for reforming courts of justice
and the criminal ordinance of August 1670. Colbert, however, oversaw
everything. His nephew Pussort, a member of the council, orchestrated the
whole proceedings, arguing against the council president, Lemoignon,
who defended the feudal justice system and the pretensions of parliament.[63] The French state contrasts with the English system, in which the
same tribunals judged cases between individuals as well as disputes between an opposed individual and the administration. In France conten-
tions between individuals and administrations were decided by the administration. In the last resort, a body of functionaries, the council of state,
decided the case. The same situation obtained in such countries as Spain,

Portugal, and Austria-Hungary, which were becoming states in much the same way France was.

The legists revived Ulpian's principle that the prince is bound by the laws, *princeps legibus solutus est*, in order to serve the sovereign's interest, but in the end it benefited the administration. It freed the monarch of the juridical formalities that the chancery or the courts, its competitors in appropriating the principle of equality, employed to enforce their will. It dissolved the legality that served the prince's whim, but more than that it established a new kind of legality, the administration's. Administrative law, which some competent historians of administration believe was influenced by canon law, is indeed a law. But this law, like the centralized administration bearing the same name, had great drawbacks. With the judge as legislator, the civil state's juridical institution entailed political action, decentralization, and community participation. With the administrator as the legislator, the bureaucratic management of the social sphere encouraged clandestine operations, centralization, and elitism. If one adds to this the monarchs' confiscation of sovereignty, which the Edict of Nantes allowed for in France, one can understand the risk the state ran of a drift toward despotism in the age of Louis XIV.

These sketchy remarks for a juridical and institutional study of the French state have been guided by a principle that reverses the conventional approach to the subject. It is customary to incriminate French power in order to glorify French civilization, to accuse the administration so as to defend social groups, to run down ministerial despotism to exalt the triumphant bourgeoisie, and to stigmatize the state in order to praise society. But what if it was not all that simple? What if civil society bore some measure of responsibility for the turbulent events of French history? What if society was not in the lead but rather was led along? What if, as historians have subtly demonstrated, it was older, more aristocratic, and more reactive than the state? These questions are not easily answered, but they surely ought to be raised.

The juridical and institutional history of the state may have in it something of the mystery of what Theodore Zeldin calls the "French passions" that divide Frenchmen between those who are obstinately fixed on privileges, hierarchy, and an aristocratic society, and those who are compulsively inclined to yearn for equality, revolution, and a plebeian nation. Perhaps juridical history, too, holds its share of secrets about the *mal français*.

Three lessons can be drawn from this partial inquiry into the state under the rule of law. The first is a lesson regarding method. The reevaluation of juridico-institutional analysis that relegates social analysis to a transitional preoccupation did not stem from an arbitrary bias but from a requirement that is intrinsic to the nature of the classical state itself. The truth is that, although the instruments forged by the nineteenth-century social sciences showed their heuristic value and their fruitfulness as long as it was a matter of understanding the workings of the economy or of social customs and of quantifying the morphology of society, they reveal themselves to be somewhat inconvenient when it comes to studying the formation of the modern state. They skirt around the principal objective of the very people who constructed this state: the process of the juridification and administrative management of society.

The second lesson is a lesson in political history. It concerns the emergence of an original form, the state under the rule of law, which did not perpetuate but rather modified the ancient forms of the city-state and the empire. By dint of eliminating every difference under the paradigm of the unique state, nineteenth-century political theory, so keen when it came to differentiating types of society, passed over a massive phenomenon. The difference between the ancient and the modern forms of the state led to our becoming blind to the perennial character of empires in one place or to the disappearance of ancient forms elsewhere. Evolution is never an ineluctable phenomenon, and the state ruled by law did not appear everywhere. Moreover, it constituted a transitional form that preceded the form of the liberal democracies, a coat of mail between the old feudal forms of the state and its modern form.

Third, this inquiry teaches us a lesson in modesty. The essence of representative government—the division of powers and the bearing down of the law on their spirit, or, more broadly, the dissolution of the state into the civil—does not constitute the most expedient way to account for the formation of modern states. Once one recognizes this, one must also admit that not much is known about what is really at work in the formation of states. At most, we can recognize a few important traits that distinguish states ruled by law—the juridico-judiciary tandem in England, the juridico-administrative tandem in France—and to point out a few paths. It seems to us that the path of analyzing the workings of associative government holds some promise.

# CHAPTER VI

# Inflections

Iᴺ ᴛʜᴇ second half of the eighteenth century and the early nineteenth, the doctrine of the state under the rule of law progressively declined, overshadowed by the novel doctrines of liberalism and democracy. This break with the early modern period was long neglected but today is the object of renewed interest and commentary.[1] Here we can only deal with it in summary fashion. What is important is to see how these liberal and democratic doctrines may have deviated from the early modern teaching and to note the inflections they brought to political right. Of course, we do not intend to deny the immense emancipation that liberalism and democracy have brought, but it is also important to observe that they have erased from our memory the origin of the state under the rule of law. What must be discovered is why they had this effect.

## Liberalism

We are indebted to liberal thought not only for its serious consideration of economic activity, its interest in the evolution of social life, and its concept of civil society as a society of needs, but also for its early anti-statism. The argument for "society against the state" goes back to the eighteenth century, when the French Enlightenment distanced itself unnoticeably from earlier legal thinkers. On the one hand, the interest in the state once shown by such thinkers as Boulainvilliers, Montesquieu, Voltaire, and Mably shifted to society. On the other, the attention formerly lavished on law was transferred to the individual, while the admiration once accorded to politics was now conferred on the rights of man. It is not that this civilist ideology, as it could be called, was anti-juridical. It did not contest law but grounded it on individual consent. Nor did it question sovereignty but rather assigned it to the people. How then was personal liberty reconciled with the claims of power? How were society and the state harmonized? New problems appeared regarding the balance of power and political representation. Such was the starting point of Enlightenment liberalism. Naturally, it then did battle with the sacred authorities of throne and altar, developed the optimistic idea of progress, and ended up glorifying an organic society in which individuals pursuing only their own interests contribute naturally to the harmony of the whole and to the general prosperity.[2]

The physiocrats, like the philosophers, saw liberalism as a gift of the state under the rule of law and the only form of power that affirmed the individual and the autonomy of civil society. Hegel understood well that the sphere of private relations attains independence when the individual ceases to be the mere shadow he is in ancient or oriental despotism and once subjective rights are at last affirmed:

> [T]he principle of the modern state has this enormous strength and depth, that while it allows the principle of subjectivity to evolve itself into the *autonomous extreme* of personal particularity, it at the same time reintegrates all this in to *substantial unity*.[3]

The modern state's opposition to slavery fosters the development of a liberal economy. It was quite natural for Quesnay and Turgot, the founding physiocrats and apostles of "laissez-faire, laissez-passer," to be functionaries in state governments. A state under the rule of law—even in France, where the initial failure to get it started delayed its development—moves in the direction of liberalism as rivers flow to the sea.

But it is also possible, paradoxically, for liberalism to oppose the state. The Enlightenment concept of civil society's self-institution has nothing to say regarding the state and, more broadly, the theological and political authorities. Solzhenitsyn was not the first to tell American liberals that liberalism lacks ideas of transcendence and community. However liberal they may be, men of faith and men of power cannot help but find liberal philosophy incomplete. It is no wonder that it generated mistrust among Christians throughout the nineteenth century. Liberalism's limitation was not its preoccupation with economic problems, since political liberalism could coexist with economic liberalism. But the liberal teaching on politics was reducible to an individualist philosophy of human rights restricted to the guarantee of these rights. No doctrine can be both statist and liberal. Liberalism simply has nothing to say about the state.[4]

Liberalism was consistent in economics, where it always called for a relaxation of state control and a defense of free enterprise, but it was equivocal in politics, where the state could mean different things depending on the will of the states. The anecdote about the brief exchange between Quesnay and the future Louis XVI epitomizes the liberal teaching neatly. When the prince asked, "What is there to be done?" Quesnay replied, "Nothing." There is an ambiguity in this "nothing" on which

Ferguson and Smith would later base their thinking. Once it was grafted onto the crisis of the state in eighteenth-century France or onto the crisis of national identity in Germany, statist nihilism produced some astonishing antiliberal reversals: in France, Jacobin ideology, and in Germany, nationalism.

*Democracy*

The end of the eighteenth century saw the rise not only of liberalism but of the democratic ideal as well.[5] The two movements had different origins, and they arose in England through evolution and in France through revolution. Liberalism stemmed from the modern development of civil society, the fruit of the state under the rule of law that blossomed with modern capitalism. It resulted from the division between power and property that allowed each individual to acquire property without seizing power and called for power to respect ownership of property. Democracy, on the other hand, came from the ancient city-states, where it was linked to slavery. Democracy's ancient legacy weighed heavily on its modern ideal.

Ancient democracy was direct, self-constituted democracy without any division between the state and the citizen, government and individuals. Hobbes had noted this trait,[6] which was vigorously emphasized by the nineteenth-century liberal school obsessed with the perils of democracy. Benjamin Constant and Alexis de Tocqueville each for his own purposes developed the view later expressed by Fustel de Coulanges that "it is a singular error . . . among all human errors, to believe that in the ancient cities men enjoyed liberty. They had not even the idea of it."[7] The ancient democratic ideal was communitarian rather than individualist. The liberals defended individual rights, interest, and will, and showed no concern for the state, whereas the democrats stood for the power of the people and the general interest and will and were not concerned with the individual. On this score democracy ran a risk. The ancients knew well that democracy was the form of government most conducive to tyranny and most compatible with dictatorship. The notion of the people was a fluid notion and even in the smallest republic a change in population often led to one man's rising up to speak deceptively in the name of all. It was not easy to determine just who was governing. Unlike the aristocratic and monarchical governments that could exercise their power directly over small communities confined to one place, the power of the people always entailed distribution or delegation. A tyrant always claimed to rule in the name of the people. This particular weakness of democracy explains why it was compatible with slavery. The citizens of antiquity were not obsessed with human liberty, but they needed to have slaves.

The democratic ideal completely politicized the life of citizens in the ancient city, whose political hypertrophy undoubtedly accounted for its economic atrophy. The "power of the people" defined exclusively the ways in which power was to function, government in action, in a word, the executive. The ancient democratic ideal had none of the modern mechanisms for checking power, because all the people held and exercised power at all times. There was no abstract form of power, because there was power only in action. Every citizen belonged both to the governed and to the governing. Ancient democracy invented "the primacy of the political" and the self-institution of the city that the French conventionalists sought to revive.

Herein lay the antinomy of democracy. The best thing about it was that all it needed was the people's direct exercise of power. The worst was that it showed no concern for individual rights. Liberalism overlooked the state, whereas democracy neglected the individual. As Giovanni Sartori has aptly remarked, Greek democracy rested more narrowly on the equality of all before the law (*isonomia*) than on liberty (*eleutheria*). Democracy tended to promote equality in the same measure that liberalism tended to promote liberty. The first, Hannah Arendt observed, led to a revolution of liberty in America, and the second to a revolution of equality in France.[8] If liberalism neglects the role of the state and buries the political in the civil, the democratic ideal remains indifferent to individual action and immerses the individual in the populace. Liberalism and the democratic ideal are responsible for the blossoming of civilism and populism, two ideas that are foreign to the classical doctrine that in the past they had rejected.

### Civilism and Populism

The problem of reconciling individual liberty and political alienation lies at the heart of Enlightenment political philosophy. It was resolved by reconciling the particular and the collective in the civil sphere, leaving behind any concern with the state. Civilism, however, was a new departure and not an outcome of anything preceding it. Such partisans of the civil as Mably and Boulainvilliers were already moving toward new ways of constructing the body politic's identity. Instead of founding the state on law, as did classical political theory, they went about the task by appealing to the conquests of past eras recorded in history. Their return to historicist phantasms about origins inaugurates the great drift toward nationalism.

Populism as a way of looking at society arose when the notions of popular sovereignty and the general interest achieved their definitive triumph with Rousseau. Populism did not concern itself with the relationship between the state and the citizen any more than did civilism. Both overlooked the individual, and in so doing both forgot the political.

Inasmuch as they both developed within states under the rule of law, liberal civilism did not show signs of explicit anti-statism any more than democratic populism diffused virulent anti-individualism. Paradoxically, however, in a different setting in which there was no state, these latent tendencies could make themselves felt and even destroy the ideologies that spawned them. Such a surprising but not unforeseeable consequence had already been perceived by a French precursor of political Romanticism whose work Karl Marx read avidly and held in high esteem—Simon-Nicolas Linguet, the author of the *Traité des lois civiles*, published at London in 1774. Linguet shared liberalism's ideas on the inconsistency of the law and the exclusive importance of economic organization. It was he who coined the phrase, dear to Marx, that "the spirit of the laws is property."[9] He also shared romanticism's antipathy toward Enlightenment philosophy, which he expressed in a venomous pamphlet entitled *Le Fanatisme des philosophes*. Linguet believed in the supremacy of private right over all kinds of rights before the rise of the historical school of law.

Linguet drew different political conclusions from the same premises as those of liberalism. His defense of property and negative view of power led him to extol slavery and Oriental despotism. Long before Karl Wittfogel's comparison of socialist regimes with oriental despotism drew a skeptical response, Linguet based his thinking on the oriental form of government and restored the word "despotism" to the political vocabulary. Linguet was able to calculate, and to reconcile himself to, the high price of despotism. The great would be unhappy, but that did not matter, since the people would be freed of petty tyrants. Nor did it matter that freedoms would disappear, since liberty was only a mirage. Power would be absolute, but power was always essentially oppressive and all governments were despotic. These considerations, together with Linguet's superb command of language and his presocialist railings against exploitation make his work a convincing demonstration that the progress from popular sovereignty to the despotic state is a move in the right direction.

These new doctrines did away with the classical notion of the body politic in which both sovereign power and individual rights played a part in the institution of society. Along with it, the concept of juridical transcendence was also swept away. The anti-statist character of civilism and populism may well have spawned the Jacobin revolutionary spirit of the general will embodied in the quarrelsome rabble. But beyond the brief period of the revolution, liberalism and the democratic ideal promoted individual economic initiative and democratic freedoms within states that were already under the rule of law. There they strengthened the economy and gave political life a broader foundation. Outside these states, however, they had altogether different consequences. Before long, the revolutionary French armies would spread new ideas along the roads of Europe, and an anti-statist civilist and populist ideology would arise in Germany. Fichte was just around the corner.[10]

# PART TWO

# The State and Despotism

"I was already tolerably well aware that what is called liberalism—individualism, the humanistic conception of citizenship—was the product of the Renaissance. But the fact leaves me entirely cold, realizing as I do, that your great heroic age is a thing of the past, its ideals defunct, or at least lying at their last gasp, while the feet of those who will deal them the *coup de grâce* are already before the door. You call yourself, if I am not mistaken, a revolutionist. But you err in holding that future revolutions will issue in freedom. In the past five hundred years, the principle of freedom has outlived its usefulness. An educational system which still conceives itself as a child of the age of enlightenment, with criticism as its chosen medium of instruction, the liberation and cult of the ego, the solvent forms of life which are absolutely fixed—such a system may still, for a time, reap an empty rhetorical advantage; but its reactionary character is, to the initiated, clear beyond any doubt. All educational organizations worthy of the name have always recognized what must be the ultimate and significant principle of pedagogy: namely the absolute mandate, the iron bond, discipline, sacrifice, the renunciation of the ego, the curbing of the personality. And lastly, it is an unloving miscomprehension of youth to believe that it finds its pleasure in freedom: its deepest pleasure lies in obedience. . . . No," Naphta went on, "Liberation and development of the individual are not the key to our age, they are not what our age demands. What it needs, what it wrestles after, what it will create—is Terror."

—Thomas Mann, *The Magic Mountain*

# CHAPTER VII

# Romanticism and Totalitarianism

The Germans are the people of the Romantic counter-revolution.
Against the philosophical intellectualism and rationalism of the
Enlightenment, one finds in them a revolt of music against literature
and of mysticism against clarity.

—THOMAS MANN

### The Origins of Totalitarianism

THE METAMORPHOSIS of the state under the rule of law into the state
under despotic rule would not be so pernicious if the number of states
currently belonging to the first category were not so small and uncertain
and if the mutant of the totalitarian system had not appeared in the growing swarm of new states.

The post-1968 generation that awoke from the Chinese dream, as others
had from the Soviet dream, has tried to understand the dark workings of
totalitarianism. One recent writer, André Glucksmann, went searching in
Germany, the nation that begat the fundamental doctrines of totalitarianism's two forms, fascism and communism, and turned the first into reality.
In probing the origins of totalitarianism in the thought of Fichte, Hegel,
Marx, and Nietzsche, Glucksmann went back to the Enlightenment to discover how "the rationalist principles of Fichte and the new sun of science
was already high on the horizon when the second stage was about to un-
fold, the terror and the struggle unto death."[1] Fichte, the herald of Hegel
and of rationalism, would thus have led Germany to what we have wit-
nessed. Glucksmann's accusation, which rests on the alleged scientific
character of Marxism-Leninism and on the official account of the young
Marx's formation in the course of which he returned to Enlightenment
thought thanks to Feuerbach's influence, deserves more than annoyed rid-
icule. It calls for examination and discussion. The same applies to what
can be called the stakes for Germany.

### The Stakes for Germany

Just as there are stakes—and mystery—in Russia's fate, so there are stakes
and mystery in Germany's fate. After three wars, today's democratic Germany, affluent, lulled, and united against its terrorism, bears no resemblance to its nineteenth-century forebear. But as long as there remains
some uncertainty regarding the obscure genesis of German nationalism, of
Nazism and the socialism of the concentration camps, the question raised
by William Schirer will come up again and again: how did Germany go
mad? The question is not resolved by appealing to some racial or cultural
principle. What must be understood is not what is German in totalitarianism's destiny, but what was totalitarian in Germany's history. If in recent
times there were two Germanys, it is perhaps because in the past there
were two roads for Germany to take.

A previous generation's inquiry into Germany's fate produced *The German Crisis of French Thought*, as Claude Digeon called it.[2] The aftermath
of the wars of 1870 and 1914 unleashed an attack on the whole of German
philosophy, particularly on the work of Fichte. French university professors had to fight on two fronts. They locked arms on the first front because
the popular chauvinistic rejection of German culture posed a threat to the
progress of scientific research and university work, which had much to
learn from Germany's example. On the second front, however, the professors were divided when it came to searching for the roots of Germany's
fate. Beneath nationalism and Pan-Germanism, French thinkers could see
traces of a more dreadful origin, but they differed in their opinions when
they came upon Fichte.

Generous minds, such as Victor Basch and especially Xavier Léon in his
monumental dissertation, sought to exonerate Fichte of any responsibility
in the rapid development of German nationalism, whereas Boutroux and
Andler, receptive to the calls of the Pan-Germanists who invoked him as
their patron, indicted him straight out.[3] The quarrel took shape over
whether there was continuity or change between the author of the *Contributions towards the Correction of the Public Judgment on the French Revolution* and the author of the *Addresses to the German Nation*. Some held
that Fichte's position had remained unchanged, whereas others saw an
irreversible break.

Fifty years later, however, the debate no longer had any significance. In
a 1946 article, Martial Guéroult paid homage to Xavier Léon but was concerned to explain that

> it is more difficult to defend Fichte now than it had been in the past, because
> since the death of Xavier Léon, we have once again suffered from that spiteful

nationalism that the founder of the University of Berlin was, in whatever sublimated form, among the first to embody.[4]

One might see a mitigating circumstance in the fact that mysticism and nationalism never fully replaced rationalism in Fichte's thought and democracy, yet the later elements were incorporated in the dominant current of German thought, whereas the earlier ones were obliterated.[5] Fichte's ideas became flesh and the truth came into being. The *Addresses to the German Nation* were inscribed into popular memory, but Fichte's other works remained largely unread.

Today, the debate has come to life again. German history has undergone a double metastasis under Nazism and, more recently, socialism, the latter under the indirect influence of Marxist allegiance. We now know de facto, but not yet de jure, that these regimes, which put aside habeas corpus, set up a political system that differed greatly from that of the state under the rule of law. How did this upheaval take place? What intellectual developments prepared this change? In dealing with these questions, there is a strong temptation today to blame the old culprit, nineteenth-century German philosophy, which our elders were too quick to absolve. Such a quick reflex overlooks the early-nineteenth-century debate between those who held on to the principles of classical legal doctrine and those who relegated them to the dustbin. Today we need to avoid a one-sided judgment against the whole of German philosophy and to assess more precisely in what way it abetted the genesis of totalitarianism.

The dramatic confrontation between the Enlightenment and romanticism in early-nineteenth-century Germany that ended in the latter's victory was a far greater conflict than the battle of Hernani. It was a drama more vast, a more lavish and ghastly tragedy, because in the theater of the world of that time, romanticism set the stage for the nation-state. But the clash between the Enlightenment and romanticism escaped the notice of a sincere contemporary such as Mme. de Staël, or an otherwise profound thinker such as Dilthey. Mme. de Staël's *De l'Allemagne*, published in 1801, is filled with journalistic information and instant analyses, but in her passion to get the chauvinistic and close-minded French to see that something new was happening in Germany and to give the soul of Germany a voice, she missed the battle of the hour. Later Dilthey reconciled within himself Hegelianism and romanticism, without ever saying a word about the conflict that pitted the one against the other. In our own time, however, such scholars as Henri Brunschwicg, Jacques Droz, and Roger Ayrault, building on the earlier research of Georges Gurvitch, Charles Andler, and J. E. Spenlé have uncovered the details of the struggle in which German romanticism overcame Enlightenment rationalism and the foundations of classical political philosophy were uprooted.[6]

### From Rationalism to Fideism: Prolegomena to a
### New Political Doctrine

German romanticism was a multifaceted movement with major figures in every sphere of culture: in literature, with Klopstock, Novalis, Herder, Jean Paul, the Schlegel brothers, and others now forgotten; history, with Wackenroder and Tieck; linguistics, with Justus Möser; philosophy, with Fichte, Schelling, Schleiermacher; law, with Hugo and Savigny; politics, with Friedrich von Gentz; not to mention what was done in other fields as well. Our aim here is simply to recall precisely what in the events, manners, and debates of that time prepared the way, through a teaching that did not directly concern itself with politics, for a political transformation.

More than anything else it achieved, romaniticism brought to an end the brief reign of the Enlightenment. Between 1740 and 1780, two generations were reared in the Enlightenment spirit, but the Sturm und Drang already sounded with the publication in 1773 of three articles, "Von Deutscher Art und Kunst," signed by none less than Justus Möser, Herder, and Goethe.[7] These first stirrings of romantic feeling invoked sentiment against reason, exalted the Middle Ages against antiquity, and valued Germany over all things foreign. The episode might have passed without any consequence. After all, Goethe later declared that classicism was healthy and romanticism disease. By the turn of the century, the salons were spreading a cosmopolitan spirit and a taste for reasoning à la française in all the larger cities of Germany. In Berlin, Rahel Levin, like Henrietta Hertz, Sarah Mayer, and Madame d'Arnstein before her, hosted a rationalist circle frequented by Gans and Heine as well as the youthful admirers of Goethe, Friedrich Schlegel, Schleiermacher, and Friedrich von Gentz.[8] Later, as the wife of von Vanhagen the diplomat, she met them again in the corridors of the Congress of Vienna, but by that time they were altogether different men.

In the intervening years, the tide of romanticism that had ebbed made a sensational comeback under the banners of war and religion. The first stage of the French Revolution appeared to the young German intellectuals as the fulfillment of the Enlightenment's rationalist and universalist ideas. When he heard of the victory at Balmy, Kant interrupted his rigid work schedule, and Goethe proclaimed the start of a new era in world history. In the Revolution's second stage, however, Napoleon's victories unleashed in the defeated lands of Eastern Europe a resistance that took the novel form of a war of national liberation. What starts as a tear, soon becomes a rip. In Berlin in 1799, then at Jena in 1801, a small group founded *Das Athenäum*, a review in whose pages the Schlegel brothers,

Tieck, Novalis, and Schleiermacher cast the seeds that spread the prodigious and troubling blossoming of new ideas in Germany.

In the sphere of religion, pietism was undermining the institutional, Masonic, and political foundations of the Enlightenment from within. When rationalists and mystics confronted each other head-on at the Congress of Wilhelmbad in 1782, the pietist movement centered in Berlin assumed leadership over a significant portion of Freemasonry. The Prussian ministers Woellner and Bischoffwerder, implacable enemies of the Enlightenment, secured their influence on Frederick-William II, a man of mystic bent and irreproachable morals. Only the despot remains of enlightened despotism. A new tone, new customs, new ideas were abroad in the land.

A new tone, first of all. One testimony to the new tone of conviction that finds debate annoying and commands a faithful following is the model proposed by Novalis's *Die Lehrlinge zu Sais* (*The Novices of Sais*). Another is the aged Kant's indignant reaction to the air of superiority affected by younger philosophers. Kant could sense in their partisan spirit the dangers of terror lurking in the republic of letters. In giving precise formulations to culturally correct speech, the young romantics were conducting verbal experiments on the guillotine that had only a short time before toppled heads in France. Militant and arrogant young men like the Schlegels, Novalis, Tieck, and Schleiermacher were the avant-garde of romanticism.

New customs, too. Friedrich von Schlegel imagined a "symphilosophy," and, together with his group, he drew up a mini "countersociety" that broke with the Enlightenment. In his *Origines de la France contemporaine*, Taine described the desiccation of feeling fostered by salon life that had stifled and revolted Jean-Jacques Rousseau. Pleasure replaced love. Friendship was constrained by the tempests of politics, hampered by the calculations of social life, and supplanted by the courtesies of buddy-buddy relationships. Cliques, groups, even parties would form by chance around some idea and just as quickly dissolve by some quirk of fate. To the soul athirst for the absolute, like the author of the *Confessions*, such people were nothing but playful chums ready to betray one another at the least breath of wind. As in all court societies, even among the bourgeoisie, the only bonds among people were services rendered and returned in the form of dinners and exchanges of information. The infamy of philistinism attached itself to bourgeois civil society. A whole new way of life began when the young romantics met, formed friendships, lived together, reinvented Montaigne and La Boétie, made marriages of love, and exalted women like Caroline, Dorothea, and Sophie. The genesis of their work is the story of their lives. Their biography is the key to their thought. Theirs was a time of elective affinities and privileged places, among Hegel, Schelling, and Hölderlin at Jena and in Berlin among the Schlegels, Novalis, and Tieck. The romantic air they breathed in their youth no doubt accounts for Marx's and Engels's voluntary marginalization and their undying friendship.

New ideas also. The banner of the German language was flying high. In his *Fragmente* of 1767, Herder wrote a defense of the new German literature, and Klopstock rebuked learned Germans who disparaged the mother tongue that Fichte extolled above all other languages. Was this a new pleiad, a German renaissance three centuries late? Not exactly. Rather than think of establishing a German state through political institutions, the romantics dreamed of the nation developing through its soul. The language of state meant nothing to them compared to the national speech. In France, Francis I's ordinance of Villiers-Cotterêts made French the language of government and the Académie thereafter kept the state's language pure. But Germany did not follow the French example of a state under the rule of law that first formed its speech and then made it the official language. Instead Germany innovated by making the living language of the people the sacred source of the nation that defined its civil society.

The nationalist movements of the nineteenth century followed the model established by Germany. The Hungarians, the Poles, the Serbs—each sought to legitimize the essence of Hungary, Poland, and Serbia. Such a linguistic politics had inverse geopolitical consequences, however. It accompanied the irresistible rise of Pan-Germanism and Pan-Slavism and provided arguments for a policy of annexation, but it also became the ancestor of regionalism based on a given territory's dialect and so furnished grounds for secession. Everywhere it poisoned the process of establishing modern states.

In their high regard for feeling, the romantics looked on reason with disdain. They opposed a materialist intelligence with a living and dynamic nature, endowed with memory and mobility. Their terminology—matter and memory, thinking and moving, and the like—anticipates Bergson. Yet in this shift the romantics did not rest content with passive experience. They took the offensive, too. The new value they gave to feeling and the forces of instinct led German thinkers to new kinds of knowledge and Germany itself to new heights of power. The German masters of knowledge saw new things, as though they were looking from the other side of a mirror, in the deepest recesses of the body. It is not the least paradox of intuitionist idealism that it explored the new continent of materialism and observed the workings of the economic, cultural, and psychological forces that shape Western civilization. Soon after, Marx, Nietzsche, and Freud scrutinized the entrails of capitalist economy and class struggle, of the religious genealogy of morals, of psychic drives and their fates. With the instruments of misery, folly, and solitude, the realm of matter conducted live experiments on its very self. All at once the "other side" of politics, culture, and consciousness revealed itself in these great discoveries.

Increased value was also placed on power, and to such power! Thomas Mann once observed with bitterness and lucidity that, in signaling the return of primal energies long repressed, romanticism unleashed the great newfound force of the instincts by opening up a world "intoxicated with death and beauty—a world of pessimism, of intimate acquaintance with exotic drugs and an overrefinement of the senses that indulges rapturously in all manner of synaesthetic speculation."[9] At the end of his life, Freud came to the conviction that the force at work in Nazism was the will unto death. Beneath the Novalis of the *Hymns to the Night* and of the desire for death, the romantics invented what can rightly be called thanatopolitics. Romanticism in Germany was not, as elsewhere, a passing phenomenon or a fresh but gentle breeze. From 1850 to 1890, Germany, in contrast to France, further developed the philosophical reaction to the Enlightenment that had marked early-nineteenth-century Europe. While reason slept, monsters were being conceived.

# Anti-statism and Nationalism

People and fatherland . . . , as a support and guarantee of eternity on earth and as that which can be eternal here below, far transcend the state. . . . That is why this love of fatherland must itself govern the state and be the supreme, final, and absolute authority.

—JOHANN GOTTLIEB FICHTE

*The Development of Anti-statism*

Sოცი against the state!" Before wasting one's effort in reviving this generous slogan, it might be good to reflect on its fate in Germany, where this rallying cry arose from the rude awakening that everyone felt after Napoleon's defeat of the German armies. As Hegel put it in the opening sentence of *The German Constitution*, "Germany is a state no longer."[1] In Germany the state became everyone's enemy and all were crying, "Society against the state!" The country's backwardness, caused by the prejudicial balance between the strength of the multiprincipalities and the weakness of the emperor, who had kept the trappings but lost the authority of Charlemagne, at first provoked a sense of inferiority. The young turned their sights abroad and admired France. They were anxious over how to remedy Germany's weakness and how to rebuild Germany's unity.

Then everything happened as though Germany could not become a Western-style nation-state. The majority of Germans stepped back in order better to jump ahead. Like the fox in the fable, they made a virtue of necessity.[2] The annoyance about the absence of a state gave way to compulsive rejection of statism.

That inflexibility only developed further. In his 1792 essay, *The Limits of State Authority*, Humboldt was concerned only to defend the state under the rule of law against absolutist deviations, to protect the individual rights of citizens, and to harmonize the application of the law with the exercise of liberty. But barely ten years later, in his *Addresses to the German Nation*, Fichte fulfilled Hölderlin's prophecy that in seeking to make of the state a paradise the Germans had made it a hell. Anti-statist ideas made their way into Germany through the writings of such French and English political thinkers as Montesquieu, Voltaire, Ferguson, Burke, and others who taught that civilization meant more than political power and that society was superior to the state, something that Althusius had already defended. From a tendentious reading of *The Spirit of the Laws*, the Germans took the anti-juridical argument that maintained that the laws should be dependent on the people, whose "last avatar," according to Roger Ayrault, is "the populist mentality," the *Volkgeist*, the collective soul that participates in a direct and mystical way in the divine scheme of things.[3] They read Ferguson, too, Adam Smith's teacher whose *Essay on the History of Civil Society*, published in London in 1767, came to the attention of Marx and Hegel through the romantics.[4] Ferguson maintained the idea of the consistency of civil society and emphasized the influence of property on law. In a slight alteration of Rousseau's thought, Ferguson stated that the first man who said, "I take this field as my own and bequeath it to my heirs" had no idea he was making ownership the foundation of civil law and political institutions. Laws and constitutions, Ferguson thought, simply grew out of the struggles of civil society.

The Germans especially read Edmund Burke, whose *Reflections on the French Revolution* was translated by Friedrich von Gentz, later Metternich's mentor, and termed "a revolutionary book against revolution" by Novalis. At Göttingen University, two high-ranking Hanoverian functionaries, Brandes and Rehberg, adapted Burke's ideas, attenuating his historicism and his critique of natural right. In removing the law, in this instance English common law, from the will of the legislator and placing it in the successive decisions of the English people, Burke transformed the notion of contract into a doctrine on covenant, a twofold covenant with God and with history. Without being openly anti-statist, Burke inverted the link between the state and the nation in the interest of the nation.

In Germany, where a nation-state did not exist, the influence of liberalism, rather than making itself felt only in industrial development or a relaxation of the regime, came to bear on the question of how Germany should be unified, whether through legal or military means, constitutionalization or nationalization, society or the state. In states under the rule of law, liberal doctrines—except during the brief period of the French Revolution—strengthened economic liberties and citizens' initiatives, but in the beginnings of the German nation, they cut off access to the constitutionalist route and opened the way to despotism.

The success of the slogan, "Society against the state!" ruled out unification though state juridification and in its place promoted a nationalist unification. In the latter half of the nineteenth century, Germany's unification was achieved by military means, with iron and blood, according to Bismarck's implacable scheme. Following Prussia's lead, Germany offered the world a new statist paradigm of the nation-state that reaped the nationalist drift impelled by the Revolution's aftermath of terrorism and Bonaparte that, in France itself, the Restoration broke up. But before military victory came the decisive force of words. Nationalism had already won over people's minds in the first half of the nineteenth century. Its victory came in two stages, the first marked by the success of Fichte's *Addresses to the German Nation*, whose call was heard with enthusiasm, and then by the defeat through the unconditional surrender of its supporters of Hegelian political right, the only serious resistance to political romanticism. The victory of the one and the defeat of the other encouraged the spread of both anti-statism and anti-juridism.

## *The* Addresses to the German Nation

Composed of public lectures given at Berlin in 1807, *Addresses to the German Nation* is not just an idealistic polemic against the Enlightenment or a glorification of Germany or even, as in the case of Fichte's earlier writing, a panegyric on society against the state. This last idea Fichte shared with Herder, Justus Möser, Schleiermacher, and Novalis, but he felt it in a more enduring way than they did. Despite the striking evolution that led him from admiring France to defending Germany, Fichte's original conviction of the primacy of society grew deeper throughout his life. Xavier Léon, Georges Gurvitch, and Martial Guéroult have all observed how sociability was from the very start one of Fichte's key ideas.[5] From the *Foundations of Natural Right*, in 1796–1797, to the *Considerations Destined to Rectify Public Opinion on the French Revolution* to the *Addresses to the German Nation*, published in 1812, and *The Theory of State*, of 1813, one and the same conviction bore its ever-deeper furrow. For Fichte, society was distinct from the state, it held greater value, it embodied the people. Sovereignty, with its duties and its rights, belonged to society. Fichte was among the first to conceive of the withering away of the state.

He was also more implacable than his contemporaries in developing the consequences of society's primacy over the state. The appeal of *Gesellschaft* (society) could have resulted in favoring *Gemeinschaft* (community). The love of community could have become lost in esotericism or stuck in short-term associations. It could have fragmented the unity of power. The young romantics dreamed of bringing back the houses and the guilds. They loved fireside chats, small gatherings, intimacy. Fichte, however, was of another mold. He had no interest in remaking the world starting from small, close-knit communities. He was not for self-made societies. His genius was to take stock of the nation in one fell swoop and, by avoiding destruction and the impasses of criticism, to rebuild his country's house on its original foundations. Beyond his controversies with the romantic generation and despite the unbridgeable gap that separated the philosopher who was devoid of mysticism and aesthetics from the admirers of Jakob Boehme and the renovators of German art, the nationalist teaching of "the greatest metaphysician of the age," as the grateful young romantics called him, gained a hearing. Fichte became the godfather of German patriotism.

The classical teachers spoke to the political animal, the citizen and the legislator. Fichte addressed the social animal, the nation, the people. He proclaimed that

> people and fatherland . . . as a support and guarantee of eternity on earth and as that which can be eternal here below, far transcend the state. . . . That is why this love of fatherland must itself govern the state and be the supreme, final, and absolute authority.[6]

Fichte's teaching resolutely contradicted the classical teaching that law alone was needed to found a state. Abandoning the classical constitutionalism that the French revolutionaries had at first adopted, the convention and its successors bore a greater influence on him. Fichte was a conventionalist to the same extent that Kant was constitutionalist. He was unflinchingly revolutionary in the sense that for him revolution meant eliminating constitutions, the Supreme Being, and the world soul. Instead of deploring the state's absence and scheming to fashion the social compact needed for its creation or imagining the conditions for the future body politic's legitimacy, Fichte filled the void left by the nonexistent state with ravings about the fatherland. A withdrawal into the dark of night, a hurried flight to ancient Germania with its forests and lakes, its savage, primitive men with their tresses that Boulainvilliers in his feudal reconstruction of the French nation had gone looking for. But instead of creating a power vacuum, as in France, and reversing, even if only for a moment, the great idol of the absolute state through the terrorist politics of the popular will, the nationalist drift in Germany gave rise to the political theory of the nation-state in Germany. It did so by locking arms with the movement to shape Germany's character through three decisive changes.

A change of identity. There was no need for the state to come into being, since the nation has always existed. It did not derive from any legislative process, the painful birth pangs of internal peace. It was not born when private wars were replaced by lawsuits regulated by tribunals and legal codes. It had been nurtured instead on foreign wars and resistance, and it only needed to be strengthened and revived. Fichte forged Germany's identity by forsaking juridical procedures for ahistorical phantasms. He exchanged the legitimacy of a state founded on law for the vitality of a people fed on love of country.

A change of reference points. Germany had already become incarnate and its law was inscribed in the heart of the people. The German people was the new chosen people that carried the seed of human perfectibility destined to blossom in a new humanity. In Germany's "election" there was also latent a nexus of forces foreshadowing the Holocaust in that Germany's ascendancy entailed a denial of the Jewish law. The Jewish law also broke with classical philosophy, but Fichte made no mention of it at all. For him, the Jews, the bearers of a divine covenant, disappeared before the true destroyers of Roman culture, the German patriots destined to regenerate the modern world.[7] A new kingdom was at hand, the reign of the nation-state.

Was this founding the nation through territorialization rather than establishing it through legislation? Choosing empire, settling down to a quiet home life instead of making laws? Not exactly. Fichte kept the idea of law, but he embodied it. He accepted territorialization, but he embodied it in a symbol.[8] The French hymn extolling the law of the heart found new life on the lips of Germany's nationalist philosopher, who taught that a German should be willing to die for the fatherland.[9] Fichte embodied the law in the German people, and then he annulled it by replacing it with faith, for the law of the heart is faith, as Saint Paul holds. Yet Fichte's incarnation had nothing in it of Christianity, since it entailed neither grace nor divine mercy. In place of a recognition of transcendence and faith in the resurrection, it substituted an immanent love of the nation, a call to survival, and the expansion of the country. With the *juris consensus*, the guarantee of transcendent laws disappeared, and any form of private trust was dissolved in the immanence of the nation-people. Nationalism absorbed all forms of transcendence, and the fatherland became the Christ. Fichte boldly preached a new religion.[10]

A change of perspectives. Germany's horizon was no longer the horizon of past and present civil peace but of once and future foreign war. Fichte taught that

> it must be love of fatherland that governs the state by placing before it a higher object than the usual one of maintaining peace, property, personal freedom, and the life and well-being of all. For this higher object alone, and with no other intention, does the state assemble an armed force.[11]

This threefold shift, which did away with state, law, and peace in each instance, made society more and more a subject unto itself. The enhanced status of the civil realm and the elevation of the citizen transformed human beings at their deepest level. In this, too, Fichte broke with classical thought, since he did not aim to form a state but to educate citizens.

Hence the didactic tone of his *Addresses*, which sought to overcome the resistance of society. For Fichte, the key to Germany's regeneration lay in national education.

Was this a fatal accident that in one fell swoop brought classical politics to ruin? Unfortunately, this was not the case. Fichte knowingly overthrew the ideals of the state under the rule of law: the state, justice, law, peace, the rights of man. His attack was measured, point for point. He decried a mechanistic and individualistic society founded "on the assumption that everyone seeks his own well-being, to compel everyone against his wish and will to promote the general well-being."[12] Maintaining peace and protecting property were for him secondary goals that imposed limits on the natural freedom of the individual. "It would be well," he thought, "to limit individual liberty as much as possible, to bring all their activities under a uniform rule, and to keep them under unceasing supervision."[13] Fichte may not have known where he was headed, but he knew where he was coming from. The new idols took a heavy toll on the old political ideals. Fichte spoke not of the state, but of the nation; not of justice, but of education; of foreign wars instead of internal peace; of faith, not of law; and of the dictates of society rather than of human rights.

The impact of this shift was great. Fichte lost his friends, but in return he won over his enemies. This revealed the meaning of his transformation. He had earlier in life won over a portion of the young romantics but at the same time suffered the betrayal of his Masonic supporters. This time, he scored a triumph with the conservative political ideologues. It was ironic that the charge of atheism that forced him to leave Jena was made and executed by the Weimar court that had embraced the Enlightenment. The Weimar rationalists returned to their abandoned convictions and decided on banishing him, while the romantic neomystics applauded the onetime disciple of Spinoza.

Novalis asserted that "the good Fichte is fighting for us all." Friedrich von Schlegel planned to write a pamphlet to show that Fichte's great merit lay precisely in his having rediscovered religion and that his teaching was nothing other than true religion in philosophic form. Even Friedrich von Gentz was won over by the *Addresses*. The counterrevolutionary who fought with all his might to defend Burke had held that Fichte's philosophy was a chimera, a hardened idealism, shallow and contradictory, and Fichte himself a discredited charlatan who just kept on peddling his panaceas. All that changed when von Gentz enthusiastically proclaimed that no one had ever spoken of the German nation so nobly and so profoundly. For him, as Xavier Léon notes, all the literature of the age bore the marks of Fichte's *Addresses*.[14]

Anti-statism was the prolegomenon to every form of nationalism to come. But it was only a beginning.

# CHAPTER IX

# Anti-juridism

Law . . . is *par excellence* the shibboleth which marks out these
false friends and comrades of what they call the "people."

—HEGEL

I am a profoundly anti-juridical man. . . . I have neither any
sense of law or need for law.

—NOVALIS

## *Hegelianism or Romanticism*

THE ATTACK on law follows in the wake of the assault on the state. In
view of the disproportionate place law occupies in early-nineteenth-century thinkers, such as Fichte, Krause, and Hegel, and the bitter debates
that resulted in the establishment of a new school of legal thought, the
historical school of law, one hesitates to take the pulse of anti-juridism.[1]
One is especially reluctant to do so since the questions raised by romanticism about law, society, and sovereignty all fall under classical categories
without getting any closer to the heart of the matter.[2] The definition of law
engages the modalities of legislative construction and determines whether
states should fashion a common civil code and adopt, with appropriate
nuances, the French code, or keep their ancient legislations, which are in
a shambles and out of date but nevertheless Germanic. The matter cannot
remain undecided for long. Outside Hegel's stronghold, the classical concept of right as law is fractured and the rights doctrine challenged. It all
comes down to either Hegelianism or romanticism. The latter's success
inclined the majority of minds to oppose law and constitution and to favor
the communitarian ideal and feudal theory of power that Hegel revised or
rejected.

Let us go out on a limb and consider that, more so than Marx, Hegel is,
at least in his quarrel with romanticism, at the end point and not at the

beginning (lest we give him too much credence) of recovering the break of his thought with the works of his youth, the writings of Frankfurt and Jena that run the risk of inclining us, following Dilthey and Meinecke, to overlook his opposition to romanticism. Hegel took Schleiermacher to task in *Faith and Knowledge* (1801), and in *The System of Ethical Life* (1802–1805) he attacked Fichte, but his thought evolved considerably from the political writings of his youth to his masterwork, the *Principles of the Philosophy of Right* (1821). The Thomas Aquinas of Protestantism, to use Chamberlain's spiteful phrase, prepared slowly but surely for the battle against romanticism, which he fought well enough for Friedrich von Schlegel to condemn his "satanic philosophy." When one is tempted to indict German political philosophy for its perversions, Hegel and Fichte should not be named together in the same suit. They had neither the same accomplices nor the same disciples. As wise observers among their contemporaries noted, the two thinkers turned their backs on one another.[3]

## The Definition of Right: Right as Law?

For a German thinker of the first two decades of the nineteenth century, to give a definition of right meant pronouncing himself on current political-juridical questions, whether he was for or against the constitution or the civil code based on the French model. To the abstract and theoretical code of law, the jurist Hugo had opposed popular customs and traditions of the people, to which he gave the name of positive law.[4] The new terminology soon became standard, but neither the idea nor the controversy were anything new. Justus Möser and Rehberg had already provided grist for Savigny and Puchta to grind. Möser had proclaimed that if he had to erect a general code, "it would be that every judge decide cases on the basis of those usages and customs which the parties on trial would assert to be binding on them."[5] This stiffened opposition to constitutionalism marked the rejection of revolutionary and French codification. How could one not fear the terrorism of the will of the people stemming from the abstractions of the general will and the occupier's *jus francorum*? That fear was widespread and encouraged a rethinking of the nature of law. One of the first objects of Hegel's reflection was to reject subjective law and to repudiate the individualist conception that had prevailed in the late eighteenth century. In its place Hegel conceived of a law that would regulate the modes of balancing power and the organization of the people. In short, Hegel countered abstract and individual law with concrete and collective law. He stuck to his guns in energetically opposing artificially constructed constitutions imposed on the people from the outside, such as the legislation Napoleon imposed on the Spaniards. In his *Principles of the Philosophy of*

*Right*, Hegel stands by the conception of law rooted in the historical traditions and the spirit of the people, the *Volkgeist*.[6] But in his view the
*Volkgeist* flows from the effort made by the state to give a law to society
and to bring about an ethic of law. The *Volkgeist* is in fact identical to that
effort. Hegel asserted that "right must become law."[7]

The historical school of law, on the other hand, gave preference over
codified law to customary law, the expression of the *Volkrecht*, an immanent law that lies dormant in the bosom of the spiritual community, the
*geistige Gemeinschaft*, deep beneath the countless layers of rules that govern usages and traditions. The consequence of this dramatic shift is more
than a drift in the direction of legal positivism and the exaltation of social
law, whose importance in the nineteenth and twentieth centuries Gurvitch
and Duguit have underscored. The shift results in the emergence of a
strong anti-statism. As Puchta observed, "the law does not originate in the
state . . . it springs up apart from the state."[8] This anti-statist position is
also the start of a drift toward three consequences: the rejection of an ethic
of law, the rise of populism, and the return to Roman law.

## Opposition to an Ethic of Law

The historical school of law immersed law in the sea of customs and traditions. It justified doing so with the shock argument that a law imported
from the outside could have only a fragile hold.

> If, in conformity with public opinion, the civil law of a people is seen as the
> product of an arbitrary will at whose pleasure it can at any instant disappear
> to make way for another, it belongs to the history of the people and of the
> state only by a very weak accident.[9]

Filled with "civilist" ideas, the school thus sinks constitutional law in the
strict sense, since it bursts the legislative hull that kept it afloat on the sea
of customs and traditions. It plunges law into the depths of organic spiritual life, buries it in tradition, drowns constitutional law in private law.
Law becomes the primal and flaky reef of moral concretion that calcifies
society. As Puchta says forcefully, "morality and law point in the same
direction, but morality goes further than law."[10] Puchta's observation
would carry little import if it did not lead to making law inferior to morality and incapable of grounding any form of transcendence.

Herein lies anti-juridism. The refusal to grant any moral eminence to
law at the very moment it dissolved into the people robs law of any force
it could have as a political and collective catalyst for morality. This view
comes close to joining hands with pietism, which looks down on law as it
looks ahead to a world in which transparency and love will make duty

superfluous. In destroying the ethic of law by situating law in the realm of custom, the historical school of law sowed the seeds of a yet more dangerous weed in the political community and opened the way to a secularization of faith.

## Populism

The metallurgy of terror during the Revolution had already experimented with this point of fusion in which the will of the people is transformed into the whim of the despot once all juridico-legal and mediating guarantees of representation are eliminated and the popular will is taken over by an individual who acts as though he were its oracle. It now became clear what "serving the people" meant. Yet Savigny maintained that "the necessary origin of law rests with the people itself."[11] More populist than the people, Savigny was less concerned with the popular origin of sovereignty than with the security of this juridical property, which he exalted to the point of plebeianism and anti-individualism. As though he had always recognized his indebtedness, he took from Fichte, the onetime admirer of the Revolution, an exaggerated estimation of popular community that Hegel himself had rejected. Hegel had steered clear of individualist exaggerations of natural right, but he also was on guard against communitarian and societist abuses. In his *System of Ethical Life*, he railed against Fichte's coercive and mechanistic doctrine of collectivity. He accepted that membership in a community is what constituted an individual at his deepest level, but he rejected the elimination of the individual and the paring of personal liberties through social law. Hegel critiques the tyrannical and despotic morality summed up in the phrase *"Fiat justitia, pereat mundus!"* ("Let justice be done and the world be damned").[12]

In the guise of a conservative traditionalism, there is nothing ostentatious in the populism of Savigny and Puchta. Yet it nonetheless contains the dangerous and virulent idea of an immanent *juris consensus* that does away with problems regarding representation and the democratic delegation of individual rights to the community. Once the law's collective dimension is undermined straightaway in customs and traditions, the complex and nuanced mechanisms of the sovereign and legislative power, which the classical theoreticians conceived as the controls and limits within a pact, are invalidated. When these mechanisms are gone, democratic security is nullified and has no future. But let us not go overboard. Savigny and Puchta sense very well that the *Volkrecht* is only a sketch of the law that jurists alone would be apt to bring about perfectly and thus make of the *Juristenrecht* the universal heir of the *Volkrecht*. Unfortunately, law is too serious a matter to be placed in the hands of jurists. As with local *self-government*, the prerequisite of *self-justice* is the state under the rule of law.

Hence the ambivalent character of the historical school's populism. It is readily presented, as the Marxists and positivists do, as a gain in rationality for the juridical conception. The school would have added something to law by substituting a social and collective conception for an individual and subjective doctrine. In recalling that law is the manifestation of relations within a social group and the historical web of social regulation, it would have definitively surpassed the most recent construction of classical natural right, which claimed to rebuild the whole juridical order from the starting point of supposedly free individuals voluntarily binding themselves in a contract. Better yet, in rediscovering law's natural social dimension, the historical school would have perfected legal thought by logically uniting Roman law and positive law.

But is this really a gain? There is some reason to ask whether this new social conception of law did not entail a loss of something, whether it did not at the same time take away some ideas from legal science by remaking the definitions of individual and society that govern classical political right.

The definition of the individual: besides countering classical political right by giving the individual autonomous status, the physiocratic and liberal shift in political theory asserted that power must respect individual rights, assure legal security, guarantee liberties, those same subjective rights the Franciscan nominalists had affirmed long before, but which were recognized only much later. Such a requirement was obviously not to be found in ancient, pro-slavery Roman law, not for the slaves, obviously, but not any more for the citizens. A Roman must die for the city and even, if necessary, sacrifice his life for the city. But the requirement is also lost, deposed in the romantic political right that inaugurates modern despotic right. An individual life is but a feather against the weight of collective, patriotic, or social demands. Mao Zedong would later write one of his "bestsellers" on this theme. There was a surreptitious shift in principle in exchanging the contract between state and citizens for the people's self-establishment and the patriotic or social requirements of the collectivity. In short, there arose a new definition of society.

## The Social Is Not the Whole

The word "social" would from now on cover everything. In romanticism, it meant simply chucking out individual rights. Social transcendence, or what earlier thinkers called the common good, was no longer thought of *here and now* in terms of individual rights grounded in a juridico-political contract. It was instead conceived of *before and after* as the historical tradition of a people, in Savigny's view, or as the futurology of the proletariat, as Marx saw it. Individual life is left without any support once the age-old transcendence of the group is cast into the supra-individual graveyard of history.

Romanticism breaks with the biopolitics of the present to build a "thanatopolitics" of the past before constructing a still more deadly politics of the future. It constructs a politics made not for the living but for supermen and dead souls. We have gone from the classical theorem according to which society comprises a juridico-political transcendence to the romantic theorem of an immanent society. It might come as a shock to learn that there is such a thing as a classical idea of society. That seems to be a contradiction in terms, since everyone knows and agrees that there is no notion of society in the classical era.

In the heyday of structuralism, it was drummed into us again and again, with the fans of Marx and Freud joining in the chorus, that at the heart of early modern culture that atomized individuals into discrete entities and thought in terms of resolutive-compositive logic, it was in no way possible to have any idea of anything social. Classical thought might describe love, sing the praises of friendship, classify the passions, in short, analyze a nature's immediate attributes. But it could not understand class struggle, probe neuroses, explain madness—in a word, it could not interpret the distinctive traits of an organized social order. The knowledge of society as the analysis of the intersubjective and historical dimension of the psyche required other postulates: a logic of relation that swept away the doctrine of identity, an *ordo rerum* that bypassed the individual. Those who searched for evidence of society's natural foundations joined in discrediting the myth of Robinson Crusoe. We were repeatedly told that the evidence of human nature has thickened the mystery of culture, that the "cogito" had veiled the thinking of society, that the classical writers had neglected to do sociology. Of course, it might be noted that eighteenth-century ideas are not the whole of classical thought. That would preserve the social element found in earlier thinkers. But it would only be taking a step back in order to jump ahead.

Perhaps it is better to change the terms of the discussion altogether. It is not enough to observe that there is a collective and historical conception of power as well as a classical politics in thinkers like Machiavelli, Bodin, Loyseau, Hobbes, and Locke, and learned historians like Pasquier, Mabillon, and le Nain de Tillemont. It is also necessary to emphasize, without branding it straightaway, that this view of politics is not a civilist or social thought. Why should it be? Ever since the days of political romanticism, collectivity has been reduced to society and politics seen as nothing if it is not social. We have lost the understanding of the classical political principle that society is encompassed by a law that transcends it. We have forgotten that the social is not the whole.

### The Return to Roman Law

"Our present law which owes its origins to the Romans has arisen out of Western civilization by a succession of modifications and uninterrupted changes."[13] Is there anything to the historical school's return to Roman law? Does it represent a return to tradition against nationalism—or is it merely a conservative preference for private law?[14]

When German thinkers took up Roman law, long after the annotators and commentators, the works of such Romanists as Budé and Cujas, they were not content with a mere scholarly restitution of Roman law.[15] Neither were they concerned, in the way Michel Villey is today, to let the echo of a law conceived in terms of relations within a group rather than as the attribute of a subject resonate above the deafening demands of subjective law, or to highlight the supple gymnastic of the spirit of equity in the face of the unmovable rigidity of regulations. In Roman law, the historical school was not looking for a general science and a natural history. Its members were much more concerned with the Romans' conception of politics and the state and on this point, along with their early modern predecessors, they sought to revive a political right. It does not matter here that, in search of this nonexistent political right, the historical school turned the texts around and produced a heretical and unfaithful Romanism. By proceeding this way, they nonetheless invented a new political law along with a myth of Romanism.

In his book on the spirit of Roman law, Jhering systematized the themes that Hugo, Savigny, and then the commentators on the *Pandectae* had already taken from Roman law.[16] Point for point they opposed modern law on two scores: first, that right is founded on might; and second, that politics is war. They called into question the views that held that in its origins ownership is a takeover and that the state is merely the sum of its citizens standing behind the people, which is the sole subject of public law. They looked beyond the ideas that there is no distinction to be made between private and public law and that private law reigns supreme. Beneath all these theses, the scholars of the historical school discovered another concept of law in ancient Rome: the political law of an imperial and pro-slavery system.

On that basis, the biblical strain in early modern political law gave way to the Roman strain that weighs on German political philosophy. Rediscovered, or rather invented by the historical school of law, Roman political law acquired a permanent place in German thought. Fifty years later, the *iimperium romanum* became one of the principal reference points of Nietzsche's politics. The anticlassical thinker par excellence ceaselessly exalted the Roman Empire against the Judeo-Christian heritage.

> That which stood there *aere perennius*, the *imperium romanum*, the most magnificent form of organization under difficult circumstances which has yet been achieved, in comparison with which all before and all afterward are mere botch, patchwork, and dilettantism . . . Christianity was the vampire of the *imperium romanum*."[17]

Nietzsche also legitimated and called for slavery—nothing less—and analyzed morality in the light of the Roman penal system in *The Genealogy of Morals*. In a word, Nietzsche rethought history, the state, and justice, with Rome as his starting point.

It is not out of place here to summon Hegel to pass judgment on this amalgam of "master thinkers." The Roman state, the prose in the life of the spirit, is for Hegel a state of thieves, formed by violence and maintained by force, whose principle is abstract domination and military power. Hegel does a careful analysis of the opposition between imperial and modern power as the difference between *domination* founded on naked force and *government* established on law and morality. "The emperor *domineered* only, and could not be said to *rule*; for the equitable and moral medium between the sovereign and the subject was wanting."[18] What a subtle dissociation of the political mechanisms of a despotic state and a state under the rule of law! Far from forging a path in the direction of traditionalist universalism, the return to Roman law paved the way toward the political law of the nation-state.

What about modernism? Is this modernism? Is this really promoting a bourgeois political form with a new kind of law when couched beneath the ancient ideal lies the reality of empire suddenly come to life again? If the abdication of Francis II in 1806 brought the Holy Roman Empire to an end after the deadly blow Napoleon dealt the German Empire, the Austrian Empire, not to mention the phoenix of the great Reich, did not collapse until the First World War. To measure the romantics' attachment to the Holy Roman Empire, one should read the preacher of its revival, August Wilhelm von Schlegel, who proclaimed that it was Germany's mission to restore the moral and political unity of Europe after the fall of the Roman Empire.[19] That mission is in the tradition of the Holy Roman Empire, which, at its founding in 962 with the crowning of Otto, saw itself not as a new beginning but as the heir of Charlemagne and of Rome. It also preserved the idea of empire and colonialism. The empire grounded its *dominium* in *imperium* and prolonged the conquest and servitude of Germany. This was not a concentric domination from Rome as its focal point to the periphery of possible conquests, but rather an extension of the superficial and capillary symbolism of the ancient imperial ideal. The perpetuation of the empire preserved the ideal of the military camp within the body politic and fostered the waging of ever-renewed wars wherever possible. Imperialism (the use of the substantive in this instance is not a whimsical choice to designate the imperial regime's bellicose inclinations) was a system designed for war, domination, slavery. Although it was linked in Germany to the early beginnings of bourgeois law, in Napoleon's France the rise of Roman law was also connected with the reactivation of ancient imperialist politics. Novalis unlocked the door to this connection:

> As a land, Germany is Rome. . . . The tendency and inclination of the Romans for universal politics also lies in the German people. The best that the French achieved in the Revolution is a portion of the German heritage.[20]

## *Return to the Feudal Doctrine of Power*

As for the other route, it was clearly and repeatedly articulated by the German jurists and philosophers. Perhaps it is true that Germany pursued another route because it was falling behind. Perhaps one needs to understand literally what Nietzsche said regarding the other route, that Germany willed the eternal return. Perhaps one needs to take Nietzsche's word as it applies to what runs through Germany's history, even if its process of maturation and laboring, the torrential current, had gone underground and was hidden from what the nearsighted could perceive. That was indeed the case with Karl Ludwig von Haller, author of *Restauration der Staatswissenschaften (The Restoration of Political Science)*, published in 1816 and afterward translated into French.[21] It is a landmark work in the panorama of anti-juridism. Written soon after the author's dramatic conversion to Catholicism, it sought to critique classical political philosophy from Bodin to Rousseau as one and the same system to be rejected as a whole. Haller held that the classical theory's unity rested on the doctrine of sovereignty.

When one sets Hegel against Haller, one sees that, once again, the philosopher who remained faithful to the classics is an iconoclast clashing with the swordblades of romanticism. The arguments Hegel set forth in his *Principles of the Philosophy of Right* articulated precisely what was at stake in the debate with romanticism. Hegel maintains that "the functions and powers of the state cannot be private property."[22] To emphasize the modern character of sovereignty, he adds that "in feudal times the state was certainly sovereign *vis-à-vis* other states; at home, however, not only was the monarch not sovereign at all, but the state was not sovereign either."[23] Hegel explains that it would be a mistake, again to the extent that "the sovereignty of the state is the ideality of all particular authorities," to confuse it with arbitrary power and to amalgamate it to despotism, the state that is without law.[24] In the constitutional monarchy that Hegel supports, the monarch is the opposite of a master, and the bond of state never encompasses conquered subjects and their invaders. On the morrow of the Erfurt meeting of 1808, about which Hegel wrote an article in the *Bamberg Gazette*, had not Napoleon told the German emissaries: "I am not your prince. I am your master!"? It is precisely the sovereignty theory that Haller attacks, where Rousseau, he holds, follows logically from Bodin, since according to the system of sovereign power

> the source of power is in the people, that is, in the body of subjects . . . , for it is they who had to establish the state by their joining together. The mass of the people is the true sovereign, the real master, the *summus imperans*.[25]

The fact is that in this system, as Haller no doubt sees clearly, the mass of the people is assimilated to a bourgeoisie or a free corporation, "and the model of the social pact is the corporation and the guild-mastership." Given this, how can one escape this proposition on sovereignty whose consequence is that empire ceases to be a function and becomes a duty and that instead of expressing the desire of a leader, the will becomes embodied in the general will?

What else did Karl Ludwig von Haller have to propose? Nothing less than a restoration. This project was more than a simple and rather material operation of fixing and rebuilding a damaged political reality. It was rather a matter of reaching back into the past to an original privilege. The romantic love of ruins, antiquities, and archaisms became in Germany the lovingly contemplated archaism of the political civilization of feudal domains, states, and serfs.

Haller did not conceal his admiration for Roman law. His restoration entailed nothing less than a restitution of ancient natural right, where he saw proof that humanity did not leave the state of nature to enter the state of civil society because human relations are founded on might rather than right. That was nothing less than the destruction of the state's autonomy. The definition that modernizing Marxists whisper as their latest and boldest theory, that the state is merely a social relation, was blatantly trumpeted by Haller, who aimed at nothing less than reinvigorating the patrimonial and dominial theory of power.[26] This novel thinker scornfully swept away the distinction dear to the classical legists between royalty and lordship, that "the prince is an independent lord who commands others and himself serves no one." This is the motto of the new kind of power, where authority precedes independence and jurisdiction follows welfare.

With it came a new conception of law that turned the classical perspective on its head. Whereas in the past a number of social acts that fell under the heading of charity were transformed into public acts and placed under public administration, Haller reversed the process in restoring to welfare what the law had taken from it. Right must be bestowed as a benefit, a protection, and cease being public in order to become social again. Social right is the regulated and well-ordered charity of superiors toward their inferiors. The development of Bismarck's "state socialism" and the welfare bureaucracy organized by German Prussia probably stems from this inversion. It was a disaster that it was so quickly exported elsewhere.

The argument invoked to maintain that "restored" power was a domination of the feudal type rests on the restriction that the execution of laws imposes on those in power. On that score, in Haller's view, all administrators could be called sovereigns. The prince is not he who executes laws, but he who shows force. Thus, feudal lordship again becomes the model for all forms of power and mastery, the essence of every kind of domination. The state is one form of lordship among others, established not to defend citizens' rights or social justice but to execute a master's authority. This is nothing less than a justification of serfdom.

There is a disturbing coherence in the reasoning of this author, who shows the way to the new direction of German political right. Haller extolled feudalism and ancient imperialism for their relations between dominators and dominated. If these relations are unjust, at least they are direct and human. One comes to prefer the sacred bond of dependence to the independent rigor of law and to preach a return to the village and the flock, with human lives hemmed in together, with instant order and obedience. This is nothing less than the phantasmatic restoration of slavery. The program of *Mein Kampf* calling for the subjugation of the Slavs and the taming of the Latins was no more novel in contemporary politics than the enslavement of prisoners in concentration-camp socialism. A hundred years earlier, romantic political right had "restored" their justification.

# CHAPTER X

# The Secularization of Faith

For religious we must once again become if politics is to be our
religion. But this can be achieved only if we possess the highest point
of reference within ourselves as the condition for making politics
our religion.

—LUDWIG FEUERBACH

Every POLITICAL experience is to a certain degree a religious experience. Who does not already know that? The early modern thinkers understood well that the recognition of religion's part in politics and of theologico-political authorities was a necessary condition of the new historical spirit. In our time, however, it is no longer a sufficient condition. We want to know more: from what type of religion does such and such a politics derive its dynamic, its collective unconscious, its morality, and its consensus? What is it that leads men to live and die for it?

The early nineteenth century was a time of intense theologico-political reflection in Germany and, as elsewhere in the early modern period, of efforts to forge social consensus by appropriating religious ideals. But these efforts took a different course in Germany. Instead of elaborating an ethic of individual right and of right as law along the lines of the nominalists and the *Decalia*, the German romantics focused on the secularization of faith.

### Spinoza's Legacy?

Spinoza, of course, had already sought in his own way to secularize faith, by changing one aspect of theological authority into political reasoning and by making of man a god for man. Whatever influence Spinoza had on

German idealism, it was very discreet and subversive. The clandestine Spinozism of Leibniz, who refused to acknowledge meeting with Spinoza, is an early instance of the shameful mentality Spinoza induced in classical German philosophy. Herder fashioned an image of Spinoza as a counterfeit that was later altered so as to make Spinoza compatible with a religious syncretism in which Christianity could have a part. Add to this Jacobi's outcry over Lessing's admission to following Spinoza, and one can see how no debate of Spinoza's ideas ever developed. The question simply was not raised.

Something else happened instead. A more private and passing acquaintance with Spinoza became a part of everyone's philosophical formation that, one after another, Lessing, Fichte, and the Schlegels had all taken in before disavowing it when they began to publish. Nonetheless, something was digested in this hidden rumination: Spinoza's monism, rather than remaining on the plane of metaphysics as its author conceived of it, in a strange way found its way into theology and politics. In these areas Spinoza had been liberal and tolerant, not at all monistic. Even if Spinoza is reproached with forgetting conscience, his monism did not entail a reduction of political realities to natural phenomena, a leveling of civic life, or the erosion of political passions. Spinoza did not dream of a uniform, empty society but of a restoration of man's humanity in clear and forthright speech and writing, with the proper distinctions being made once again. The world would not be impoverished by removing the moral and theological lens that reduces and deforms what simply needs to be understood. On the contrary, what the prophets and priests had unduly taken as their own was now restored to the domain of learning and learned inquiry.

Spinoza's assessment was simple: excessive moralizing about nature, society, and man demoralizes knowledge, because it consigns what the soul could otherwise grasp and master to the barbarous enclaves of pompous and officious discourse within disciplines that shackle and hurt the body. Spinoza sought to open the gates that keep the soul of the man-beast lying in his prison. In fostering the development of rationalism, Spinoza limited monism to the realm of metaphysics so as to keep an ethical perspective in the theologico-political sphere. But German political philosophy transplanted his ontological monism into the theologico-political sphere and subjected final causality to rationalism.

Perhaps the absence of any reflection on the role of the subject encouraged this anti-individualist and immanentist shift in Spinoza's own work. In any event, one ought to note the gap between those who, like Novalis, pronounced him intoxicated with God, and Spinoza himself, the sober teacher of the intellectual love of God.

*A Time of Conversions*

The young romantics had a passion for politics and revolution, but they were also taken up with revelation and mysticism. Yet in the conversion they experienced, there was a strong element of tradition. Political spirituality and spiritual politics were nothing new in Germany. Twice in her history, Germany had made it clear that national sentiment was not to be separated from religious sentiment. First, Otto's successors, the restorers of the Holy Roman Empire, claimed they were acting in the name of Christ to impose spiritual unity on Europe by means of the sword. Gregory VII put an end to their claim by denouncing caesaropapism and asserting the division of the two powers. Later, the Lutheran reformation favored the formation of a religious state by severing Germany from the grip of Roman Catholicism. The break-up of the land and the triumph of the *cujus regio ejus religio* principle put a limit on this ambition.

The young romantic writers extolled their political mystical past in prose and poetry. A. W. von Schlegel recalled how the Holy Roman Empire colonized the whole of Europe with its spiritual politics. Novalis celebrated the Middle Ages as Germany's greatest era. Others wrote in *Das Athenäum*, the journal of the romantic circle gathered around Friedrich von Schlegel, who urged that "the model of Germany . . . doesn't lie behind, but before us" and asserted that "the revolutionary desire to realize the kingdom of God on earth is the elastic point of progressive civilization and the beginning of modern history."[1] They agreed with Fichte, who saw Germany's territorial fragmentation and historical backwardness compensated in her being chosen for a Pan-European spiritual mission. They foreshadowed Wagner, for whom Germanic blood was mystical, its vital powers spiritual. Tradition lived again in the romantics' sensing in their formative stages the inspiration of the medieval mystical ideal. Franz von Baader and Claude de Saint-Martin rediscovered and commented on Meister Eckhart and Jakob Boehme.[2] The Swabian brethren Bengel and Oetinger, of the Protestant theological seminary at Tübingen, taught a mystical pietism with gnostic overtones to their students, among whom were Schelling, Hegel, and Hölderlin. Hegel's own theology, however, took an altogether different direction.

*Hegelian Theology*

Although it is not readily manifest, one striking indication of the distinctiveness of Hegel's thought is its theological character. The effect of romanticism on the thinking of this young man immersed in his own time was to sever objective, popular religion from subjective, personal religion. The first, Hegel maintained, encompassed understanding and memory and was dead matter, but the second was a living force that brought the imagination and the sensibility into play and wove people together in the bonds of friendship. Like his contemporaries, Hegel took a stand against the Old Testament, but he did so for reasons that were entirely his own. The demands of Jewish formalism seemed to him exaggerated and asocial. The religion of Abraham broke with domination and the dialectic of master and slave. In leaving behind family and homeland, Abraham turned his back on nature and humanity and, refusing the logical fate of mastery, reoriented himself toward a transcendent God. The young Hegel, firmly opposed to the individualistic empiricism of natural right, suddenly realized that men must be dealt with as they are with their feelings and passions. The morality of law forged a chasm between what ought to be and what is. Hegel consequently repudiated Kant's *Religion within the Limits of Reason Alone*, in which he saw the formalism of the morality of law extolling conciliation by faith at the cost of love rooted in life. Law broke and wounded human existence, but life sealed the breaches and bound the wounds.

With this starting point, the young Hegel, somewhat in advance of the romantic generation, was well on the way to a political morality and a secularized religion. But he made it clear just where he was inclined to part with romanticism. Instead of severing the sequence of Judaism and Christianity and choosing between the Old and the New Testaments, Hegel evoked a third party others had excluded—Hellenism. The politics of Hellenism attenuated the tension that grips the two alternatives of Old Testament commandments and New Testament counsels. Hellenism was something else, a different form of secularized religion. The Greek ideal subordinated private right to public right and made civil liberty dependent on political liberty.

Instead of borrowing from Christianity an ethos of reconciliation whose secularization would lead to theocracy, Hegel dreamed of a political religion that was nowhere to be found. The bright sun of the Greek deities was forever extinguished and the agora of men assembled in political faith, Greece itself, a lost continent. There remained only fragments of broken myth to be pieced together. Plato's *Republic*, which Hegel compared to modern political orders, was not only utopian but anachronistic as well, forever gone from modern historical experience. But thanks to the Holy Roman Empire, to the church, and to the Italian city-states, Rome still existed in the nineteenth century. To choose Rome was to stand by an abiding entity; to turn to Greece was a pure dream. There was no harm in living in the dream of Greek political religion, since a dream is recognized as only a dream. Thus the Greek model was suitably tempered so as to avoid the appearance of a secularization of faith.

Hegel adapted its outward trappings so well that, once he had arrived at the mature thought of his *Principles of the Philosophy of Right*, he was free to advance beyond his earlier repugnance for the morality of law and to reinject Kantian morality into the heart of his own thinking. In the meantime, Hegel had come to think that right must become law, and he had defined the state in terms of self-knowledge rather than of life. That shift was hidden from the eyes of his contemporaries, who thought that the separation of the morality of faith from the morality of law was no longer a matter of concern to Hegel. The shortcut through the Greek world had closed the political prospect of a secularization of faith and erased the traces of a return to Kantian morality. The young Hegelians saw only fire in all this. Bruno Bauer thought he remained faithful to Hegel in formulating a revolutionary political theology founded on the New Testament.

Novalis and Schleiermacher developed their religious thought among the Moravian brethren reformed by Count Zinzendorf. The brethren had made its own Saint Paul's understanding of faith as "the evidence of things not seen" (Heb. 11:1). Novalis, Wackenroder, Tieck, and Schleiermacher all penned religious writings in this era of great theological commitments, which was also an era of conversions.[3] Görres, Adam Müller, Friedrich and Dorothea von Schlegel (the daughter of Moses Mendelssohn) all converted to Catholicism. Among his numerous projects to transform life, love, and society, Friedrich von Schlegel was particularly successful in his mission to transform religion, in which he imagined Novalis to be Christ and himself Saint Paul.

A massive reformation was slowly taking shape. The return to faith preached by Novalis and Schleiermacher was not a return to the fold of Roman Catholicism or of traditional Lutheranism, but the search for a reformed religion and a church of the new age. As Novalis proclaimed bluntly, Christianity's "accidental form is as good as annihilated. The old Papacy lies in its grave and Rome for the second time has become a ruin. Shall Protestantism not cease at last and make way for a new, enduring Church?"[4] The traditional Christians who rejoiced in this religious ferment ought to have been more cautious, and they should have listened more closely to Schleiermacher's stretching the definition of religious sentiment so that it could be put to strange and pernicious uses and eventually inform not only the social realm, as is normal, but also the civil and be taken over by the political realm. Romanticism was consciously preparing the way for a rediscovered but revised faith to be committed to the new goals of the fatherland and the people. It was concerned to relax and reorient religious sentiment itself, uproot its traditions, and sow the seeds of new plantings. It pursued that effort in a twofold direction of opposing faith to law and of disparaging transcendence.

## Faith against Law

On the heels of the Reformation and Counter-Reformation, traditional theology was overshadowed by a renaissance of biblical studies and the elaboration of a canon of Scriptures that gave renewed emphasis to the unity of the Old and New Testaments. But something unexpected took place in Germany at the start of the nineteenth century among both Protestant and Catholic romantics. They turned their backs on the Old Testament and severed Christianity from its Jewish roots. They severed the Judeo-Christian tradition and rejected the early moderns' agreement with Hobbes's assertions that the mark of the New Testament was "the preaching of (the) doctrine, that Jesus is the Christ, that is, king of the Jews, promised in the Old Testament" and that "there is nothing done or taught by Christ that tendeth to the diminution of the civil right of the Jews."[5] Schleiermacher taught that the law is useless and inferior to love in that it did not reveal the goal of sanctification. Faith and law were opposed. A doctrine that rests only on the Old Testament has no credibility in the new dispensation. "Judaism has been a dead religion for a long time. . . . The fact that I want to say something about this formation of religion has nothing to do with its being the 'forerunner' of Christianity."[6] A return to the New Testament by itself alone is necessary.

But what was meant by faith? What Schleiermacher called "the shibboleth of faith," purposely taking up the word and giving it new significance, "is the feeling of absolute dependence on Christ." Hegel replied that a dog would then make the best Christian. Hegel aside, however, this reevaluation of faith could have led the romantics to a revival of evangelical charity, the greatest of Christian virtues. In those times of war and misfortune, of illness and social inequality, faith could have offered the healing and the peace that can alleviate suffering and illness. It could have reminded people that charity transcends a city torn apart, because man is more than a political animal.

But romantic faith turned its back on charity, as can be see in the gnostic twist Friedrich von Schlegel gave the Gospel teaching on love in *Lucinda* and the influence of quietism and the doctrine of pure love in Herder, Jacobi, and Jean Paul.[7] More telling is the important essay Novalis published in 1798, *Faith and Love*, a work whose palpitating beauty masked disturbing theologico-political ambitions. The poet made known his religious preferences in politics and secularized his faith, which now becomes the essential civil bond.[8] Society must be united by love, a bond more solid than law, since law has no force unless it is the expression of the will of one who is beloved and worthy of reverence. Novalis's fervent defense of the mystical political faith that would move mountains all the way to Caesar went to great lengths. Not only did it raise the monarch above the traditional conception of divine-right kingship, but it also revealed the great servitude that political faith warranted. It would be wonderful, according to Novalis's view, to have a regime in which peasants would more willingly eat a morsel of bread than roasted meat and thank God for being born in such a country. What a strange premonition!

### Immanence

The political appropriation of faith inevitably led to the emergence of the doctrine of immanence. Words like "transcendence" and "immanence" may appear barbarous to the secularized, who see in such words an esoteric or terrorist jargon that philosophers and theologians use too freely. Yet these words hold meaning for everyone. To acknowledge that there is such a thing as transcendence is simply to recognize a universal experience and not only the experience of faith. Even if the believer's faith in the invisible divine reality is a matter of choice and transcendence, there is more to faith than that. Every individual who lives by religious, moral, and logical ideals that he receives and passes on in some way experiences transcendence. Faith, morality, and science all remain when individual lives end, as the ancients discovered. To the Greeks we owe mathematical and logical concepts. Traces of Thales and Pythagoras disappeared in the sand they wrote on, but mathematics remains. To the Jews, we owe theological and moral ideals. The people of the Diaspora has lost its land, but, thanks to the law, the nation's identity holds firm. Our existence endures far longer than our meager individual chronology, and our culture holds greater knowledge and ideals than do our obscure personal lives.

The recognition of transcendence is not without its dangers. It can inflict an excess of humility or uncalled-for humiliations on individuals, empty individual lives of meaning in the name of an inaccessible universal, celebrate culture and death to the detriment of life and the body. But the denial of transcendence, especially the romantics' denial of theological transcendence, entailed greater perils. The overvalued individual lost his sense of humanity, distances and differences were obliterated, and otherness abolished. Every form of mysticism that leads to ecstatic intimacy with the living God produces a kind of private prophecy conducive to the sentiment of immanence. Stirred by heavy doses of the strong drug of medieval mysticism, romantic theology surrendered to immanence. The young romantics were fond of meditating on Meister Eckhart's famous saying that carried in it the temptation to assimilate man to God: "[T]he eye with which God sees me is the eye with which I see Him. My eye and His are identical. . . . If God did not exist, I would not exist; and if I did not exist, neither would He." From such a starting point, romantic theology produced both naturalism and historicism.

*Naturalism*

Schelling's 1797 essay, *Ideas for a Philosophy of Nature*, is a striking formulation of the immanentist representation of nature. Schelling later made of himself "an irreplaceable being," and his evolution led him further eastward and further back in time toward Oriental mythology and paganism. But this work, the kin in many respects of Novalis's *Novices of Sais* or of Ritter's physics in the conception of nature that it develops, was hailed by A. W. von Schlegel as the orthodox expression of the romantic physics.[9] The naturalism of Schelling's essay and of romantic, poetic physics is of a different sort than the naturalism that produced the apologia of country life, frugal living, and English gardens that mark British and French naturalism. It is more violent, more ambitious, more profound. It uproots man from the city to transplant him in a cosmic, dynamic nature filled with symbols and squalls. It grafts the individual onto telluric and chthonic forces that plunge Germanic man into the nocturnal depths of his forests and past dreams. Inevitably, it moves in the direction of mythology and certain brutal forms of paganism. Wagner is just around the corner.

Romantic physics rejects the partial perspective of classical physics and chemistry that formulated laws of precise relations, which allowed the mind to move from one compartment of reality to another according to predetermined rules. Instead, it views nature as a whole regulated by the action of opposing forces that combine with, interpenetrate, and displace one another. It sees nature as a perpetual creative force animated by the world spirit (*der Weltgeist*), the soul of the universe (*der Geist des Universums*). Schelling sees the world soul as moving from the particular to the whole, from the air to the vegetal, culminating in the grand encounter of man and the universe.

Faith, creativity, and theology no longer refer to God but to the body, to every material form and morphological appearance (and soon also to obsessions, such as race and naturalness). The direction of finality, which Spinoza sought to abolish and which the romantics played down, is inverted and reordered into the realm of matter.

To arrive at this fusion of the human spirit with the spirit of God that is the intuition of the divine, naturalism beckons everyone to enter deep within himself and at the same time into the most fragmented surface of things. *Naturphilosophie* is monistic, unifying soul and body. It culminates in a mystical eroticism that synthezes the finite and the infinite. The paradox of this synthesis is that it can be realized only in an infinity of particularized forms. The absolute is attained only in an infinity of relative connections, the divine apprehended only in an infinity of terrestrial relations. Once it is forsaken, transcendence yields to a fragmented body whose materiality is the logical consequence of immanence. "One day," Novalis says in his *Hymns to the Night*, "everything will be body." This fixation on bodies and material things, this gnostic exaltation of the body does not arise because bodies reveal the continuous creation of the universe that Descartes perceived, but rather because bodies reveal the ongoing incarnation of God. When this fixation is joined to an obsession with death, it provokes a phobia of corpses decaying in the shadows.

The experience of death was central for the young romantics. The deaths of Sophie von Kuhn or Caroline Schelling were occasions for profound meditation in which one denied the death of the departed, but at the same time allowed oneself to be won over and tempted by death. In the last poem of Novalis's *Hymns to the Night*, "Yearning for Death," one senses a demiurgic and nocturnal force, a reactive energy, emerging from the past, a force bent on destruction. Freud and Thomas Mann, each in his own way, identified that force as the death wish.

## *Historicism*

The dialectic of nature extends into a dialectic of history that is already present, before Schelling or Hegel, in the Swabian teachers who formed the romantics. For them, theological knowledge is historical knowledge. They saw history as intimately linked to the Scriptures, as the unfolding of the providential divine plan, the sphere in which revelation develops in the course of the ages. Bengel conceived the idea of a spiritual kingdom in which the Lord will pour his Spirit over all flesh, and all forms of knowledge will be reconciled. Oetinger is responsible for the idea of a golden age whose social order is democratic. In the early nineteenth century, the world of tomorrow sang forth, and eschatology mixed with utopian socialism. The ultimate outcome of a vision of history from the perspective of the end of time is a society rooted in the equality of all its members, in brotherhood and the community of goods.

With Schleiermacher, one can assess how unrealistic things can become once eschatology is transposed into history and salvation is expected not in another world but in a better world that lies just ahead. A self-proclaimed "prophet-citizen of a world to come," he asserts that "what the present world is doing leaves me unmoved; far below me it appears insignificant."[10]

The idea of a continuous epiphany and incarnation of Christ might have stayed confined to mystical ecstasies. Instead, it took root in the cosmos and set itself up in history. It did even more than that: mysticism joined hands with nationalism. Here the romantics concur with Fichte, who proclaimed that Germany is the incarnation of Western spirituality and the German people is Christ. Such is the conclusion of Novalis's *Die Christenheit oder Europa* (*Christendom or Europe*). Henceforth Germany's mission is to save the world. The doctrine of immanence and the secularization of faith gave birth to a monster, the people as Christ. Feuerbach was to be its tutor.

## Ludwig Feuerbach

The myth of a rationalist Feuerbach whose influence brought Marx back to eighteenth-century Enlightenment thought derives from the notice on Karl Marx that Lenin penned in his biography of Feuerbach. Ever since, Feuerbach has been taken to be a thoroughgoing critic of religion, the systematic atheist and enemy of faith. But Feuerbach's critique of religion is not in the straight line of the Enlightenment and Spinoza. It is not rationalist but romantic.

There is a great difference between Spinoza's crtique and Feuerbach's. Spinoza's atheism led to the elimination of the theologico-moral perspective and the deliberate replacement of commands and obedience with understanding and tolerance. Spinoza never thought of establishing himself on the plane of religion. He gave no thought to usurping what to him was of so little value. Feuerbach's atheism proceeds in the opposite way. For him it is a matter of injecting the forces of religious sentiment into political action. In exalting the value of religion, Feuerbach's dream is to appropriate it. *The Essence of Christianity* proclaims the need to give back to man what man has alienated from himself in his representation of God. It is not a manifesto against religion but a theoretical coup intended to turn religion away from its theological uses. Strictly speaking, it is a religious perversion.

Although Feuerbach's project caused scandal upon its publication, the young Hegelians greeted it with applause from the very first, because its author had formulated it in the language they knew best, the language of romanticism. Feuerbach fulfilled more than he abolished romanticism, with which he shared the same enemies and the same ideas.

Feuerbach and romanticism above all have a common enemy in Hegel. Despite his shortcomings regarding religious sentiment, which he rationalized in the extreme, Hegel kept himself from the deadly sin of secularizing faith, which Fichte preached in the name of rationalism. According to Hegel, the state rightly requires that citizens fulfill their legal obligations, but it is not concerned with their salvation. Beyond that, Feuerbach and romanticism share the same concerns to defend love against law and to exalt immanence. The truth of the new philosophy is love, sentiment. "Only in feeling and love has the demonstrative this—this person, this thing, that is, the particular—absolute value; only then is the finite infinite."[11] To the circle that is emblematic of Hegel's philosophy, Feuerbach prefers the ellipse to symbolize the philosophy of sensation rooted in intuition. "The heart is not a form of religion which could also exist in the heart; it is the very essence of religion."[12] This new value placed on sensation entails a disparaging depreciation of the understanding and of science. "By the understanding an insect is contemplated with as much enthusiasm as the image of God-man. . . . It is the enthusiasm of the understanding that we have to thank for botany, mineralogy, astronomy, zoology, physics, and astronomy," but the understanding forgets what is essential for man: man himself. "The Christian thinks only of himself!"[13]

With respect to immanence, Feuerbach adapts a naturalist philosophy and critiques Hegel's timidity on this score. To Feuerbach, nature is not in contradiction with moral freedom. Its constructs include not only the elementary mechanism of the stomach but the temple of the mind as well. Here Feuerbach, carried away by the doctrine of immanence, goes a step further and crosses the Rubicon. If there is no more law, there is no more transcendence. If there is only a continuous incarnation, if, as Nietzsche will say, God is dead, then what point is there in maintaining faith in a world beyond, in keeping a separate realm of religion? None whatever. Since man is God, God is no different than man, and since the infinite is in the finite, the infinite must be abolished. In declaring that the authentic essence of religion is anthropological and not theological, Feuerbach simply sums up the central intuition of romantic theology that, man being God, God must dissolve into man.

Should religion then be abolished? By no means, since religion is "the solemn unveiling of a man's hidden treasures, the revelation of his intimate thoughts, the open confession of his love-secrets."[14] Religion ought to be preserved, to be appropriated and transformed. Feuerbach asserts that man is a religious animal and his whole project is to elevate anthropology to the status of theology, "for religious we must once again become if politics is to be our religion. But this can be achieved only if we possess the highest point of reference within ourselves as the condition for making politics our religion."[15] As the apostle of sentiment who disparaged science and intellect, Feuerbach did not mount a rationalist critique of religion. His was a romantic critique. He fulfilled the romantics' dream of transfer-

ring the forces of religious sentiment to the life of society and injecting the
mighty forces of religion into politics. That project held the young Hegelians in thrall.

Romanticism's handling of the theologico-political realm called for the
secularization of faith and the divinization of the nation and the people.
From that point onward, the salvation of the individual rests in the hands
of political forces. In the words of Alain Besançon,

> thus formulated, this religious thinking is the matrix of a conflicting revolu-
> tionary thought that eliminates religious elements while keeping a social and
> political ideal. . . . The ground of their opposition is atheism, and nothing
> else. . . . Their common ground is a hatred of the world, the gnostic tinge of
> romantic Christianity.[16]

# CHAPTER XI

# Marx's Romanticism

### The Marxist Critique of Political Right

THE EXISTENCE of the concentration camps in *all* the soviet regimes under the banner of Marxism imposes an obligation on the partisans of socialism to undertake a critique of Marxist notions of political right. The historical record summons us to understand the move from Marxism to the gulag. Oddly enough, however, Marx's political thought remains an uncharted no-man's-land.

The same critique that Marx levied at others all his life needs to be applied to Marx himself. Not a criticism in its immediate and brutal form, "criticism in a hand-to-hand fight," since, as Marx says, "in such a fight it is of no interest to know whether the adversary is of the same rank, is noble or interesting—all that matters is to strike him."[1] It is not our intention to "attack" Marx, or basely to tarnish his reputation, as was done recently, by peering under his covers.[2] Althusser has very rightly observed that, generally speaking, concepts are not to be found in people's bedrooms. It is rather a question of examining how Marx's political theory, his teaching on the withering away of the state and on the reconciliation of society divided into the social and the political, was able to inspire a system that brings into being political institutions of unprecedented repression and massacres. It is a matter of discovering what, by excess or by default, could permit or could fail to stop the antiliberal and antidemocratic drift toward the concentration camps in those systems that are indebted to Marx's thought. Marx knew that the route goes from "the arm of criticism to the criticism of arms," and Lenin understood that Russia's future hung on "the slightest nuance, the most obscure comma in the ideological struggle." Once words become material forces, they exert their pressure on things. There is no point in going back indefinitely; the fate of Marxism needs to be sought out and analyzed in Marx himself.

### The Formation of Marx's Doctrine

There exists an official catechism on the genesis of Marxism. One of its most persuasive preachers is Lenin, who made Marx the heir of the three "most advanced" movements of his time: German philosophy, French socialism, and English political economy. The rationalist genesis of Marxism lies in the first of these movements. Cast out from Hegelian idealism, Marx would have returned, thanks to Feuerbach, to Enlightenment materialism, which he would have reworked and improved into dialectical materialism. This impeccable biography in the past had the considerable advantage of substantiating the Communist Party's claim to the Jacobin legacy, and today it has the added benefit of consigning every form of rationalism to the same disgrace. It has but one flaw, however: it is false, both chronologically and epistemologically. Marx's notion of political right does not stem from the Enlightenment.

It is first of all false chronologically. As Auguste Cornu's careful research shows, the father's reasoning is not always the better reasoning.[3] The myth of Marx's spontaneous adherence to Hegelianism—that he stayed closer to the Enlightenment than to romanticism—is indeed confirmed by the Voltairean culture of his father, Heinrich Marx. But what about Marx's father-in-law? About him, Marx's daughter, Eleanor Marx, informs us that

> the Baron of Westphalen, half-Scottish by birth, filled Marx with enthusiasm for the Romantic school. While his father read Voltaire and Racine with him, the baron read Homer and Shakespeare, who remained his preferred authors throughout all his life.[4]

In 1835–1836, Marx came to Bonn, the home of the romantic school, where he heard the lectures of one of its leading figures, A. W. von Schlegel. Already prepared by Jenny's father, he conceived a passion for the movement and even became a novelist and poet. For Christmas 1836, he gave Jenny three notebooks of his poems. Was this a mere passing fancy, a must-do for a German student taken up with the *Zeitgeist*? The following year in Berlin, the influences were more divided, since Marx followed the lectures of Gans, a disciple of Hegel, along with Savigny's. But romanticism stayed with him, and he composed in turn the first act of a fatalist drama, *Oulanem*, and a satirical novel, *Scorpion and Felix*, this time offering his father the fruits of his inspiration, much to the elder Marx's chagrin.

Did Marx's break with literature also mark a parting of ways with romanticism? Not quite, since, after following in the winter term 1836 lectures on the *Pandectae* by Savigny, on criminal law by Gans, and on anthropology by Steffens, Marx undertook to compose a vast work on the philosophy of right wherein Savigny's influence is clearly manifest in the attention Marx gives to Roman law, the great value he places on private right, and his refusal to see political life regulated by law.[5] Yet in 1838 Marx joined the young Hegelians' club and in fact turned to Hegel by the end of 1837. And so Marx became a Hegelian. But for how long?

Five years, if one goes as far as the final reckoning in *The Critique of Hegel's Philosophy of Right* (1843); three years, if one considers the serious reservations contained in Marx's dissertation, *Democritus and Epictetus* (1841); but barely one year, if, along with the other young Hegelians, he read the sensational article Feuerbach published in their own journal, *The Halle Annals*. Engels said of its effect that "at once we all became Feuerbachians!" Feuerbach's article, "The Critique of Hegel's Philosophy," appeared in September 1839. Earlier, Friedrich Strauss in his *Life of Jesus* (1835) and A. von Ciesztowski in his *Prolegomena to the Philosophy of History* (1838) had attacked Hegel so forcefully as to leave the younger generation dumbfounded. Hegelianism's influence on Marx thus came to an end, while romanticism, through Feuerbach, stayed with him.

The official view of Marx's formation is also false epistemologically. It holds that the second and firmer bond between Marx and the Enlightenment would be Feuerbach, the materialist enemy of religion. In the second official stage in his formation, Marx is guided by Feuerbach, who would have opened up the royal road to materialist rationalism. Feuerbach the materialist is the avowed enemy of the Enlightenment, the high point of romantic spirituality, the founder of the program for secularizing faith. The break with Hegel by way of the detour through Feuerbach did not bring Marx closer to Enlightenment thought. It led him away from the Enlightenment.

What strikes Feuerbach's readers is the extent to which Marx took in his ideas. One senses how deeply Marx was moved by Feuerbach's text through the tempo of its phrasing, the prophetic inspiration of its message, and the theologico-political resonance of its thought. Feuerbach's writing combines elements of the sermon and the rally, in which the preacher's homiletic strains merge into the leader's marching orders to the new recruits. The style is the man. The master's commanding phrases and polemic aggressiveness are also to be found in the disciple. In search of a philosophy-program and a practical theory, Marx could not remain indifferent to the alternative Feuerbach sketched between

> a philosophy that owes its existence to a philosophical need . . . and one that corresponds to a need of mankind. . . . There is a world of difference between a philosophy that is related to mankind only indirectly by virtue to its belonging to the history of philosophy and one that is directly the history of mankind.[6]

Marx aimed at fashioning a philosophy that could leave its mark on history and transform the world rather than only understand it. Even when he chides Feuerbach for not attaining such a goal, he shows his fidelity to the master.

### Marx's Political Teaching

Does Marx have a teaching on politics? Those who argue that the author of *Das Kapital* is slavishly mired in economics claim never to have seen such a thing in Marx. Immersed in analyzing production and party activity, Marx would have had no time to articulate the essentials of his political thought; in fact, he never even finished the final chapters of *Das Kapital*. But perhaps this omission, deduced from an order of theoretical priorities, is more intentional than it at first appears to be. Marx's political right is indeed nowhere to be found, but that is not the case with a teaching on politics that can vie with any and that can be found in the specifically political writings of his youth as well as in the proliferation of observations on power in his philosophical and economic writings.

It is a mistake to assert that "Marx has no political theory." One should rather observe that there is a political theory according to which politics does not exist and does not have any existence of its own. With Marx, politics exists only as an illusion, an appearance, an alienation. On this score, one finds continuity in the language of the youthful philosopher and the mature economist. A few expressions from his writings reveal much more than the trite refrain that repeated use has rendered unintelligible. In *The Jewish Question*, Marx speaks of "the religious paradise of politics," in *The Holy Family* of "the surface of politics." In *The Critique of Hegel's Philosophy of Right*, he declares that "political life, in the modern sense of the word, is the people's school of life." Finally, in *Das Kapital*, he speaks of "the nebulous regions . . . of politics." In these definitions Marx explicitly grounds the division of state and society that makes politics an autonomous realm in the theological division of the heavenly and the earthly cities. From his youth, Marx held the conviction that politics was a form of mysticism, which, like all religious phenomena, came under Feuerbach's critique. Marx believed that politics had to be secularized and dissolved into the human community. Very early on, he denounced the split between society and state as pathological, and as early as *The Jewish Question* he saw human emancipation as the end of the political realm, the end of the separation of society and state, when man and citizen would be reconciled and abstract man become concrete again.

Marx's political teaching was thus established at an early point in his career. As a young man, Marx decided, in *The Critique of Hegel's Philosophy of Right*, to forsake political thought as a domain unto itself. He arrived at this conception by abandoning Hegelian thought, a break that he formulated in terms of three romantic principles, which he never called into question: opposition to the state, to law, and to individualism.

*Anti-statism*

Taken up as we are with the outcome of Marxism, we are influenced by the dichotomy separating words and deeds when we see Marxist socialism's doctrinal opposition to the state locking arms with a despotic buildup of the state. As a result, we willingly take Marx's critique of the state to be a patchwork, a superficial and last-minute addition to his system. Marx, it seems, would have fallen under the influence of the anarchism surrounding the insurrection of the commune and so decided that the state had to be completely destroyed, as he asserted in *The Civil War in France* (1871). Perhaps a little earlier, Marx's encounter with liberal economics might have inclined him to be suspicious of superstructures. The evidence would be there to see in the cavalier acknowledgement of his indebtedness:

> My investigation led to the result that legal relations as well as forms of state are to be grasped neither from themselves nor from so-called general development of the human mind, but rather have their roots in the material conditions of life, the sum total of which Hegel, following the example of the Englishmen and Frenchmen of the eighteenth century, combines under the name of 'civil society,' that, however, the anatomy of civil society is to be sought in political economy.[7]

Marx would be indebted to Ferguson and Smith for the reevaluation of civil society.[8]

All of this, however, is an optical illusion, looking at things from the perspective of a *terminus ad quem*. Even though he brushed with anarchism and associated with liberalism, Marx's anti-statism was a genuine, profound, and original sentiment. It was for him a *terminus a quo*, a gift of sorts, the legacy of his predecessors, which he assimilated. Marx's anti-statism is romantic.

Therein lies the reason for his different views. When Marx wrote in 1843 that "family and civil society appear as the dark natural ground from which the light of the state emerges," he was not taking up the strict "civilist" position of the Enlightenment and the liberals.[9] For the liberals, political nihilism is the consequence of deliberate neglect and feigned indifference. They seek not so much to destroy the state as to do without it and less to do away with politics than to subordinate it to economy. But for Marx, anti-statism is something very different from the start. It is the heart and soul of struggle. Marx seeks to destroy the state, not just to forget it, to abolish politics rather than detach himself from it. And so he has different motivations to oppose the state. Liberalism's concern is with economics, whereas the young Marx's perspective is moral and theological. This is thanks to the influence of romanticism, something that no one has been concerned to look at closely, with the exception of Kostas Papaioannou. Marx is no longer a civilist but already a socialist.

Marx himself at least is aware of the change: "The standpoint of the old materialism is 'civil' society; the standpoint of the new is *human* society, or socialized humanity."[10] Marx transfers the line of argumentation that Feuerbach had developed on the plane of theology to the realm of politics. He denounces the illusion of the state as a manifestation of the illusion of transcendence. "The critique of heaven is transformed into the critique of the earth, the critique of religion into the critique of law, the critique of theology into the crtiqiue of politics."[11] Feuerbach emphasized that religion alienated man by having him project his genetic identity onto the world beyond, the world of faith. Religion sunders and impoverishes man. Marx observes that the political state divides the individual between his being a citizen and a man:

> The members of the political state are religious because of the dualism between individual life and species-life, between the life of cvil society and political life. They are religious in the sense that man treats political life, which is remote from his own individual existence, as if it were his true life."[12]

Hence for Marx "the political state, in relation to civil society, is just as spiritual as is heaven in relation to earth."[13] Under such conditions, the state is not an essence but an appearance, the pernicious illusion and opium of society. Opposed to this "abstract pole," "only the people is concrete." From this "pure representation," there is only one remedy, to give to civil society what the state took from it, to purge society of politics, to return to immanence, where the social is everything.[14] Such a program presupposes a critique of right.

*Anti-juridism*

Marx's opposition to right is much less subject to debate than his opposition to the state, because it is as much an influence on his heirs as it is an element of his own thought. No orthodox Marxist today would not hold the doctrine of right to be a capital sin. The defender of political liberties is roundly told that he is taken up with mere formal rights. The Chinese on Beijing's Chang-an Avenue seeking legal protection after Li Yizhe— "right, not rite!"—dissidents who, like Sakharov and Pluyusch, invoke the rule of law, can rail all they like against those who cry that "a bowl of rice is all the people need!" or "freedoms made in the West, all rights reserved!"—Marxism maintains firmly that rights are a useless luxury or an outdated antique.

There is not a socialist regime that does not take right to be a practice suited to states under the rule of law. Although a thorough study remains to be done on the subject, the descriptions of Solzhenitsyn, the claims of human-rights organizations, and more recently the analyses of Aleksandr Zinoviev have acquainted us with this observation. A society of terror, Zinoviev tells us in *The Yawning Heights,* that *Phenomenology of the Spirit* of soviet socialism, is a "civilization without law." To ground the truth of his remark, Zinoviev readily invokes the principles of classical political right in conflict with romantic principles. The presence of a code and regulations is not enough to constitute a civilization of law (on this score, the society of terror has nothing on anyone else). Other conditions must also be met. First, the equality of all under law, regardless of the place they hold. Next, the exercise of the principle of legality: no one should be prosecuted for a deed whose criminality is not established a priori in a code and apart from the legal procedures set forth in the penal code. Finally, the people's interests must neither invalidate nor annihilate the interests of the individual. Without these conditions, Zinoviev observes, a society may have a code of laws, but it lacks a bill of rights, a legal system that articulates and balances the reciprocal rights and duties of authorities and citizens. It does not have, we would say, a political right.[15]

This legal void or alteration of the law is not accidental. The society of terror's practical opposition to law flows from Marx's doctrinal opposition to law. It was Marx who declared that "man does not exist because of the law but rather the law exists for the good of man."[16] It was Marx, too, who denounced the idea of the transcendence of law as the juridical illusion par excellence:

> What then is the content of political adaptation, of the political end: what is the end of this end, what is its substance? Primogeniture, the superlative of private property, sovereign private property. . . . What then is the power of the political state over private property? Private property's own power."[17]

Marx's teaching is opposed to the constitutionalism supported by Hegel but not to the view of Savigny, whose saying that "one does not make a constitution, it makes itself" turns the law's transcendence on its head. Marx's implacable undertaking reduces all public law to private right, the whole of law to the system of ownership, and makes it the prisoner of the axioms of the historical school of law. It was this conception of law that dictated the prohibition in *The German Ideology* against eleborating an autonomous history of law and that nurtured Marx's enthusiasm for Linguet.

Since it followed Savigny's critique, there was nothing original in Marx's opposition to law save that he called into question the doctrine of the rights of man. That he did so in *On the Jewish Question* only makes it more ironical. But we must not be unfair toward Marx on this score. The work written in 1843 to answer Bruno Bauer's pamphlet, also entitled *On the Jewish Question*, was not born of any anti-Semitism. Against his opponent armed with theology and fond of the New Testament, whose thought Marx followed with great interest, Marx seeks first of all to defend the Jew by indentifying him with the bourgeois of civil society, an egoist and huckster.[18] Marx feigns to discover the essence of Jewishness in the real Jew beneath the Sabbath-observing Jew. To anyone who takes civil society to be the sole reality, this identification is nothing less than infamy. Contrary to Bauer's eager denunciation of Judaism's archaic character over against the modernity of Christianity, Marx's identification asserts that the Jew is the very embodiment of the times. But in doing so, it also rejects the Jewish law and denies it any role in the legal construct of the state.

From that point onward, the critique of the rights of man is inspired by Feuerbach. What is the origin, Marx asks, of the distinction between the rights of man—equality, liberty, security, property—and those of the citizen? It arises out of the separation of civil society and the state. "The so-called rights of man, as distinct from the rights of the citizen, are simply the rights of a member of civil society, that is, of egoistic man, of man separated from other men and from the community."[19] Man is divided, alienated between the bourgeois subject of human rights, passive but alone real, and the citizen who is active in the political state yet remains abstract and unreal. Marx readily recognizes that the bond between the egoist individual of civil society and the generic being, that is, between man and citizen, is fashioned by the right to protection and by juridical security. But he deprives this right of any value whatever to the extent that it preserves the division between society and the state. The right to security is, he holds, a *formal* right, only "the concept of the police," that restores and sanctifies the division, just as religion brings comfort and fosters alienation.[20] It is not a matter of expecting emancipation from these formal rights but rather of abolishing the difference between the social and the individual through the rediscovery and redeployment of the human being as a generic being. "Human emancipation will only be complete when . . . man . . . has recognized and organized his own powers (*forces propres*) as *social* powers so that he no longer separates this social power from himself as *political* power."[21]

The young Marx's anti-juridism thus results in a twofold liquidation of law. First, constitutional law is eliminated once it is made to remove its disguise so that the ugly face of property relations at last sticks out. Second, human rights are eliminated so that the wound that separates man from citizen might heal. Marx denies the ideas of right as law and of subjective right, the juridico-political transcendence and the rights of the individual that were the pillars of the early modern teaching on political right. In the name of the democratic ideal, Marx, too, rejects classical political right. With a keen intuition that shows just how well he has understood Bruno Bauer, Marx goes on to say that democracy is much like the New Testament:

> Democracy relates to all other forms of the state as their Old Testament. Man does not exist because of the law but rather the law exists for the good of man. Democracy is *human existence*, while in the other political forms man has only *legal* existence. That is the fundamental difference of democracy."[22]

Marx does away with law to the tune of Feuerbach's anthropology, to the accompaniment of a Romantic political theology eager to secularize faith and take the place of religion.

## Anti-individualism

The critique of the rights of man inevitably leads to calling the individual into question. If the political state separates abstract humanity from concrete man, severs political citizenship from economic activity, and in the end sees in man only the truncated shadow of an individual cut off from other individuals, individualism appears as a mutilation to be overcome.

Marx's principles, which reject the very idea of political right—anti-statism, anti-juridism, anti-individualism—are by no means the whole of his social teaching. They rather constitute a starting point from which Marx, once he had done away with rights, could devote himself exclusively to the social realm and conceive of politics itself, including his theory of the state, which he later revised, from the perspective of social conflicts. Very early in his career, Marx, who had an education in law and had read Hegel, turned his back on the Hegelian conception of right, on politics conceived on the basis of right. Despite his harsh words in referring to the historical school of law as "a servile Shylock," he nonetheless felt its influence, just as Friedrich Engels attended the aging Schelling's lectures and still pursued the dialectic of nature.[23] Marx never went back on his definitive position against giving any place to thinking about political right. Political right is completely absent from Marxism. On that score Marx is a romantic.

# CHAPTER XII

# The State under the Rule of Despotism

*Nation-State, Party-State*

Is THERE anything left now that the principles of the state under the rule of law are despised and its foundations are destroyed? Nothing, unfortunately, for the critics of romanticism did not preside over the disappearance of the state. They rather oversaw the erection of hitherto unseen and gigantic monoliths, the nation-state and the party-state, the modern and arrogant forms of power. Much more than the states under the rule of law, they have sown their seeds throughout our world and have reawakened despotism.

Fichte made for the nation-state; Lenin followed Marx's lead in the direction of the party-state. But that is another story. To study how the nation-state arose, one needs to go back to the rebirth of ancient forms of political life in the period of conquests and the emergence of imperial powers. But to study the genesis of the party-state, one would have to take an altogether different route than the one we have followed. One would have to start with society. Long before Lenin elaborated the canonical doctrine of the revolutionary party, some of its elements had already been gathered in the learned societies, Jacobin clubs, and Masonic mysteries.[1] But one could already show that the varied forms of the contemporary state owe to their one origin a preestablished harmony and a common mechanism.

A preestablished harmony can be seen in the astounding apparent congruence of Marxism and nationalism. Between Fichte's and Marxism's opposition to the state, there is no real common ground. The first is an incomplete political system that leads to nationalism. But the same cannot be said for Marx, for whom the proletariat has no country. The author of the *Communist Manifesto* is no less antinationalist than anti-statist. Against the state Marx does not pit the nation as does Fichte, nor the people as Savigny does, but rather the proletarian class that will emancipate the whole of humanity. There is a difficulty with this, however, since the working class is not spontaneously political. That, of course, is the cross that Marx's heirs had to bear—how to rally the working class to politics—until Lenin at last discovered the answer in *What Is to Be Done?* The party will do it.

Stated in other terms, Marx's system, unlike nationalism, is not steeped in politics. From this follows either a necessary prolongation or an inevitable regression, a going back and forth between the party-state and the nation-state. Planting the seed of Marxism often entailed grafting onto an already-existing growth, onto the nationalist revival in Germany, onto the Pan-Slavic movement under the Slavophiles in Russia, onto the Chinese nationalism of Kang Yu Wei and Sun Yat-sen or that of Nguyen Ai Quoc, the future Ho Chi Minh who learned about European nationalism from his Franco-Vietnamese mentors.[2] Despite appearances to the contrary, nationalism is not a problem for Marxism. Far from being an adversary that needs to be confronted, nationalism is an ally that can always be mobilized, since it nurtured Marxism from early on. Between Marxism and nationalism, both derivatives of a common root in romanticism, there is a preestablished harmony in their common patrimony.

A common mechanism is to be found in the manipulation of opinion that passes for political action at its best. This mechanism stems from the secularization of faith, which replaced the vanished legal system of the state under the rule of law with another technique to obtain consensus, the public-opinion machine.

## The Public-Opinion Machine

Once the legal concepts of power were watered down and the state under the rule of law called into question in the early nineteenth century, the next step was to shift the way authority is exercised from the sphere of law to the realm of public opinion so as to control opinion. Wherever there is morality of law, limited power, and abstract sovereignty, disputes are heard and regulated according to precise procedures set by laws that mandate and administer a process of deliberation together with instruments for distribution and representation. But wherever there is secularization of faith, absolute power, and concrete sovereignty, hearings are set aside, since the case is taken as decided beforehand. The precise role of power is no longer to regulate disputes or to punish crimes as specified by law, activities that rest on a preexisting legal foundation. Rather power is concerned with controlling opinion, with watching over and correcting the mind by a set procedure that scrutinizes the most intimate and minute details. The modern despotic state functions in part as a machine to control and produce opinion and as a force to distill and watch over orthodoxy, as Aleksandr Zinoviev's astonishing disclosures reveal. In examining its bloody consequences, Solzhenitsyn assessed the savage surgery that concentration camps performed on living flesh, the ritual marks and painful wounds, all the physical tortures of the gulag. Zinoviev reports the less visible workings of ideological production, which are more destructive of the soul. He shows how ideology is constructed, squared off, set afloat, and piloted. A tyrant at work in the form of the public-opinion mechanism.

Is this raison d'état? The power of science? Enlightenment terrorism? The image of a Faustian state provides an attractive explanation of the rise of the public-opinion machine. According to the latest theories, the totalitarian state is the offspring of an excess of rationalism that split the swollen head of positivism, just as Athena did to Zeus's headache. The promotion of Lysenkoism, the ridiculing of biologists, the sealing up of archives, the detention of dissidents in asylums under the iron sky of concentration-camp socialism are all ascribed to learning and seen as the result of science. But this is to confuse pretense and reality and to take ideology at its own word. This is to condemn science in two ways: first, in the name of the opinion machine, which, as experience shows, saps knowledge of its vigor and wreaks terror on the scientists; and second, in the name of the errors of ideology purged of everything save its curious conception of knowledge.

This secularized faith that passes for science, this fetish of a conviction christened as knowledge, should not be compared to science or religion generally. It is much more the kin of a particular religion, of Gnosticism, which is at one and the same time the most obscurantist and the most theoretical antithesis of Christianity. Alain Besançon's penetrating analysis of the similarities between the gnostic *ideal* and the militant *ideal* of Russian intellectuals in the 1880s provides a much more solid foundation for examining the differentiated processes of the raison d'état and the scientific establishment in different types of states.[3] One might also discover that states have the sciences they deserve.

Ideology abhors a vacuum, as everyone knows. Once law disappears, a substitute takes its place. Politics itself does not disappear, nor is the state destroyed. Instead, the forms of political life and of the state undergo a metamorphosis once the despotic state is established.

## The Despotic State

Political romanticism likewise produced only one paradigm or ideal-type. Between this paradigm and its embodiment lie the intrusion of history's sidetracking jolts and the spectacular reversals to which history is so susceptible. Let us consider just one such reversal that has marred the way. At the end of the nineteenth century, the shotgun wedding of Hegelianism and romanticism gave birth to a new theory of the state. The majority of German commentators and legal theorists took up the idea of the power-state. Instead of distinguishing the nation from its representatives, such theorists as Gerber affirmed that the original and sole titleholder to sovereignty is simply the state. They maintained that the state is indivisible, subject to law that is at the same time the public force.[4] Thus they broke with the earlier teaching in that for them force itself produces right rather than power's being subjected to, and limited by, power. This novel "statism" was assumed to be the view that always held sway in German public law.

It did take time, of course, for all of this to sink in and be mulled over so that the irrational could become real. Yet we agree with Thomas Mann's intuition that gives primordial responsibility to political romanticism for the genesis of totalitarian political forms, those societal forms opposed to the law and that have embodied the program of the secularization of faith to a hitherto-unforeseen degree. Mann's intuition is shared by another, but unduly discreet observer, Georg Lukacs, who, in *The Destruction of Reason*, takes great pains to show the frightening coherence of romanticism and Nazism.[5] But this is just a story of the pot calling the kettle black, since Lukacs refrains from disclosing where he gets his sharp perspective on things and from confessing that he himself came to Marxism by adhering to the tenets of romantic philosophy.[6]

If one takes stock of political romanticism, one finds that it not only modifies the code of the state under the rule of law, it also paves the way for a transformation of the human condition. The state under the rule of law is characterized, as we have seen, by an anti-imperial and antifeudal conception of power and by the regulation of suits according to law—that is, by the development of a process of lawmaking within society that guarantees individual rights while at the same time promoting a juridical consensus. Romanticism, on the contrary, conceives of politics as being of society's own making. In such a society, the distinction between individual rights and the requirements of authority is invalidated, since the two are held to be reconciled beforehand in the nation, the people, or the proletariat. Henceforth, the legal apparatus regulating lawsuits gives way to means of unifying opinion, and the process of lawmaking disappears in the face of the advances of the opinion machine that avidly elicits and manipulates men's convictions. Now made the object of scorn, personal security, the fundamental right of the early moderns, vanishes and with it the free disposition of the body, which again becomes a wandering, uncertain object subject to the designs of the powers that be. With it, too, human liberty, the *status libertatis*, disappears, since the conditions under which a body is another's possession are slavery, war, and sacrifice. In the modern despotic state, the horizon of the human political condition is the condition of sacrifice in the militant's patriotic fervor, the military condition of the soldier, the condition of the enemy of the people's subservience. The only exception to this horizon is the condition of the despot himself.

Can the modern state still be a state under the rule of law, as Jean Rivero asked in 1957? And are we headed toward the end of the state under the rule of law, as Jean-Pierre Henry asked in 1977?[7] If, twenty years apart, two legal thinkers raise the same question, it is because grounds for concern over the evolution of such states have not gone away. On the one hand, Henry maintains that juridical inflation through the multiplication of laws at the end of a process of political grandstanding together with the confusion of norm and law discredit the use of law. On the other hand, Rivero observed that the tendency to place in the hands of technicians, such as administrators and managers, what would be better handled by law restricts the sphere in which laws are applied. The truth is that the state under the rule of law can be maintained only if society accepts and revives an ethic of law.

# The State and the Slaves

WﾠHAT IS the way out of slavery? The only way is through law, the way discovered over two thousand years ago by a shrill and impassioned people who had been slaves themselves. No better way has yet been found. There are other ways and means to build a nation, to pursue a conquest, or to fortify an empire, but the chains of oppression can be broken and a community of men freed from bondage only by passing through a narrow gate. Other doors open and close to the rhythm of feudal regimes.

In the end this is what we have learned from reading the royal jurists and the German romantics and from comparing theologies of law and theories of knowledge. It is not by chance that romantic socialism produced slaves and masters or that its ruling class constitutes an imperialist and messianic caste that calls forth and dismisses prophets. It is not accidental that the members of political bureaucracies are feudal lords. The concentration-camp socialism found only in struggling feudal systems did not appear all of a sudden. Seek out the standards, the arms and the armor of feudalism. Listen to its voices; follow its footsteps; observe its ways. Allow yourself to be guided by the images it conjures up—the noises, the woods, the fears. Everywhere you see the fortress and the men within its walls, the siege and the final struggle, the terror over the onset of combat—everywhere feudal socialism.

There does not exist "the state" but rather many states. No matter how rancorous the cries of anti-statism, nothing will obviate the division between states under the rule of law and states under despotic rule. It is said that those states under the rule of law, currently limited to Western Europe and North America, established their principles before capitalism's revolutionary movement against feudal society and slavery. The early modern jurists and doctrinarians defined a slave as a man deprived of right by virtue of being dispossessed of his right to own property and above all his own life. They held that a free man is a man who has rights, because he is subject to neither the *imperium* nor the *dominium;* he is neither dominated nor subjugated, because he is a subject, a citizen, a person. Indeed, the states under the rule of law did more than bring law to feudal society or civilization to warrior communities, more than replace private wars with civil peace, more even than change might for right. They brought law to political life and bound power under a constitution.

It is a mistake to place responsibility for the emergence of this movement on the rediscovery of Roman law. No doubt a society that was in the process of juridification and searching for a model found an unexpected teaching in Roman law. That explains the blossoming of Roman schools and the teaching of Roman law. But in order to leave the slave society that produced Roman law itself, in order to break at last with the political antiquity that survived in feudal serfdom, another example and model was needed. One had to look somewhere else than to a legal system that took master-slave relations to be a matter of fact and concerned itself only with the use of property. Roman law does not point to a way out of a slave-based mode of production or political theory. The main artery, the necessary passage because it was the one route that was taken out of slavery, is religious. Its course is charted in the Scriptures. The Bible is the book of liberation from slavery, and it is to the Bible that the states under the rule of law turned when they chose emancipation through law.

We maintain that the states under the rule of law are governed by an ethic of law and that for that reason they secure a private realm to faith. Against both feudalism and slavery, early modern political philosophy gave birth to biopolitics by legitimating individual rights, security, and—at a later date—liberty, by subjecting the sovereign to law.

On the other hand, the modern states ruled by despotism, which were born of imperialism and socialism and which along with colonialism and totalitarianism exported or imported a new slavery, stem from the reawakening of feudalism in civil society and from the secularization of faith. The two great versions of modern totalitarianism, Nazism and communism, grew out of the common planting of romantic philosophy and the monstrous hybrid concocted by political romanticism in the compost heap of the nation-state, made up of the grain of liberalism and the recycling of a feudal politics antagonistic simultaneously to the state, to law, and to the individual. The project of German romanticism, which Thomas Mann understood and denounced so well, was to secularize faith, to transplant religious enthusiasm to politics, to make the German nation the new Christ. Once Marx joined ranks with Feuerbach and broke with Hegel, he took up the same project—this time for the sake of the proletariat—and the same political philosophy that again and again has yielded nothing but servitude.

The history of slavery is a watermark on the fine vellum of the world history of states. Imperialism makes a mockery of the state under the rule of law, because it reinstates the slave trade against the founding principle of early modern politics, the abolition of slavery. As Solzhenitsyn showed in *The Gulag Archipelago*, concentration-camp socialism reinvented slavery in the condition of the *zek* who has no recourse to law. We should be fully aware that the prisoner of the camps is a slave and nothing else. Of course, the old feudal notion of power goes along with this. Slavery obtains wherever the shoe pinches the Third World. There are no formal liberties in states in which the slave trade goes on, in which women suffocate beneath the veil, in which the leader-prophet is not bound by law.

Hegel stated that the world's future belonged to the slaves. Marx took up Hegel's idea, but he forgot that the slave must first break with slavery, and so Marx perpetuates the system of domination. The classical thinkers had a good grasp of this problem. Locke and Rousseau had shown that the despot, too, is a slave trapped in the pure relation of power in the state of nature. Locke held that the despot remains in the state of nature, and Rousseau taught that the man who thinks he is a master over others is even more a slave than they are. The reverse case needs to be shown as well. The classical writers pitied the despot, but the slave also needs to be pitied. They denounced despotism's slave mentality, but the despotic character of the slaves' prejudice needs to be underscored. It is not, as some maintain, because Marx's political philosophy upholds the state and the law that it can pave the way to state despotism. It is instead precisely because it opposes the state and the law, because it is for the oppressed who are burdened by oppression and for the offended who are ravaged by offense. It seeks to avenge the slaves and serve the people, when slavery itself ought to be abolished and servitude eliminated.

The way out of the slave mentality was discovered when a small, lost people emerged from the wilderness over three thousand years ago. There is always only one route to take to dispel the raging waters of bondage, and that route is law. Contrary to what some think, more is needed to assure socialism's future than democratic guarantees. From its ancient past, democracy has retained a perfect compatibility with a tyrannical or oligarchical exercise of power. The people is always blind to the bondage it can produce above and beyond what defines it. Yesterday the people had its slaves; today it has its enemies. What is fundamental for the future of socialism is that it function according to law, along the lines of the states under the rule of law. Socialism must become legal socialism.

The present essay is not rooted in a choice for or against the state. Rather it arises from a concern to highlight a few historical observations. Our research has sought to shed a partial but less biased light of historical investigation on a common question. If it succeeds in marking out the way for a history of states unencumbered by our current preoccupations and free of the pitfalls of economic theory, it will not have been entirely useless.

FOREWORD

1. Four essays published in the *Fortnightly Review* (1860),the second of which was entitled "The Coming Slavery."

2. Published in 1988 in four volumes: *Jean Mabillon, La Défaite de l'érudition, Les Académies de l'histoire*, and *La République incertaine.*

3. On which, see Kriegel, *Les Droits de l'homme et le droit naturel* (Paris, 1989).

4. For a contrasting view, see James Q. Whitman, *The Legacy of Roman Law in the German Romantic Era* (Princeton, N.J., 1990).

5. See R. J. Smith, *The Gothic Bequest: Medieval Institutions in British Thought*, 1688–1863 (Cambridge, 1987).

6. Leonard Krieger, *The German Idea of Freedom: History of a Political Tradition* (Boston, 1957).

7. Klaus Epstein, *The Genesis of German Conservatism* (Princeton, N.J., 1966), 376ff.

8. See Sunil Khilnani, *Arguing Evolution: The Intellectual Left in Post-War France* (New Haven, Conn., 1993), 136.

INTRODUCTION
THE PARADOXES OF ANTI-STATISM

1. Pierre Viansson-Ponté, "La Crise de l'état-nation," *Le Monde*, July 9–10, 1978.

CHAPTER I
PROBLEMS FOR A HISTORY OF THE STATE

1. Emmanuel Le Roy Ladurie, *The Territory of the Historian*, trans. Ben Reynolds and Sian Reynolds (Chicago, 1979), III.

2. Louis André, *Les Sources de l'histoire de France* (Paris, 1934), 7:147.

3. François Furet, *Interpreting the French Revolution*, trans. Elborg Foster (New York, 1981), 164–65.

4. This is the case in France, at any rate. Elsewhere, the situation is different.

5. Alexis de Tocqueville, introduction to *Democracy in America*, trans. George Lawrence (Garden City, N.Y., 1969), 19.

CHAPTER II
SOVEREIGN POWER

1. Jean Bodin, *Six Books on the Commonwealth*, ed. and trans. M. J. Tooley (New York, 1967), bk. 1, chap. 1.
2. Charles Loyseau, *Des Seigneuries*, chap. 2 in *Oeuvres*, ed. Claude Joly (Paris, 1606).
3. Jacques Maritain, *Man and the State*, chap. 2, sec. 7 (Chicago, 1951), 53.
4. See Henri Arquillière, *L'Augustinisme politique* (Paris, 1934).
5. This is the thesis of André Glucksmann in *La Cuisinière et le mangeur d'hommes* (Paris, 1975).
6. See the discussion in R. Carré de Malberg, *Théorie générale de l'état*, 2 vols. (Paris, 1920), vol. 1, chap. 2.
7. Georg Jellinek rightly emphasizes the historical character of the nation. See *L'État moderne et son droit*, trans. G. Fardis, 2 vols. (Paris, 1904), 1:102. Carré de Malberg, for his part, demonstrates how the royalty sought to co-opt this notion of sovereignty in a negative effort to free itself from feudal power. See *Théorie générale de l'état*, 1:49.
8. Montesquieu, *The Spirit of the Laws*, trans. Anne M. Cohler, Basia Carolyn Miller, and Harold Samuel Stone (Cambridge, 1989), foreword to the posthumous edition, xli.
9. Ibid., bk. 2, chap. 1.
10. Ibid., bk. 3, chap. 9.
11. "Monarchical government does not admit of such simple laws as does despotic government." Montesquieu, *Spirit of the Laws*, bk. 6, chap. 1.
12. "The more peoples the prince has to govern, the less he thinks about government, the greater the matters of business, the less deliberation it is given." Montesquieu, *Spirit of the Laws*, bk. 2, chap. 5.
13. Montesquieu, *Spirit of the Laws*, bk. 5, chap. 14.
14. Ibid., bk. 5, chap. 16.
15. E. La Boétie, *Discours sur la servitude volontaire* (Paris, 1976), 212.
16. Montesquieu, *Spirit of the Laws*, bk. 5, chap. 16.
17. Paul Vernières, *Montesquieu et l'esprit des lois, ou la raison impure* (Paris, 1977), 65.
18. A. H. Anquetil-Duperron, *Législation orientale* (Amsterdam, 1778), 9.
19. See R. Koebner, "'Despot and Despotism,' Vicissitudes of a Political Term," *Journal of the Warburg and Courtauld Institutes* 14, no. 3 (1954): 270; and J. Franco Venturi, *L'Europe des Lumières* (Paris, 1971), sec. 131ff.
20. Karl Marx and Friedrich Engels, *Manifesto of the Communist Party*, pt. 1.
21. Loyseau, *Des Seigneuries*, 9.
22. Dareste de La Chavanne, *Histoire de l'administration en France et des progrès du pouvoir royal depuis le régime de Philippe Auguste jusqu'à la mort de Louis XIV*, 2 vols. (Paris, 1848).
23. These books of customs, or etiquette, were compiled privately in the thirteenth century. The citations are taken from J. Declareuil, *Histoire du droit français des origines à 1789* (Paris, 1925), 432–33.

24. Declareuil, *Histoire du droit français*, 431, n. 209.

25. Georg Jellinek, *L'État moderne et son droit*, 1:101–2.

26. Bodin, *Six Books on the Commonwealth*, bk. 1, chap. 8.

27. Duplessis-Mornay, *Vindiciae contra Tyrannos*, French translation (Paris, 1581), 24.

28. Bodin, *Six Books on the Commonwealth*, bk. 2, chap. 2.

29. Loyseau, *Des Seigneuries*, 16.

30. J. N. Moreau, *Leçons de morale, de politique et de droit public* (Versailles, 1787), 80–81.

31. Bodin, *Six Books on the Commonwealth*, bk. 2, chap. 2; Loyseau, *Des Seigneuries*, 16.

32. Bodin, *Six Books on the Commonwealth*, bk. 1, chap. 9.

33. Loyseau, *Des Seigneuries*, 9.

34. Jean-Jacques Rousseau, *On the Social Contract*, ed. Roger D. Masters and trans. Judith R. Masters (New York, 1978), bk. 1, chap. 3.

35. Charles Dumoulin, *Traité de l'origine, progrès et excellence du royaume et monarchie des François et couronne de France* (Lyon, 1561).

36. Claude de Seyssel, *The Monarchy of France*, pt. 2, chap. 15, 89–90.

37. For these, one needs to read Guibert de Nogent and Pierre le Vénérable. See the material quoted in Glasson, *Histoire du droit et des institutions de la France*, 8 vols. (Paris, 1887–1903).

38. See C. A. Davoud Oghlou, *Histoire de la législation des anciens Germains*, 2 vols. (Berlin, 1842).

39. Loyseau, *Des Offices* (Paris, 1666), 143.

40. M. Foucault, *Discipline and Punish: The Birth of the Prison*, trans. Alan Sheridan (New York, 1977); and *La Volonté de savoir* (Paris, 1977), chap. 5.

41. Marc Bloch, *La Société féodale et la formation des liens de dépendance* (Paris, 1939).

42. Bodin, *Six Books on the Commonwealth*, bk. 2, chap. 2.

43. Ibid., bk. 2, chap. 2.

44. Samuel von Pufendorf, *De jure naturae et gentium libri octo*, vol. 2 (translation), trans. C. H. Oldfather and W. A. Oldfather, *Classics of International Law* (New York, 1964).

45. Loyseau, *Des Offices*, 12.

46. "As a matter of good jurisprudence, neither an officer nor even a prince or sovereign monarch has property in an office; the matter has only a right of conferment. . . . The true property of offices and benefits is public and belongs to no one; it is not a commercial entity, although one can say that the property of offices belongs to the state. . . . It cannot, short of absurdity or dismemberment, be posited absolutely in isolation, or separated from the state." Loyseau, *Des Offices*, chap. 1, 145.

47. Moreau, *Leçons*, 105.

48. Simon-Nicolas Linguet, *Traité des lois civiles*, 2 vols. (London, 1774), 1:7.

49. "For several centuries, all the problems that have arisen in the principal states of Europe have been nothing but conflicts between the power of government as it made demands, and the power of property as it defended itself." Moreau, *Leçons*, 105.

50. Locke, *Second Treatise*, chap. 9, par. 124.

51. Locke, *Second Treatise*, chap. 6, par. 59, and chap. 15, par. 173.

52. Rousseau, *Lettres écrites de la montagne*, no. 8.

53. See Michel Villey's notes on the concept of property in *Critique de la pensée juridique moderne* (Paris, 1975), 195.

54. André Duchesne, *Les Antiquités et recherches de la grandeur et majesté des roys de France* (Paris, 1609).

55. Bodin, *Six Books on the Commonwealth*, bk. 1, chap. 1.

56. "Besides sovereign power there must also be something enjoyed in common such as the public domain, a public treasury, the buildings used by the whole community, the roads, walls, squares, churches, and markets, as well as the usages, laws, customs, courts, penalties, and rewards which are either shared in common or of public concern. There is no commonwealth where there is no common interest [no republic where there is nothing public]." Bodin, *Six Books on the Commonwealth*, bk. I, chap. 2.

57. "Sovereignty is so inseparable from the state that if the former is taken away, the latter vanishes." Loyseau, *Des Seigneuries*, 9.

58. See B. Plongeron, *Théologie et politique au siècle des lumières* (Paris, 1973), 62, 78, passim.

59. "Sovereignty consists in absolute power, that is, power that is perfect and complete in every respect, the power that the canonists called plenitude of power, a power that permits no superiority to itself." Loyseau, *Des Seigneuries*, 12. "In every City there is some *one man*, or *Councell*, or *Court*, who by Right hath as great a power over each single Citizen, as each man hath over himselfe considered out of that civill state, that is, *supreme* and *absolute*, to be limited onely by the strength and forces of the City it selfe." Hobbes, *De Cive*, chap. 6, par. 18. Jean Domat (1625–1695), whose *Les Lois civiles dans leur naturel* was published by order of Louis XIV, expresses the same theory of absolute sovereignty. See Jean Domat, *Droit public*, in *Oeuvres complètes*, ed. Joseph Rémy (Paris, 1828), 3:6. In addition, among seventeenth-century French jurists and historians, see Guy Coquille, *Institution au Droict des François* (Paris, 1608); Duchesne, *Les Antiquités;* and Jérôme Bignon, *De l'Excellence des roys et du royaume de France* (Paris, 1610).

60. Bodin, *Six Books on the Commonwealth*, bk. 1, chap. 8.

61. "Since then the nature of things is not changed by their accidental properties, we conclude that there are only three types of state, or commonwealth, monarchy, aristocracy, and democracy. A state is called a monarchy when sovereignty is vested in one person, and the rest have only to obey. Democracy, or the popular state, is one in which all the people, or a majority among them, exercise sovereign power collectively. A state is an aristocracy when a minority collectively enjoy sovereign power and impose law on the rest, generally and severally." Bodin, *Six Books on the Commonwealth*, bk. 2, chap. 1. "Sovereignty, according to the diversity of States, is communicated to the diverse possessors of it: in democracy to the people, as in Rome where majesty was attributed to the people as a whole. . . . In aristocracy, sovereignty resides with those who are in dominant roles. . . . Finally, in monarchy, it belongs to the seignor." Loyseau, *Des Seigneuries*, 12.

62. Domat, *Les Lois civiles dans leur naturel*, 6.

63. "If we insist however that absolute power means exemption from all law

whatsoever, there is no prince in the world who can be regarded as sovereign, since all the princes of the earth are subject to the laws of God and of nature, and even to certain human laws common to all nations." Bodin, *Six Books on the Common-wealth*, bk. 1, chap. 8. "Since only God is all-powerful, and since the power of human beings cannot be completely absolute, there are three types of laws that constrain the power of the sovereign without calling sovereignty into question: the laws of God, the natural rather than positive rules of justice. . . . And finally the fundamental laws of the state, since the prince must enjoy sovereignty according to its proper nature, and in the form and under the conditions that it has established." Loyseau, *Des Seigneuries*, 12.

64. "Here we find the foundation and the first principle of all the duties of sovereigns, to establish the reign of God himself, to arrange things according to his will, which is none other than justice." Domat, *Les Lois civiles*, 21.

65. Ibid., 67, 71, 92.

66. Claude de Seyssel, *La Grand' Monarchie de France* (Paris, 1519).

67. On this point, see the discussion by R. Derathé, *Jean-Jacques Rousseau et la science politique de son temps* (Paris, 1974), 307–28 and passim.

68. Jurieu, *Lettres pastorales*, 3:375. See Derathé, *Jean-Jacques Rousseau*, 320.

69. "It is one thing for a government to be absolute, quite another for it to be arbitrary. It is absolute to the extent that no thing has the power requisite to force the sovereign's hand; such a sovereign is independent of any human authority. Yet it does not follow that such a government is arbitrary. In addition to the fact that all is subject to the judgment of God . . . [t]here are laws in any empire violations of which are bereft of any legal standing." Bossuet, *Politique tirée de l'Ecriture Sainte*, bk. 8, art. 2. See Élie Carcasonne, *Montesquieu et la constitution politique de son temps* (Paris, 1927).

70. Massillon, *Sermons et Morceaux choisis* (Paris, 1863) 96–97.

71. Bodin, *Six Books on the Commonwealth*, bk. 2, chap. 3.

CHAPTER III
HUMAN RIGHTS

1. See Michel Villey, *La Formation de la pensée juridique moderne* (Paris, 1968).

2. The greatness of a writer like Tocqueville consists in his having anticipated this distinction without limiting individual rights to civil liberties. George Lefebvre has remarked on this: "For Tocqueville, liberty cannot shed its aristocratic aspect. Love of liberty presupposes the presence of a kind of virtue of which the proud independence of feudalism was an anticipation." Yet Tocqueville himself wrote that "liberty can appear to the human mind in two different forms. It may be seen as the enjoyment of a common right, or as the power of a privilege." *L'Ancien Régime et la Révolution*, 2 vols. (Paris, 1952), vol. 1, introduction, 12.

3. See Michel Villey, "Les *Institutes* de Gaius et l'idée de droit subjectif," in *Leçons d'histoire de la philosophie du droit* (Paris, 1957).

4. These liberties were severely restricted under the empire and did not reach their full development before Christianity and the abolition of slavery. See Eduard Gans, *Das Erbrecht in weltgeschichtlicher Entwicklung* (1824–1835) (Berlin, 1926)

and *Histoire du droit de succession en France*, trans. Saint-Marc Girardin (Paris, 1845).

5. Montesquieu, *The Spirit of the Laws*, bk. 17, chap. 5.

6. See É. Carcasonne, *Montesquieu*, 674.

7. Notably Tocqueville, *The Ancien Régime*, pt. 2, chap. 11.

8. Marc Bloch, *Feudal Society*, trans. L. A. Manyon (New York, 1961), pt. 2, bk. 2.

9. Beaumanoir, *Les Coutumes du Beauvoisis* (Paris, 1842), 2:33.

10. See Gabriel Ardant, *Histoire de l'impôt*, 2 vols. (Paris, 1971–1972), 1:232.

11. See Aristotle, *Politics*, bk. 1, chaps. 1–4.

12. Antoine Loysel, *Instituts Coutumières* (1536), ed. E. de Laurière (1710), 7.

13. "Yet the serfs are similar to the colonial and ascriptive servitudes that attached persons to the domain in whose fields they worked." Guy Coquille, *Institution au Droict des François*, 183.

14. In France, it never even affected arbitrary detention, as it did in England in the form of habeas corpus.

15. In France, the most prominent have been Robert Derathé, Raymond Polin, and Simone Goyard-Fabre.

16. Hobbes, *Elements of Law*, chap. 14; *De Cive*, pt. 1.

17. See, for instance, Hobbes, *Elements of Law*, pt. 1, chap. 14, par. 6, where "RIGHT, or *jus*" is defined as "blameless liberty of using our own natural power and ability. It is therefore a *right of nature*: that every man may preserve his own life and limbs, with all the power he hath."

18. Ibid., pt. 1, chap. 14, par. 6.

19. "Union thus made is called a City, or civill society, and also a civill Person; for when there is one will of all men, it is to be esteemed for one Person. . . . A City therefore . . . is one Person, whose will, by the compact of many men, is to be received for the will of them all." Hobbes, *De Cive*, chap. 5, par. 9. "This union so made, is that which men call now-a-days a BODY POLITIC or civil society . . . which may be defined to be a multitude of men, united as one person by a common power, for their common peace, defence, and benefit." Hobbes, *Elements of Law*, pt. 1, chap. 19, par. 8.

20. Hobbes, *Leviathan*, pt. 1, chap. 14.

21. "Security is the end wherefore men submit themselves to others, which if it be not had, no man is suppos'd to have submitted himselfe to ought, or to have quitted his Right to all things, before that there was a care had of his security." Hobbes, *De Cive*, chap. 6, par. 3.

22. "(Power) is a god, yes, but a god crafted by human hands and a god who disintegrates if human hands withdraw. If those who are equals by nature choose to elevate one among them to extraordinary heights, it is not out of idolatry, but to shelter themselves beneath him, and thereby to enjoy the benefits of peace." Georges Lyon, *La Philosophie de Hobbes* (Paris: F. Alcan, 1893), 210–11.

23. William Blackstone, *Commentaries on the Laws of England*, 5 vols. (Chicago, 1979), 1:123–25.

24. Ibid., 125.

25. Hobbes, *Leviathan*, pt. 2, chap. 20.

26. The Roman *mancipatio* was originally a form of punishment, and later the

process by which a son, upon reaching majority, was freed from subjection to his father.

27. "Those who accurately reflect the fundamental categories of the classical juridico-political ideology in the seventeenth century reply clearly and in good conscience: slaves and salaried workers are in all important respects indistinguishable. Members of both groups contract freely with their masters; once the contract is concluded, and so long as it remains in effect, members of neither group are free, even formally." Alexandre Matheron, "Maîtres et serviteurs dans la pensée classique," *La Pensée*, April–June 1978.

28. Pierre Charron, *Of Wisdom*, trans. George Stanhope (London, 1729), bk. 1, chap. 48.

29. "Hired laborers have the exact same status, within their work environment, as slaves. . . . 'All men are born free,' to be sure, but there is a critical juridical difference between those who have freely retained their liberty, at least in the private realm, and those who have freely abandoned all control of an entire sector of their existence to others, even if they 'remain free' in other respects." Matheron, "Maîtres et serviteurs," 13.

30. "That is complete slavery which owes lifelong service in return for nourishment and other necessaries of life; and if the condition is thus accepted within natural limits it contains no element of undue severity. For the lasting obligation to labour is repaid with a lasting certainty of support." Grotius, *On the Law of War and Peace*, trans. Francis W. Kelsey (Oxford, 1925), bk. 2, chap. 5, sec. 27, par. 2. "Upon the offer of submission by one person and its acceptance by another, there at once arises for the latter the right to command the former, that is, sovereignty. And as pacts can confer upon another a right over some possession of ours, so submission can give him the right to dispose of our liberty and strength." Samuel von Pufendorf, *The Law of Nature and Nations*, bk. 7, chap. 3, sec. 1. See Derathé, *Jean-Jacques Rousseau*, 196–97.

31. Derathé, *Jean-Jacques Rousseau*, 199.

32. Ibid., 200–202.

33. Rousseau, *Social Contract*, bk. 1, chap. 4.

34. François Guéry and Didier Deleule, *Le Corps productif* (Paris, 1973).

35. Rousseau, *Social Contract*, bk. 1, chap. 4.

36. See François Olivier-Martin, *Histoire du droit français* (Paris, 1948), 246, 257; Guy Fourquin, *Lordship and Feudalism in the Middle Ages*, trans. Iris Sells and A. L. Lytton Sells (London, 1976), chap. 5, especially sec. 5.2.A and 5.3.A.1.; Charles Perrin, *Le Servage en France et en Allemagne*, in *Xo Congresso Internationale di Scienze Storiche* (Florence, 1955), 213, 245; and *Recueil de la Société Jean Bodin* 2 (1937).

37. Pierre Chaunu, "L'État," *Histoire économique et sociale de la France* (Paris, 1977), 1:67.

38. Declareuil, *Histoire du droit français*, 303.

39. Olivier-Martin, *Histoire du droit français*, 146–57.

40. Gabriel Lepointe, *Manuel d'histoire du droit français* (Paris, 1939), 272.

41. These actions were limited, in keeping with the doctrines of early modern political right, to the realm. Louis XIV's promulgation of the "black code" made these limits of royal power quite clear.

42. Olivier-Martin, *Histoire du droit français.*

43. See "Le Vilainage anglais," *Recueil de la Société Jean Bodin* 2 (1937).

44. See Gabriel Ardant, *Histoire de l'impôt*, 604, 613; and Miller, "Considérations sur le développement des Institutions agraires de l'Ukraine au XVIIe et au XVIIIe siècle," *Revue internationale de sociologie* (1925).

45. Perry Anderson, *Lineages of the Absolutist State*, 1:195.


CHAPTER IV
LAW AND MORALITY

1. The point is well made by Bernard Bourgeois, *La pensée politique de Hegel* (Paris, 1992), and by Robert Derathé, in his introduction to the French translation of Hegel's *Philosophy of Right*, *Les Principes de la philosophie du droit* (Paris, 1975).

2. G. W. F. Hegel, *Principles of the Philosophy of Right*, trans. T. M. Knox (Oxford, 1972), par. 158, addition.

3. Ibid., par. 142 and 155.

4. See Paul Vernières, *Spinoza et la pensée française avant la révolution* (Paris, 1954).

5. See Hugh Trevor Roper, *The Rise of Christian Europe* (New York, 1965), and *Religion, the Reformation, and Social Change* (London, 1967); Bernard Plongeron, *Théologie et politique au siècle des lumiéres* (Paris, 1973); and Michel de Certeau, *The Writing of History*, trans. Tom Conley (New York, 1988).

6. See Jean Delumeau, *Naissance et affirmation de la Réforme* (Paris, 1968), and *Le Catholicisme entre Luther et Voltaire* (Paris, 1971).

7. See Alain Besançon, *The Rise of the Gulag: The Intellectual Origins of Leninism* (Paris, 1977), chap. 4.

8. Gabriel Le Bras, *Histoire du droit et des institutions de l'Église en Occident* (Paris, 1965), vol. 1.

9. Michel Villey has amply shown that mistrust of earthly justice is by no means unsupported by the Gospels. Measured against the Gospels' standard of charity, earthly justice cannot but appear imperfect and approximate, especially in its reluctance to forgive and its propensity for sanctions. See Villey, *La Formation de la pensée juridique moderne* (Paris, 1975), 91.

10. Villey, *Leçons d'histoire de la philosophie du droit* (Paris, 1957), 215.

11. "The given past—customs, Roman laws—was embellished with a catalog of rights that amount to a counterpart of power, and which are increasingly confused with power. . . . One sees throughout the Middle Ages the disorderly unfolding of individual initiative given increasingly extensive liberty: violent conquests reshape kingdoms, the feudal hierarchy is built up from contracts, vast movements of association forge corporations, communes, alliances of states. . . . A new order is being born, and its parents are liberty. . . . The meaning of the Latin word '*jus*' evolves toward the idea of power, a linguistic development that accurately reflected the practice of the Middle Ages." Villey, *Seize essais de philosophie de droit* (Paris, 1969), 156–57.

12. See Numa Denis Fustel de Coulanges, *Histoire des institutions politiques de*

*l'ancienne France* (Paris, 1875–1889), 3:463; and Henri Sée, *Les Classes rurales et le système domanial au Moyen Age* (Paris, 1901).

13. Hobbes, *Leviathan*, pt. 3, chap. 35, par. 5.

14. Bodin, *Six Books on the Commonwealth*, bk. 1, chap. 8.

15. See Glasson, *Histoire du droit et des institutions*, 8:31.

16. Guy Coquille, *Institution au Droict des François*, 39.

17. See André Jean Arnaud, *Les Origines doctrinales du code civil français* (Paris, 1969), bk. 2, chap. 2, sec. 2.

18. Plongeron, *Théologie et politique*, 38.

19. Hobbes, *Elements of Law*, pt. 2, chap. 10, par. 5.

20. Hobbes, *Leviathan*, pt. 2, chap. 26, final paragraph.

21. Rousseau, *Lettres écrites de la Montagne*, no. 6, in *Oeuvres complètes*, 3:807–8.

22. Rousseau, *Social Contract*, bk. 3, chap. 6. See Derathé, *Jean-Jacques Rousseau*, 296.

23. Rousseau, *Social Contract*, bk. 3, ch. 11; and Locke, *Second Treatise*, chap. 11, par. 135.

24. Locke, *Second Treatise*, chap. 15, par. 172 and passim.

CHAPTER V
TOWARD A HISTORY OF THE FRENCH STATE

1. See Pierre Chaunu, "L'État," *Histoire économique et sociale de la France* (Paris, 1977), 1:15.

2. Georges de Lagarde, *La Naissance de l'esprit laïque au déclin du Moyen-Age* (Louvain, 1962), vol. 1.

3. Ibid., 1:110.

4. Ibid., 1:110.

5. Perry Anderson, *Lineages of the Absolutist State* (London, 1976).

6. Friedrich Engels, *The Origin of Family, Private Property, and the State* (New York, 1969), 157.

7. See Anderson, *Lineages*, 1:33 and 41.

8. Ibid., 1:118.

9. Gradually, the Porchnevian history of the absolutist state took shape by exclusively privileging those aspects that remained feudal: the repression of peasant jacqueries by the political troup of the chancery, by civil conflicts, and the like.

10. P. A. Chéruel, *Histoire de l'administration monarchique en France, depuis l'avènement de Philippe-Auguste jusqu'à la mort de Louis XIV*, 2 vols. (Paris, 1855), 1:lxiii.

11. Montesquieu, *Notes sur l'Angleterre*, in *Oeuvres complètes* (Paris, 1964), 334.

12. Voltaire, *Letters on the English, Harvard Classics*, 52 vols. (New York, 1938), 34:86.

13. Ibid., 34:88.

14. See especially Henry Bolingbroke, *Remarks on the History of England* (London, 1743), and Sir Edward Coke, *Argumentum Anti normannicum or an Argument proving from ancient histories and records that William, Duke of Nor-*

*mandy, made no absolute conquest of England by the Sword in the sense of our modern writers* (London, 1612).

15. See Sir Edward Coke, *Institutes of the Law of England*, 4 pts. (London, 1629–1646).

16. See especially Émile Boutmy, *Le Développement de la constitution et de la société politique en Angleterre* (Paris, 1887); Edward A. Freeman, *The Development of the English Constitution* (London); Ernest Glasson, *Histoire du droit et des institutions politiques, civiles, et judiciaires de l'Angleterre*, 6 vols. (Paris, 1881–1884); F. W. Maitland and F. Pollock, *A History of English Law before the Time of Edward I*, 2 vols. (London, 1897); and the works of Holdsworth, Allen, and others.

17. Boutmy, *Le Développement*, 145.

18. See Gabriel Ardant, *Histoire de l'impôt*, 2:506.

19. Glasson, *Histoire du droit*, 2:195.

20. Boutmy, *Le Développement*, 23.

21. Ibid., 28.

22. On this point, see the fine book by Philippe Contamine, *War in the Middle Ages*, trans. Michael Jones (Oxford, 1986).

23. Alexis de Tocqueville, *The Ancien Régime*, trans. John Bonner (London, 1988), bk. 2, chap. 9.

24. Blackstone, *Commentaries on the Laws of England* (Chicago, 1979), 1:63–64.

25. See William Stubbs, *Constitutional History of England* (Buffalo, N.Y., 1987).

26. See the chapters devoted to these jurists in vol. 1 of Pollock and Maitland, *History of English Law*.

27. Bracton, *De Legibus et Consuetudinibus Angliae*, bk. 2, chap. 5. See Glasson, *Histoire des constitutions*, 2:49–50.

28. See "Le Vilainage anglais," *Recueil de la Société Jean Bodin* 2 (1937).

29. On this point, Boutmy needs to be nuanced. The medievalists did emphasize the extent to which patronages had a tendency to become independent of their feudal lords even though they did not go so far as to constitute small judiciary fiefdoms.

30. Montesquieu, *The Spirit of the Laws*, bk. 11, chap. 6.

31. Élie Halévy, *A History of the English People in the Nineteenth Century*, trans. E. I. Watkin and D. A. Barker (New York, 1949), 1:35.

32. See Charles Petit-Dutaillis, *La Monarchie féodale en France et en Angleterre* (Paris, 1933).

33. See André Luchaire, *Histoire des institutions monarchiques sous les premiers Capétiens* (Paris, 1883), 240.

34. Boutmy, *Le Développement*, 275.

35. See F. Crouzet, *L'Économie brittanique et le blocus continental 1806–1913*, 2 vols. (Paris, 1958), 1:204ff.

36. Alexis de Tocqueville, *Democracy in America*, trans. George Lawrence (Garden City, N.Y., 1969), pt. 1, chap. 5.

37. "There are two ways in which the power of authority in a nation may be diminished. The first way is to weaken the very basis of power by depriving society

of the right or capacity to defend itself in certain circumstances. . . . But there is another way of diminishing the influence of authority without depriving society of some of its rights or paralyzing its efforts by dividing the use of its powers among several hands." Tocqueville, *Democracy in America*, pt. 1, chap. 5.

38.  Glasson, *Histoire du droit et des institutions*, 8:6.

39.  "This distinction between the king and the state or the crown is tied in to the connection between patrimonial law and public law." See G. Lepointe, *Manuel d'histoire du droit français*, 537–50.

40.  See Olivier-Martin, *Histoire du droit français*, 303.

41.  The great principles of dynastic succession, inheritance according to masculine primogeniture and the exclusion of parents by daughters, came into play at the time of the succession of Philip the Fair by the invocation of the *lex Salica*. After the Hundred Years' War, Jean de Terre-Vermeille, with the intention of restoring his throne to the dauphin, the future Charles VII who had been shamelessly disinherited to the benefit of the king of England, elaborated the statutory theory of the devolution of the crown. This statute and the statute regarding royal dominion elaborated at a later date together constitute the fundamental laws of the monarchy.

42.  Guy Coquille, *Institution au Droict des François*, 2.

43.  The president of Harlay stated at the *lit de justice* of June 15, 1586, that "we have two kinds of laws: the first kind are the ordinances of kings, which can be changed according to the diversity of times and affairs; the other kind are the ordinances of the kingdom, which are inviolable and by which You have ascended the throne and this crown has been preserved by Your predecessors down to Yourself." Louis XV stated in his declarations of July 2, 1717, and April 26, 1722, that "even if this misfortune (the extinction of the dynasty) ever befell the French nation, it would belong to the nation itself to repair it in its wisdom and by its choice, and, since the fundamental laws of our kingdom happily make it impossible for us to transfer our crown's dominion, we glory in the recognition that we are even less free to dispose of our crown itself." Declareuil, *Histoire du droit français*, 392 and 394, n. 18.

44.  Jean Bodin, *Six Books on the Commonwealth*, bk. 6, chap. 5.

45.  Declareuil, *Histoire du droit français*, 410.

46.  Olivier-Martin, *Histoire de droit français*, 323.

47.  Anderson, *Lineages*, 1:40–41.

48.  J. N. Moreau, *Les Devoirs du prince réduits à un seul principe ou Discours sur la justice dédié au roi* (Versailles, 1775), 75.

49.  Linguet, *Oeuvres*, 1:23–24.

50.  See A. Bardoux, *Les Légistes, leur influence sur la société française* (Paris, 1877), 55.

51.  See Beaumanoir, *Coutumes de Beauvoisis* (Paris, 1883), preface by Comte Beugnot, 1:33.

52.  First, before all the others, came the very ancient *Coutumier de Normandie* (1200–1220?); the book of *Jostice et Plet*, from Orléans by an anonymous author (ca. 1270); *Les Établissements de Saint Louis*, by l'Orléanais and de la Touraine Anjou; the *Coutume de Bretagne* (1330); *La Somme rurale*, by Jean Boutillier; and

the *Grand Coutumier de France de Jacques d'Ableiges*. See Lepointe, *Histoire des institutions*, 220–37.

53. Montesquieu, *Spirit of the Laws*, bk. 28, chap. 45.

54. See E. Chenon, *Histoire générale du droit français public et privé* (Paris, 1926), 2:360.

55. See Georges Pages, "Essai sur l'évolution des institutions administratives en France du commencement du XVIe siècle à la fin du XVIIe," *Revue d'histoire moderne* (1932).

56. Loyseau, *Des Seigneuries*, 3:11.

57. See Roland Mousnier, *La Vénalité des offices sous Henri IV et Louis XIII* (Rouen, France, 1945).

58. See Roland Mousnier, *État et société sous François Ier et Louis XIV* (Paris, 1966).

59. Michel Antoine, *Le Conseil du roi sous Louis XV* (Paris, 1970), 52–53.

60. See Clamageran, *Histoire de l'impôt en France*, 3 vols. (Paris, 1867–1876).

61. The most recent studies on tax systems, notably those studies of Alain Guery, otherwise highlight the modern character of the fiscal techniques imagined by Colbert's administration.

62. See Gabriel Ardant, *Histoire de l'impôt*, 1:449–70.

63. See Pierre Clément, *Histoire de Colbert et de son administration*, 2 vols. (Paris, 1892), 2:291ff.

CHAPTER VI
INFLECTIONS

1. See Élie Halévy, *La Formation du radicalisme philosophique*, 3 vols. (Paris, 1895); Raymond Aron, "For Progress—After the Fall of the Idols," *In Defense of Political Reason*, ed. Daniel J. Mahoney (Lanham, Md., 1994), 157–73; François Furet, *Interpreting the French Revolution* (New York, 1981); Louis Dumont, *From Mandeville to Marx* (Chicago, 1977); Pierre Rosanvallon, *Le Capitalisme utopique* (Paris, 1979).

2. Aron, "For Progress," 239.

3. G. W. F. Hegel, *Principles of the Philosophy of Right*, par. 260. On this point, see the penetrating analysis of Kostas Papaioannu, "La Raison et la croix du présent," postface to *Écrits politiques de Hegel* (Paris, 1977), 410.

4. This explains why, in the face of Marxism, which also looks to the passing away of the state, liberalism is dumbfounded.

5. For the substance of the following reflections concerning democracy, I am indebted to remarks made by Evelyne Pisier-Kouchner.

6. Hobbes, *Leviathan*, pt. 2, chap. 31.

7. Numa Denis Fustel de Coulanges, *The Ancient City* (Garden City, N.Y., n.d.), 223. See Giovanni Sartori's bibliography of the debate in his fine book, *Democratic Theory* (New York, 1962).

8. See Hannah Arendt, *On Revolution* (London, 1963).

9. "The laws are above all destined to protect possessions. Now, since it is possi-

ble to take away much more from one who has than from one who has not, they are obviously a safeguard accorded the rich against the poor. Therein lies their true spirit, and if this is inconvenient, it is inseparable from their existence." Simon-Nicolas Linguet, *Traité des lois civiles*, 1:7.

10. On the developments of civilist thought in preparing the Revolution, see the important book by François Furet, *Interpreting the French Revolution*, and the work of Augustin Cochin, which Furet rediscovered and reexamined.

CHAPTER VII
ROMANTICISM AND TOTALITARIANISM

1. André Glucksmann, *Les Maîtres penseurs* (Paris, 1977), 146–47.

2. Claude Digeon, *La Crise allemande de la pensée française, 1870–1914* (Paris, 1959).

3. On this point, see Victor Basch, *Les Doctrines politiques des philosophies classiques de l'Allemagne* (Paris, 1927); Xavier Léon, *Fichte et son temps*, 3 vols. (Paris, 1922, 1954); and the works of Boutroux and Andler.

4. Martial Guéroult, "Fichte et Xavier Léon," *Études sur Fichte* (Paris, 1974), 278.

5. See Guéroult, *Études sur Fichte*, 279.

6. See Henri Brunschwicg, *La Crise de l'état prussien au xviie siècle et la genèse de la pensée romantique* (Paris, 1947), reprint, *Société et romantisme en Prusse au xviiie siècle* (Paris, 1973); Jacques Droz, *Le Romantisme allemand et l'état* (Paris, 1966); Roger Ayrault, *La Genèse du romantisme allemand*, 4 vols. (Paris, 1969–1976); Georges Gurvitch, *L'Idée du droit social* (Paris, 1932); Charles Andler, *Les Origines du socialisme d'état en allemagne* (Paris, 1897); J. E. Spenlé, *Novalis, Essai sur l'idéalisme romantique en Allemagne* (Paris, 1903).

7. See Henri Brunschwicg, *La Crise de l'état prussien*, 168.

8. As a matter of fact, Rahel hosted two distinct salons, one in her mansard on Jagerstrasse before the victory of romanticism and another, more fashionable, which was clearly hostile to romanticism and where Heine declared himself an "outcast of romanticism."

9. Thomas Mann, *Pro and contra Wagner*, trans. Allan Blunden (Chicago, 1985), 146.

CHAPTER VIII
ANTI-STATISM AND NATIONALISM

1. G. W. F. Hegel, *The German Constitution*, introduction, in *Hegel's Political Writings*, trans. T. M. Knox (Oxford, 1964), 143.

2. It was part of the same process that anti-statism and the impasse forced on the state in the beginning led, in the end, to a great strengthening of the state.

3. Roger Ayrault, *La Genèse du romantisme allemand*, 4 vols. (Paris, 1969–1976), 1:109.

4. See Paul Chamley, *Économie et philosophie chez Stewart et Hegel* (Paris, 1963). The author of *Das Kapital*, who took from the English the thesis of juridico-political sphere's dependence with regard to civil society, straightforwardly acknowledged his indebtedness: "My investigation led to the result that legal relations as well as forms of state are to be grasped neither from themselves nor from the so-called general development of the human mind, but rather have their roots in the material conditions of life, the sum total of which Hegel, following the example of the Englishmen and Frenchmen of the eighteenth century, combines under the name of 'civil society,' that, however, the anatomy of civil society is to be sought in political economy." Marx, *A Contribution to the Critique of Political Economy*, preface.

5. Xavier Léon, *Fichte et son temps*, 1:286; Georges Gurvitch, *L'Idée du droit social*, 411; and Martial Guéroult, *Études sur Fichte*, 69.

6. Johann Gottlieb Fichte, *Addresses to the German Nation*, ed. George A. Kelly (New York, 1968), 118.

7. "It is their (the ancient Germans') unyielding resistance which the whole modern world has to thank for being what it now is. Had the Romans succeeded in bringing them also under the yoke and in destroying them as a nation, which the Romans did in every case, the whole development of the human race would have taken a different course, a course that one cannot think would have been more satisfactory." Fichte, *Addresses*, 123.

8. "This, then, is a people in the higher meaning of the word, when viewed from the standpoint of a spiritual world: the totality of men continuing to live in society with each other and continually creating themselves naturally and spiritually out of themselves, a totality that arises together out of the divine under a special law of divine development. It is the subjection in common to this special law that unites this mass in the eternal world, and therefore in the temporal also, to a natural totality permeated by itself. The significance of this law itself can indeed be comprehended as a whole, as we have comprehended it by the instance of the Germans as an original people." Fichte, *Addresses*, 115.

9. "What spirit has an undisputed right to summon and to order everyone concerned, whether he himself be willing or not, and to compel anyone who resists, to risk everyting including his life? Not the spirit of the peaceful citizen's love for the constitution and the laws, but the devouring flame of higher patriotism, which embraces the nation as the vesture of the eternal, for which the noble-minded man joyfully sacrifices himself, and the ignoble man, who only exists for the sake of the other, must likewise sacrifice himself." Fichte, *Addresses*, 120.

10. "Such a religion (the religion of the past), which was obviously a servant of selfishness, shall indeed be borne to the grave along with the past age. In the new era eternity does not dawn first on the far side of he grave, but comes into the midst of the present life; while self-seeking is dismissed from serving and from ruling, and departs, taking its servants with it. Education to *true religion* is, therefore, the final task of the new education." Fichte, *Addresses*, 33, emphasis added.

11. Fichte, *Addresses*, 119.

12. Ibid., 96.

13. Ibid., 118.

14. Xavier Léon, *Fichte*, 3:128–29.

CHAPTER IX
ANTI-JURIDISM

1. With Gustav Hugo as its precursor and with Freidrich Karl von Savigny and Georg Friedrich Puchta as its leaders, the historical school of law exercised a fundamental influence on the whole of the romantic movement. In 1814, in *Vom Beruf unserer Zeit für Gesetzgebung und Rechtwissenschaft*, Savigny argued against his opposition to his colleague Thibault, who favored a codification based on the French model.

2. It should be noted that the doctrinarians who established the principles of political right in Germany were henceforth university professors. Unlike the French royal legists and the natural-law philosophers, whose relatively uncertain position with reference to the establishment assured them a margin of independence with regard to public authority, on the one hand, and of subjection to the body to which they belonged, on the other hand, the German thinkers of the nineteenth century belonged to the unified and normalized corporation of the university system. It should be noted that by the time these scholars were assimilated into university life, the system of German universities had become the admiration of all Europe. Germany remained as backward as ever in the process of becoming a state, and, with neither an attachment to, or a detachment from, a central authority, the universities were narrowly dependent on local principalities and fascinated by the fanciful unity of patriotism.

3. "To wish to assimilate the current of ideas stemming from Fichte to Hegelianism would be as false as not to establish any sufficient distinction between Proudhon and Auguste Comte, and more generally between the league of Saint-Simon and that of Bonald and de Maistre." G. Gurvitch, *L'Idée du droit social* (Paris, 1932), 408. See also M. Guéroult, *L'Évolution et la structure de la doctrine de la science* (Paris, 1930), 2:227, 235, and 241, who shows the irreducibility of Fichte to Hegel. Today, thanks to the fundamental research of Bernard Bourgeois, Hegelian studies in France are enjoying a renewal. See O. Poggeler, "Hegel et Machiavel," *Archives de philosophie* (July–September 1978) for the author's rigorous critique of Dilthey's abusive assimilations between Hegel's nationalist Machiavellianism and Pan-Germanism.

4. Gustav Hugo, *Lehrbuch des Naturrechts als seiner Philosophie des positiven Rechts* (Berlin, 1809).

5. See Jacques Droz, *Le Romantisme politique en Allemagne* (Paris, 1963), 49.

6. Hegel, *Principles of the Philosophy of Right*, par. 273, and *Encyclopedia of Philosophy*, par. 540.

7. Hegel, *Principles of the Philosophy of Right*, par. 218.

8. Puchta, *Das Gewohnheit Recht* (Erlanger, 1828) and *Cursus der Institutionen* (1841), 1:29, in Gurvitch, *L'Idée du droit social*, 476. "The fundamental doctrine of this school, the beginning and the end of all their knowledge . . . consists in their hostility to law, which is linked to this conception, in their hatred for the state, which is the source of all law." Gans, *Geschichte des Erbrechts*, 2:292, in Gurvitch, *L'Idée*, 473.

9. Savigny, *Geschichte des römischen Rechts im Mittelalter* (1815–1831).

10. See Gurvitch, *L'Idée*, 478.

11. See Savigny, *Geschichte des römischen Rechts*.

12. See Hegel, *The System of Ethical Life* (Berlin, 1802–1805). See also Jacques Taminiaux and Roland Maspetiol, "Droit, société civile et état dans la pensée d'Hegel," *Archives de philosophie du droit* 12 (1967).

13. Savigny, *Vom Beruf unserer Zeit*, 1:11.

14. This is notably the opinion held by A. Cornu: "In maintaining that the living source of modern law was not the old feudal law but rather Roman law, he (Savigny) in fact was defending, not the interests of the decadent nobility but those of the ascendant bourgeoisie that, with the Napoleonic Code, had just made Roman law the basis of bourgeois legislation." A. Cornu, *Karl Marx et Friedrich Engels* (Paris, 1955), 1:84.

15. Besides the writings of Hugo and Savigny devoted to Roman law, notably G. Hugo, *Geschichte des römischen Rechts;* F. Savigny, *System des Heutigen römischen Rechts* (1840–1849); and the review founded by Savigny in 1814, *Zeitchsrift für Geschichtliche Rechtwissenschaft*, a movement was established for the rediscovery and republication of Roman texts that made possible the discovery of an unedited version of the *Institutes* of Gaius and for new editions of the *Corpus juris civilis*, notably those by the Kriegel brothers (1843–1843). On this point, see the studies done by Warkoenig (1841) and Laboulaye (1842).

16. R. Jhering, *Die Geist des römischen Rechts*. But Jhering underscores that the Roman and the modern states should not be confused.

17. Nietzsche, *The Antichrist*, trans. Walter Kaufmann (New York, 1954), section 58.

18. Hegel, *Philosophy of History*, trans. J. Sibree (New York, 1956), 406.

19. See A. W. von Schlegel, *Vorlesungen über schöne Litteratur und Kunst* (1803–1804).

20. Novalis, *Pollens*, sec. 64.

21. Karl Ludwig von Haller, *Restauration der Staatswissenschaften*, 6 vols. (Winterthur, Switzerland, 1816); Charles Louis de Haller, *La Restauration de la science politique*, 5 vols. (Paris, 1834).

22. Hegel, *Principles of the Philosophy of Right*, par. 277.

23. Ibid., par. 278.

24. Ibid.

25. Haller, *La Restauration*, 1:12.

26. Ibid., 1:543.

CHAPTER X
THE SECULARIZATION OF FAITH

1. Friedrich von Schlegel, *Critical Fragment*, 38, and *Athenaeum Fragment*, 222, in *Philosophical Fragments*, trans. Peter Firchow (Minneapolis, Minn., 1991), 5 and 48.

2. See Ernst Benz, *The Mystical Sources of German Romantic Philosophy* (Pittsburgh, Pa., 1983).

3. See J. E. Spenlé, *Novalis, Essai sur l'idéalisme romantique en Allemagne* (Paris, 1903).

4. Novalis, *Christendom or Europe*, in *Hymns to the Night and Other Selected Writings*, trans. Charles E. Passage (Indianapolis, Ind., 1960), 62.

5. Hobbes, *Leviathan*, pt. 3, chaps. 36 and 41.

6. Schleiermacher, *On Religion: Addresses in Response to Its Cultured Critics*, trans. Terrence N. Tice (Richmond, Va., 1969), 305.

7. See Roger Ayrault, *La Genèse du romantisme allemand*, 4:180.

8. "As an instrument for government, faith is superior to a consitution because a political constitution is of human making, and consequently is blemished with every human imperfection. It is a product of reason and not of faith." See Novalis, *Oeuvres complètes* (Paris, 1975), 1:331.

9. In a letter to Schleiermacher, quoted by Jankelevitch in his preface to Schelling, *Essais* (Paris, 1946), 12.

10. Schleiermacher, *Soliloquies*, trans. Horace Leland Friess (Chicago, 1967), 62.

11. Ludwig Feuerbach, *Philosophy of the Future*, 33, in *The Fiery Brook: Selected Writings of Ludwig Feuerbach*, trans. Zawar Hanfi (Garden City, N.Y., 1972), 225.

12. Feuerbach, *The Necessity of a Reform*, in *Fiery Brook*, 146.

13. Feuerbach, *The Essence of Christianity*, trans. George Eliot (New York, 1957), 46.

14. Feuerbach, *The Essence of Christianity*, 13.

15. Feuerbach, *The Necessity of a Reform*, 149.

16. Alain Besançon, *La Confusion des langues* (Paris, 1978), 12–13.

CHAPTER XI
MARX'S ROMANTICISM

1. Karl Marx, *Contribution to the Critique of Hegel's Philosophy of Right*, introduction, in *The Marx-Engels Reader*, ed. Robert J. Tucker (New York, 1978), 56.

2. On this score, the publication in French of Marx's correspondence gives the lie to the truly edifying life of the Marx family. For Marx was one of those socialists, the kind the Saint-Simonians hoped for, who did not dine at the "Rocher de Cancale." The neglect of the specific impact of his life of voluntary misery and sacrifice on the workers' movement led to an underestimation of Marxism's theologico-political authority. For a serious reflection on Marxist political right, one should consult the pioneering work of Kostas Papaioannou, which unfortunately is scattered in articles appearing in such journals as *Contrat social* or in prefaces to translations into French cited above and of the writings of Werner Jaeger.

3. See Auguste Cornu, *Karl Marx et Friedrich Engels*, 4 vols. (Paris, 1955–1977).

4. Ibid., 1:67.

5. See Marx's letter of November 10, 1837, to his father, in *The Marx-Engels Reader*, 7–8; and Cornu, *Marx et Engels*, 1:91–92.

6. Feuerbach, *The Necessity of a Reform*, in *Fiery Brook*, 145.

7. Marx, *Contribution to the Critique of Political Economy*, preface, in *The Marx-Engels Reader*, 4.

8. On this point, see Chamley, *Économie et philosophie*, and Rosanvallon, *Le Capitalisme utopique* (Paris, 1979).

9. Marx, *Critique of Hegel's Philosophy of Right*, trans. Annette Jolin and Joseph O'Malley (Cambridge, 1970), 7.

10. Marx, *Theses on Feuerbach* 10, in *The Marx-Engels Reader*, 145.

11. Marx, *Contribution to the Critique of Hegel's Philosophy of Right*, introduction, in *The Marx-Engels Reader*, 52.

12. Marx, *On the Jewish Question*, in *The Marx-Engels Reader*, 39.

13. Ibid., 34. Already at this time, Marx conceived of the modern state as the perfect incarnation of the Christian state and as a more successful and more adequate embodiment of religious dualism than feudalism, which subordinated Christianity to the state.

14. "Hegel forgets that . . . the activities and agencies of the state are human activities. He forgets that the nature of the particular person is not his beard, his blood, his abstract *Physics*, but rather his social quality, and that the activities of the state, etc., are nothing but the modes of existence and operation of the social qualities of men." Marx, *Critique of Hegel's Philosophy of Right*, 22.

15. See the paragraph entitled "a lawless civilization," Aleksandr Zinoviev, *The Yawning Heights*, trans. Gordon Clough (New York, 1979), 574–75.

16. Marx, *Critique of Hegel's Philosophy of Right*, 30.

17. Ibid., 100.

18. See Marx, *On the Jewish Question*, 48.

19. Ibid., 42.

20. Ibid., 43.

21. Ibid., 46.

22. Marx, *Critique of Hegel's Philosophy of Right*, 30.

23. Ibid., 133.


CHAPTER XII

THE STATE UNDER THE RULE OF DESPOTISM

1. On this point, see Augustin Cochin, *L'Esprit du jacobinisme* (Paris, 1979); François Furet, *Interpreting the French Revolution* (New York, 1981); Daniel Lindenberg, *Le Marxisme introuvable* (Paris, 1975); and Lucien Herr, *Le Socialisme et son destin* (Paris, 1978).

2. See Renouvin and Duroselle, *Introduction à l'étude des relations internationales* (Paris, 1964), 195–200.

3. Alain Besançon, *The Rise of the Gulag* (Paris, 1977).

4. See Léon Duguit, *Traité de droit constitutionnel*, 1:612–13.

5. See Georg Luckacs, *The Destruction of Reason*, trans. Peter Palmer (Atlantic Heights, N.J., 1980). Edmond Vermeil and Roger Callois also hold this view.

6. This has been amply demonstrated by Michael Löwy in *Archives des sciences sociales et des religions* no. 1 (1978).

7. See Jean Rivero, *Annales de la faculté de droit de Liège* (1957), and Jean-Pierre Henry, *Revue du droit public et de la science politique* (1977).

# Index